The Batsford Guide to Veteran Cars

The Batsford Guide to Veteran Cars

**Compiled by
Francis Hutton-Stott
and D.G. Shapland**

**B.T. Batsford Ltd
London**

© Anthony Bird, Francis Hutton-Stott and D.G. Shapland 1978

First published as *The Veteran Motor Car Pocketbook*

First published 1963
Second Revised edition 1978

ISBN 0 7134 1182 1

Filmset in 'Monophoto' Times New Roman by
Servis Filmsetting Limited, Manchester

Printed and bound in Great Britain by
Butler & Tanner Ltd, Frome
for the publishers B.T. Batsford Limited
4 Fitzhardinge Street, London W1H 0AH

Acknowledgment

The use of the following photographs is gratefully acknowledged (those not acknowledged are from the collection of Mr Francis Hutton-Stott): p26 (top) BMC/British Leyland, p32/33 Daimler-Benz AG, p35 (top) Autocar, p42 Mr R.A. Harvey, p47 Mr William Pollock, p49 Autocar, p53 Hull Press (Photo) Agency Ltd, p54 Mr J.P. Mellish, p55 Daimler-Benz AG, p56 Mr E.A. Sollars, p58 (top) Mrs Skinner, p65 Mr J.D. Percy, p78 (bottom) Fiat Ltd, Turin, p81 Ford Motor Co, p82 Mr G.E. Milligen and Mr J.B. Mason, p90 Rootes Motors Ltd, p98 Autocar, p100 Jowett Cars Ltd, p102 Autocar, p103 Mr J.B. Mason, p106 Motor, p107 Autocar, p112 Mr F.A. Ametrano, New York, p113 Mr Charles L. Betts Jnr, p117 Daimler-Benz AG, p128 D. Napier and Sons Ltd, p133 (right) Autocar, p136 Automobile Manufacturing Association, Detroit, p145 Autocar, p150 Messrs Sennet & Spears and J. Oldham, p.154 Louis Klemantaski, p155 (bottom) Rolls Royce Ltd, p156 Mrs Skinner, p158 Rover Company Ltd, p163 Mr James Barron, p167 Mr J.D. Percy, p174 Rootes Motors Ltd, p175 Mr R.A. Harvey, p180 Autocar, p182 Vauxhall Motors Ltd, p186 Mr G.L. Milligen and Mr J.B. Mason, p195 Mr R.A. Collings.

Contents

Introduction to the Revised Edition

The Batsford Guide to Veteran Cars is in essence derived from *The Veteran Motor Car Pocketbook*, published in 1963. Obviously in the intervening years no new Veteran cars have been manufactured, but *The Veteran Motor Car Pocketbook* has been out of print for some time, and second-hand copies are hard to find, having become something of a collector's item. Consequently a second edition of the publication was indicated, in a revised form, which would accompany the other titles in the revised series: *The Batsford Guide to Vintage Cars* by Cecil Clutton, Paul Bird and Anthony Harding (1976), *The Batsford Guide to Vintage Sports and Racing Cars* by Anthony Harding (1978), and *The Batsford Guide to Racing Cars* by Denis Jenkinson (1978).

Unfortunately in the intervening years Anthony Bird died, and so D.G. Shapland was invited by Francis Hutton-Stott to co-operate with him in the task of revision. The original text was thought to have stood the test of time, and as a consequence this publication remains largely unaltered from the inimitable Bird/Hutton-Stott style of *The Veteran Motor Car Pocketbook*. Notable omissions, such as Riley, Lancia, Vulcan and Star, have been added, together with a selection of previously unpublished photographs.

The authors hope the new generation of Veteran car enthusiasts will find this book as useful and appealing as the old. They also hope that the new generation will derive as much opportunity as the old to see Veteran cars puffing, and sometimes struggling with advancing years, about the towns and the countryside.

Introduction to the First Edition
(The Veteran Motor Car Pocketbook)

The authors of *The Veteran Motor Car Pocketbook* laboured under some disadvantages not the least of which is that their work will inevitably suffer by comparison with its brilliant predecessor in this series—*The Vintage Motor Car Pocketbook*, which, despite a handful of hotly criticised (but relatively unimportant and subsequently corrected) errors of fact, remains in its sphere the finest ornament to the literature of motoring which has appeared in sixty years. Therefore the authors' introduction to this volume must be largely a plea for indulgence and an explanation of their aims.

In extenuation they can claim that the task has not been easy. The daughter of truth lives at the bottom of a very deep well, and with each year that passes the effort to disentangle her from accumulated rubbish becomes more difficult. The records of many early motor car firms have disappeared, and a great number of descriptions in early numbers of *The Autocar*, and other seemingly authoritative sources, cannot be taken without a pinch of salt. Much distortion arises from the highly vituperative and tendentious writings of such notabilities as S.F. Edge, D.M. Weigel and many more, each of whom had a different commercial horse to flog. Also, at the beginning of the century the trade of motor-journalism was quite new so it is not surprising that many of the 'expert' writers just did not know what they were writing about. A vast quantity of completely erroneous information was printed in perfectly good faith.

The task of selection, too, has been rather more difficult than that which faced the authors of *The Vintage Motor Car Pocketbook*. Not only is the period more remote and the amount of misinformation greater, but the sheer number of different makes of motor vehicle in existence (of however ephemeral a nature) between 1890 and 1916 is such as to appal the most stout-hearted. This weight of numbers is made more confusing by the fact that both here and in America, importers, agents and small engineering concerns sold motor cars, in small batches, under a great many different names. Therefore something which started life as a Renault might be sold as an Argyll or a Triumph, and the difference between a Speedwell and a Hanzer might only be one of name. There was also a tendency in England, in the early days, for cars to be advertised as 'All British' when, in fact, they were built up from imported French components. Most vehicles of this sort were extremely bad and did not stay on the market long; therefore there seems little point in wasting much space upon them—though one or two have been included to complete the picture.

In the hope of presenting a reasonably accurate picture of the development of the motor car in its early years the authors have tried to make their choice as representative as possible, though in some instances they have had to be influenced by the availability, or otherwise, of illustrations and information. Inevitably Reader A will see no point in the inclusion of the Puffhard, and Reader B will be infuriated by the exclusion of the Halfdaft. Readers A to Z will unite in groaning at the stupidity of the authors for saying that the 1903 Mikado was the first car to be fitted with elliptical friction balls, when it is well known that these were used ten years earlier by Messrs Ayres & Gracies who built two motor cars neither of which would work. To all these readers the authors apologise.

A sufficiently representative selection of American makes has been included to illustrate the trend of events in the U.S.A.; at least, such is the authors' hope, but if the American reader feels disappointed at the relative paucity of American names it must be said by way of apology that the American industry, though numerically huge, had less influence on the development of the motor car in its early years than its European and English contemporaries. This point of view is now slightly unfashionable, but it was recognised at the time by many American authorities who saw no reason to be ashamed of the fact that the most successful American cars were, in the main, derived from European rather than native sources. This must not be taken as a denigration of America's many notable contributions to the automotive scene, but if it is also thought that a pair of dyed-in-the-wool reactionary English writers are not without bias they are freely prepared to admit that they are so 'square' as to be almost cubic.

The Introductions to the other books in this series include brief background histories of the subjects dealt with. In this instance the authors feel that as they could not do justice to the early history of the automobile in a few pages it is better to be silent than superficial, and to let the individual motor cars speak for themselves.

As far as the specifications are concerned the stereotyped layout used in the other books in this series has been modified. There seemed little point, for example, in having headings for clutches or gearboxes when dealing with those cars which have none; and as, in many cases, models were available with different lengths of wheelbase, wheel diameter, gear-ratios, etc., more or less to the customer's choice, the details are confined to bare outlines of the engines and transmission systems. These details are kept to a minimum for the 'conventional' cars, but all those which do not conform to the *système Panhard* are dealt with rather more fully.

For the less important makes, the specification of only one model is usually sufficient, but for the more important (or prolific) the specifications have been chosen, as far as possible, to show the major changes in design which took place during the period under review. Some few manufacturers, such as Rolls-Royce, Lanchester, Ford, etc., produced only a few basic types and these are easily dealt with, but the besetting sin of many pre-1914 makers was the production of a staggeringly wide and wholly uneconomic variety—there are, for example, thirteen models of Panhard listed for 1910—and in the early years particularly, improvements in design often meant that the new season's model really was new. Therefore a comprehensive number of specifications for each make would be impossible in the space available, and the seeker after more detail must delve (with the authors' blessing) into contemporary journals and catalogues which he will find vague and baffling to a degree. It is all very fine, for instance, to read in the catalogue issued by the Weevil & Blight Autocar Company in 1898 that 'our carriages are propelled by petroleum oil motors of improved pattern built of the finest materials and entirely free from objectionable odour and vibration . . .' but the number of cylinders and their dimensions are secrets which Messrs Weevil & Blight carried with them to their graves or the Bankruptcy Court.

The cylinder dimensions given in the specifications (always bore given first and stroke second) are sometimes in inches and otherwise in millimetres: the reader may well suppose the authors to have been too idle to make the necessary conversions so as to have them all alike, but it will usually be found that the 'inch figures' only convert into metric with very untidy fractions left over. In other words when a particular car or model has its dimensions given in inches it can generally be taken that the makers were working in inches at that particular time, and consequently the writers have followed the usage of the contemporary catalogues or journals.

Difficulties also arise over nomenclature. For instance, some early descriptions of cars with horizontally opposed engines, but with the crankshafts in the usual longitudinal line of the chassis, refer to them as *transverse* engines. Again, 'jump-spark' ignition in American usage generally, though not always, referred to high tension coil and battery apparatus with a mechanical contact-breaker and non-trembling coil, but in English usage, at one time, 'jump-spark ignition' meant any form of H.T. ignition with spark-gaps or 'intensifiers' included in the circuit. In modern usage 'live axle transmission' means the combination of propellor shaft and bevel- or worm-geared live axle—but many chain-driven cars also had live axles of a different sort. 'Pressure lubrication' now means the usual modern system of a pump feeding oil under pressure to all engine bearings, the big-ends being supplied through a hollow crankshaft, but at one time 'pressure lubrication' merely meant that oil was lifted to, or forced through, the sight-feeds on the dashboard by exhaust pressure instead of the more usual slow-moving plunger pump. And so on. . . . In an attempt to avoid ambiguities the following usages have been adopted:

1   Unless otherwise stated engines may be assumed to have been made by the makers of the car and to have been placed vertically in front with crankshafts in the fore-and-aft line.

2   'Transverse engine' means that the crankshaft is parallel with the axles irrespective of cylinder disposition.

3   Unless otherwise stated, twin- and multi-cylinder engines may be taken to be of the ordinary 'in line' variety.

4   'Trembler coil ignition'—by contact *maker* and electric auto-trembler H.T. coil.

5   'Coil ignition'—by mechanical contact *breaker* and non-trembler coil. This being the usual modern system originated, in embryo, on the first De Dion Bouton engines.

6   'Dual ignition'—strictly speaking, originally meant a system using two (or more) sparking plugs per cylinder fired simultaneously either by two separate magnetos, by magneto and coil in conjunction, or by a single magneto with duplex distributor. In many instances the term was wrongly used for those cars fitted with two independent systems of ignition, generally a battery and coil for starting or emergency use and magneto for ordinary running. As far as it has been possible to sort out the ambiguities the term 'dual ignition' used in text or specifications means dual ignition in its full sense, and those makes or models with duplicated ignition are described accordingly.

7   Low tension, or L.T. ignition means the system using low voltage current,

without an induction coil, and with mechanically operated contact breakers inside each combustion chamber. The current for L.T. ignition was generally derived from a simple magneto but some early examples had batteries.

8 'A.I.V.'—automatic or atmospheric inlet valves. Found on many early engines and generally arranged 'inlet over exhaust' (I.o.E.).

9 'M.O.I.V.'—mechanically operated inlet valves. Specified on early examples where applicable. After about 1905, unless otherwise stated, 'M.O.I.V.' may be taken for granted.

10 'S.V.'—side valves: unless otherwise stated 'S.V.' indicates all valves or one side of the cylinder block and the T-head layout is separately indicated, where applicable.

11 Unless otherwise stated engines are assumed to be water-cooled and to work on the 4-stroke cycle.

12 Unless otherwise stated gearboxes are assumed to be of the sliding pinion, or sliding gear-wheel variety. Constant-mesh, epicyclic, and other varieties of change-speed mechanism are specified where applicable.

A.C.   England

In the early days, the motor tricycle provided cheap mechanised transport for those who could not afford a car, and before long various expedients for passenger-carrying were tried. First, the tricycle was furnished with a light wickerwork trailer which ensured the passenger (generally female) her full share of the mud, dust and exhaust fumes. Next came the quadricycle, with a passenger chair suspended between the two front wheels which replaced the single forewheel of the tricycle. Then the affair lost a back wheel to become a tandem tricar with a single rear driving wheel, and many weird machines, some effective but mostly rather horrible, were evolved on this formula. They suffered from the disadvantage that driver and passenger were not seated side-by-side, so the next stage in evolution was the 'sociable' which remained a three-wheeler but had side-by-side seats.

One of the most successful of these was the A.C. which grew up out of the Autocarrier tradesmen's box-tricycle. A passenger-carrying version of this had been made from 1907 onwards by substituting a passenger chair for the box body, but this involved the unpopular tandem seating arrangement with the

1910 single-cylinder 5/6 hp box van

passenger acting as a buffer between the driver and the mishap. So, by 1909, the machine had been re-designed as a Sociable, with a low-slung comfortable little body for two (or, at a pinch, three) between the front wheels, and with all the controls brought forward from their former position farther aft. The single rear wheel was driven by a 90 × 102 mm single cylinder air-cooled engine in the back part of the body-work. Two singularly puny little fans were driven by friction discs from the external flywheels, and despite the fact that they appeared to be so placed that their air-streams cancelled one another out the engines were never known to overheat. Transmission was by roller chain to a 2-speed epicyclic gear in the hub of the back wheel; this had the engaging peculiarity that as the machine came to a standstill, part of the gear-casing (which rather resembled a large brake drum) spun merrily backwards which made many a citizen doubt the wisdom of that last gin-and-tonic.

Steering was controlled by a side tiller and the epicyclic gear-cum-clutch control was simply operated by one lever. Petrol consumption was nearly 50 mpg, top speed about 40 mph, comfortable cruising speed 30 mph, and hills of 1 in 10 could be mastered without resorting to the slow speed—on which the creature was indefatigable. Riding comfort and weather protection were extremely good. Very similar machines (both goods and passenger types) were also made by John Warrick & Co. Ltd, and it is not quite clear who was cribbing from whom.

It is a sobering thought that the performance figures of the 5 hp A.C. Sociable were very similar to those of the 20 hp model T Ford, and still more sobering to reflect that the 20 hp Ford cost approximately the same as the 5 hp Sociable. . . . The little tricars were extremely durable and as late as 1950 at least two of the box-vans, built in 1909, were patiently performing their duties in London.

In 1913 A.C. brought out a conventional light car with a 4-cylinder Fivet engine, 3-speed gearbox and worm-gear live axle. Only 475 were made before the war stopped production, and it was not until the 'twenties that A.C. reached the height of their fame under the guidance of S.F. Edge who had, in 1912, accepted a settlement of his differences with Napiers on the understanding that he would not engage in the motor trade again for ten years.

1910 'Sociable' 5/6 hp (R.A.C. 4·9)
Engine: Air-cooled, transverse, rear-mounted, 1-cylinder, 90 × 102 mm, S.V., H.T. magneto ignition. *Transmission:* Roller chain to epicyclic gear-hub in rear wheel, clutches: contracting band for low speed, multiplate for high speed, no reverse. Tiller steering. (There were minor variations in brakes and controls and the engine bore was increased by ¼ in. in 1912 which brought the R.A.C. rating equal to the maker's rating, otherwise the box-van and 'Sociable' models remained unaltered.)

1913/14 Light car 10 hp (R.A.C. 8·6)
Engine: Fivet, 4-cylinder, 59 × 100 mm, S.V., H.T. magneto ignition. *Transmission:* Cone clutch, 1913, single plate, 1914, shaft, 3 speeds and reverse gear integral worm final drive in back axle casing. It has not been possible to determine whether the early models had the combined gearbox and back axle, but it is believed that this is so: by 1914 it was certainly so.

1913 light car, 10 hp

Adams-Hewitt England

That the early Adams-Hewitt cars have a distinctly American flavour about them is hardly surprising, because they were designed for the Adams Manuf. Co. of Bedford by Mr Hewitt, who was also responsible for a similar car made by the Hewitt Motor Co. of New York from 1904 to 1909. Hewitt had helped Sir Hiram Maxim with his gargantuan steam aeroplane in the 'nineties, and had then worked with Wolseley's who had done most of the machining for the aeroplane engines.

The 10hp Adams-Hewitt was on the market by 1905 and it was a fairly straightforward, but tougher, copy of the original Oldsmobile (qv), with the same sort of combined road spring-cum-chassis structure, and a slow-running horizontal engine amidships. The first models were fitted with 2-speed epicyclic gears, but to meet English requirements a 3-speed version was soon adopted. All gear changing was done with the feet (antedating the Model T Ford), and the firm adopted their famous slogan of 'Pedals to Push—That's All'. They managed to capture a large slice of the Doctor's Car business and many of the single-cylinder cars were fitted with closed coupé bodies which looked a little odd on the short, high-pitched chassis.

The original design continued until late 1909, alongside more conventional models, with 2- and 4-cylinder vertical engines and shaft drive, which first appeared in 1906, after which the Hewitt part of the name was dropped. The 4-cylinder vertical-engined cars had particularly handsome 'A'-shaped radiators with the number plate forming the cross-piece of the 'A'. One of the most interesting exhibits at Olympia in November 1906 was the Adams-Eight which incorporated a V-8 cylinder Antoinette type aero engine, built by the Adams Company.

This ambitious project does not seem to have been successful—at least no more was heard of it, and by 1909 production had settled down to 4-cylinder cars of 12/14 hp, 14/16, 14/18 (all very similar), a new 10 hp twin called the 'Varsity' model, and a few of the old one-lungers. In 1912 the Company had to bow to public opinion by abolishing their admirably simple foot-control in favour of a system disguised to resemble the ordinary gate-change and clutch-pedal; they also introduced a 4-speed sliding pinion gearbox as an alternative to the 3-speed epicyclic system. Of more interest to the motoring public was a compressed-air starting device which seems to have worked very well. The old-type runabout became extinct in 1910, but in 1913 the firm tried to go back to it, in slightly more modern form. Their new light car had a horizontally opposed 8 hp 2-cylinder transverse engine under the floor, 2-speed epicyclic gear and the old single-chain drive to a divided rear axle. It also had full-elliptic springs in front and a single transverse spring at the back. As with so much else the Adams cars died out after 1914.

1908 10 hp (R.A.C. 9·02) *Engine:* Horizontal, transverse, central 1-cylinder, 4¾ × 6 in., M.O.I.V., coil ignition, or H.T. magneto, or both. *Transmission:* Pedal-controlled 3 speeds and reverse epicyclic gears.

Clutches: for low speeds and reverse by contracting band brakes on gear drums, high speed by a further band brake which locked the unit solid, final drive by single chain to live axle.

1912 16hp (R.A.C. 19·3) *Engine:* 4-cylinder, 88 × 120 mm, S.V., H.T. magneto. *Transmission:* Cone

clutch, 4 speeds and reverse, shaft, bevel-geared live axle.

1912 30 hp (R.A.C. 28·9) As above, but engine 6-cylinder, 88 × 110 mm.

Albion   Scotland

Before the Kaiser's war three famous firms made cars in Scotland and they had three things in common. They all began with the letter A (Albion, Arrol-Johnston and Argyll); the cars they made were admirable, and all three firms tried front wheel brakes on one or another of their models. (A comprehensive and well-laid-out selection of these cars is to be seen in the Glasgow motor museum.)

Dr T. Blackwood Murray and Norman Fulton formed the Albion Motor Co. in Glasgow in 1899: their first car appeared early in 1900 and a horizontal-engined, twin-cylinder, chain-driven, solid-tyred 'dog-cart' was in production by the end of the year. Dr Murray designed the car throughout, including an early form of synchromesh mechanism, the carburettor, and a most reliable type of low-tension magneto ignition. The early Albions were not particularly fast but they could keep up their 20 miles an hour over the roughest roads with remarkable little trouble. An owner who entered his 1901 Albion for the

left 1900 single-cylinder station cart

right 1910 24/30 4-cylinder tourer

14

Glasgow trials reported to *The Autocar* a year later that he had covered 9,000 miles without a hitch—there were not many motorists who could say the same in 1902.

By 1902 the firm was selling cars as far afield as Malaya and Siam, and in the following year they moved from Furmieston Street to a larger factory at Scotstoun. The 2-cylinder 12 hp 'dog-cart' sold well at £440 complete with body and fittings—quite a high price for a 2-cylinder car of supposedly obsolete design. However, bowing to the critics of horizontal engines, the firm brought out a vertical-engined 12 hp model in 1903, and this was slightly enlarged in 1904 to become a lusty 16 hp car, capable of 40 mph on the pneumatic tyres which Albions had hitherto frowned upon.

This big twin model proved its worth by remaining in production, altered only in detail and body-style, for eight years. Their first 4-cylinder model, which appeared at the 1905 Show, had almost as long a life. A number of other 4-cylinder models were made but Albions kept their feet on the ground and did not weaken their finances by too much diversification. Allen-Liversedge front wheel brakes were fitted to a 16 hp Albion in 1909 but were not adopted as standard equipment; practically all the 'experts' who wrote on motor matters at that time declared front wheel brakes to be dangerous, and there is no doubt the public were influenced by these pronouncements.

One of the last Albion models appeared in 1912 to supplant the old 16 hp twin; this was a very handsome 15 hp 4-cylinder with 79×127 mm monobloc engine, in unit with a 4-speed gearbox, and worm-geared back axle. It sold for £475 complete. In 1914 the Company—perhaps frightened by the fate which was closing in on Argylls—turned their whole resources over to producing the heavy goods vehicles for which they are still famous.

1900 7 hp (R.A.C. 12·8) *Engine:* Horizontally opposed, transverse, rear-mounted, 2-cylinder, 4×5 in., A.I.V., Murray L.T. magneto ignition. *Transmission:* Cone clutch, 2 speeds and reverse with synchro mechanism, single chain, live axle, solid tyres, tiller steering. 1902/3, as above, but wheel steering and minor modifications.

1905 16 hp (R.A.C. 19) *Engine:*
2-cylinder, $4\frac{7}{8} \times 5$ in., S.V., L.T.
magneto ignition. *Transmission:*

Cone clutch, 3 speeds and reverse,
bevel-geared countershaft, side
chains, dead axle.

1909 24/30 hp (R.A.C. 28·8)
Engine: 4-cylinder, $4\frac{1}{4} \times 4\frac{1}{2}$ in., S.V.,

H.T. magneto ignition, otherwise as
for 16 hp but 4 speed gearbox.

Alda   see C.G.V.

Alldays and Onions   England

Messrs Alldays and Onions proudly trace the ancestry of their business back
to the mid-seventeenth century, and before they went in for motor cars they
were busy making pneumatic machinery in Birmingham.

Their first production model was the 'Traveller' sociable which could be
had with a large box for samples or a *vis-à-vis* front seat to choice. It was one
of the most satisfactory of the early rear-engined voiturette type of vehicle
despite the shortcoming of an unsprung rear axle. The single-cylinder 4-hp
engine had a water-cooled head and air-cooled barrel and drove through a
cone clutch and 2-speed sliding pinion gear; the first models had no reverse,
and a free-wheel mechanism in lieu of differential. Reverse gear for so light a
vehicle was something of a luxury at the beginning of the century, but the
luxury was fitted to the later examples of 1902/3.

A front-engined shaft-driven car with normally sprung back axle came out
in 1904. This was a straightforward contrivance with the then common
specification of single-cylinder engine (8 hp), automatic inlet valve, trembler
coil ignition, cone clutch and 3-speed gear. It went very well but nobody could
describe the single-cylinder Alldays as particularly refined in the manner of its
going. Whilst being conveyed on a 1904 model on the Brighton Run some
years ago, one of the authors was delighted to observe that his driver (who had
only previously driven the machine a few hundred yards) was obliged to
remove his top teeth as the car got into its stride: had he not done so, he said,
he would have lost the lot from vibration unless he kept his mouth shut the
whole way.

A 2-cylinder 10 hp model soon supplemented and then supplanted the
single; 4- and 6-cylinder models were also made later on. These, and the twins,
were notably smooth running and reliable. The 10 hp model, in particular,
had a very good reputation and stayed in production, in long or short chassis
form, from 1905 to 1913 inclusive. Many were supplied to the G.P.O. as vans
or service cars.

In addition to their private cars Alldays and Onions made chain-driven lorry and omnibus chassis. No startling technical innovation came from the firm before the Kaiser's war, and the interesting radial-engined Enfield–Allday lies outside our period.

1907 'Allday 8' 8 hp (R.A.C. 8·06)
Engine: 1-cylinder, 114 × 114 mm, S.V., coil ignition. *Transmission:* Cone clutch, 3 speeds and reverse, shaft, bevel-geared live axle.

1905 'Alldays No. 2' 10 hp   As above, but engine 2-cylinder, 95 × 114 mm.

1913 'Alldays Midget' 8/10 hp (R.A.C. 9·14)   *Engine:* 2-cylinder, 86 × 92 mm, S.V. (T-head), H.T. magneto ignition. *Transmission:* As above but worm-geared live axle. Also, 4-cylinder 'Midget' Bore and stroke 59 × 100 mm, otherwise as above.

1912/14 30/35 hp (R.A.C. 33·6)
Engine: 6-cylinder, 95 × 115 mm, S.V., H.T. magneto ignition. *Transmission:* as in 'Midget' but 4 speeds.

1904 single-cylinder 7 hp tonneau

1914 'Alldays Midget', 2-cylinder 10 hp

Argyll   Scotland

The Argyll story should be an 'Awful Warning' to all manufacturers who try to counter financial difficulties by introducing more and more new models. The first Argyll cars were indistinguishable from the first Renaults and it may very well be that Alexander Govan, having bought a Renault to copy, bought a few more to sell whilst organising his works—the Hozier Street Works of the Scottish Cycle Co. in Glasgow. This was in 1899, and by the end of 1900 the Hozier Engineering Co. were turning out a neat Renault-type voiturette, powered by a De Dion (or M.M.C. built-under-licence De Dion) 2¾ hp engine, and fitted with an ingenious 3-speed gearbox designed by Govan to avoid infringement of Renault patents.

In 1902 the Argyll models included an 8 hp car with De Dion or Simms engine (single cylinder), 10 and 12 hp twins with De Dion engines and 16 hp 4-cylinder cars with Aster engines.

Between 1902 and 1906 the Argyll concern climbed almost to the top of the automobile tree in Great Britain, production being even greater than that of Wolseley. Successful participation in trials of every kind earned valuable publicity, and the cars were well designed, beautifully finished and rigorously tested. The range comprised cars with $6\frac{1}{2}$ hp 1-cylinder Aster engines, 8 and 9 hp 1-cylinder De Dions, 11 hp 2-cylinder Clements, 14 hp 3-cylinder Argyll engines, and finally 10 hp 2-cylinder and 16 hp 4-cylinder models both with Aster engines. This frighteningly large range increased rather than diminished as time went on, with the addition of specially tuned and finished models, taxi-cabs and what-have-you. But up to 1907 business boomed and the firm prospered—enough to justify adding a fine Argyll-engined 24 hp 95×150 mm model capable of 60 mph.

Towards the end of 1904 an agreement was made with the French Aster Company to build Aster engines in the Argyll works, a splendid showroom and driving school was opened in London, a 35 per cent dividend was paid and the Company was re-formed with a capital of £500,000. Flushed with success Argylls spent £220,000 on a huge and positively palatial factory, complete with test-track and hill, at Alexandria. This was their undoing. Fine cars continued to be made, competition successes continued to be scored but the Marble Halls of Alexandria (well, terra-cotta brick actually) had been planned for a volume of business which could not be reached.

Alexander Govan died, aged 38, in May 1907 and the rifts in the Argyll lute became more apparent. The firm sank into liquidation in 1908 and was re-constructed at heavy loss to the shareholders with Alan Davidson as chief engineer and M. Perrot, formerly with Georges Richard-Brasier, as designer. Although an uneconomic number of models continued to be built some attempt at rationalisation was made in 1910/11 when the major components of six different models were largely interchangeable. It was in 1911 that 4-wheel brakes appeared on the 12 hp (72×120 mm) car. These were designed by J.M. Rubery who parted with his patent rights to Perrot for a derisory £200.

left 1902 single-cylinder 8 hp tonneau

right 1913 4-cylinder 12 hp tourer

Things seemed to be on the mend by 1912, though production was less than half the planned figure, when Argylls fell victim to the sleeve-valve mania and this, coupled with the Alexandria millstone, pulled them down again and the 10s. shares fell to 7½d. in 1914. This was a pity, for the Burt and McCullum single-sleeve Argyll engines were certainly more efficient than the Knight double-sleeve affair. The single sleeve had to make an exotic rumba-like motion, combining up-and-down with semi-rotary movements, which sounds complicated but worked admirably. Unfortunately the use of this engine for their larger models involved Argylls in litigation with the Knight patentees which cost them £50,000. This was the end; the huge factory was sold (at a huge loss) to the Admiralty and the dull stolid cars sold by a reorganised Argyll Co. from 1919 to 1931 had nothing but the name in common with their fine pre-war ancestors.

1900 2¾ hp (R.A.C. 3·03) *Engine:* De Dion Bouton, air-cooled barrel, water-cooled head, 1-cylinder, 74 × 76 mm, A.I.V., De Dion type coil ignition. *Transmission:* Cone clutch, 3 speeds and reverse, shaft, bevel-geared live axle.

1900 5 hp (R.A.C. 6·2) As above, but M.M.C. (De Dion Bouton type) engine 100 × 110 mm.

1905 10/12 hp (R.A.C. 11·2) *Engine:* Aster, 2-cylinder, 95 × 140 mm, S.V., trembler coil ignition. *Transmission:* Cone clutch, 3 speeds and reverse, shaft, bevel-geared live axle.

1911 15 hp (R.A.C. 15·84) *Engine:* Argyll, 4-cylinder, 80 × 120 mm, S.V., H.T. magneto ignition. *Transmission:* Cone clutch, 4 speeds and reverse, shaft, worm-geared live axle.

1913 25/50 hp (R.A.C. 24·8)
Engine: 4-cylinder, 100 × 130 mm,
Burt & McCullum single-sleeve
valves, H.T. magneto and coil

ignition. *Transmission:* Multi-disc
clutch, 4 speeds and reverse, shaft,
worm-geared live axle.

Ariel England

The Ariel Motor Company's first offering to the British public in recognizable
car form was produced in 1902. This was a 10 hp twin with automatic inlet
valves. The firm had, however, been active in the tricycle and quadricycle field
for some four years in the production of the ubiquitous De Dion powered
tricycle, in competition with such firms as Riley.

A 2-cylinder 10 hp water-cooled car, built on a tubular frame chassis, was
first produced in 1902. A unique feature was the design of their own float feed
carburettor. This carburettor is described as having no less than three inlets.
The first, situated near the exhaust pipe, brought in hot air, a secondary cold
air supply was regulated by means of a shutter, and yet a third, connected to
the dashboard, was for use at the highest speeds, being brought into action by
means of a second shutter. Presumably, for that little extra in acceleration,
one blew forcibly down the dashboard air supply. An optional four-speed
gearbox was also available.

A four-cylinder 16 hp car was also made at this time, in which the engine
sump supported the crankshaft main bearings. Alternatively paired exhaust
pipes were joined after separate expansion chambers.

In 1905 the company was reformed and production policy changed. The
range of cars produced expanded until in 1908 an 83·6 hp (R.A.C.) 6-cylinder
car was produced in company with cars of 31, 45, 55 and 66 R.A.C. hp. These
cars were based on continental chassis of the period, such as Mercedes, and
the marketing name changed to Ariel-Simplex.

By 1910 a range of smaller cars had been re-introduced. The 31 hp was listed for only one more year, giving way to a 25 hp, and a variety of smaller cars returned once again to twin-cylinder cars of 10 hp. An 8 hp was also listed for 1913.

1900 2¾ hp Tricycle *Engine:* single-cylinder, 74 × 76 mm, S.V. water-cooled head, automatic inlet, patent electric ignition. *Transmission:* direct drive via spur gears.

1912 25 hp (R.A.C. 24·8) *Engine:* 4-cylinder, 100 × 130 mm, S.V. Bosch Dual magneto ignition. *Transmission:* Leather cone clutch, four-speed gearbox, shaft, bevel-geared live axle.

Arnold England

Walter Arnold & Sons of East Peckham in Kent, Agricultural Engineers, imported a 1½ hp Benz in 1895. It was decided to build similar cars in their East Peckham factory, but before the work had gone very far it was also decided to improve upon the German design in various particulars—notably the not-unimportant particular of the engine which was completely re-designed with the object of having a better output than the bare 2 hp per litre of the original Benz design.

The firm was anxious to have an English-built car ready in time for the 'Emancipation' run in November, 1896, but time defeated them, and their

left 1900 single-cylinder 2¾ hp tricycle

right 1896 single-cylinder 1½ hp dog cart

Brighton entry was a hybrid with German chassis and transmission but an English engine. It was adorned with a most handsome cast-brass nameplate inscribed 'Arnold Petroleum Carriage, Benz's System'.

After building fewer than a dozen complete cars the concern found there was danger of the motor car business interfering too much with their normal affairs and they handed over their automobile interests to Henry Hewetson, who soon became the leading English agent for Benz cars. The Arnold, or, at least, *an* Arnold, earns a place in history by being, almost certainly, the first car in the world to be fitted with an electric starter; this was designed by H.J. Dowsing, and took the form of a large dynamotor coupled to the flywheel. It was intended to use this not only for starting but as a booster for steep hills and for propelling the car in traffic, or if the engine failed. This ambitious project was far ahead of battery design in 1896—or rather, a battery big enough to drive the Arnold would have been far too heavy for the Arnold to lug about.

Specification: As contemporary Benz (qv).

Arrol-Johnston   Scotland

Anybody who has had an opportunity to examine the singularly massive construction of an early Arrol-Johnston car will not be surprised to learn that the 'Arrol' part of this combination was Sir William Arrol, architect of the Forth Bridge. He and George Johnston joined forces in 1897 as the 'Mo-car Syndicate Ltd'. Their first production was a rugged, high-wheeled 'dog-cart' with the famous opposed piston engine. Even in 1899 this contrivance had an air of hippomobile antiquity, but it continued to sell quite well as late as 1906. The engine was placed transversely at the back of the chassis and was coupled via a cone clutch and Renold's silent chain to an enormous 4-speed gearbox from which a massive single central chain gave motion to a live axle of gargantuan proportions. The first few cars sold, *c*.1899/1900, had tiller steering and $5\frac{1}{2}$ hp single-cylinder double-piston engines, but wheel steering and 2-cylinder engines were soon standardised.

The horizontal engine had two cylinders, each of which contained two opposed pistons, coupled by short rods to rocking levers from which longer connecting rods gave motion to the crankshaft set below the cylinders. (This 'Scotch Motion', as it was called, has recently been revived for a 3-cylinder 2-stroke Diesel engine.) Low tension magneto ignition was used and the engine was started by hauling on a rope to which was attached a suitable handle. The rope passed through the floorboards beside the steering pillar, and was rewound upon its pulley, after each tug, by a spring. Presumably if the engine backfired the operator was yanked smartly through the floor and into the machinery. . . . With its 10 hp engine and weight of over 21 cwt, the dog-cart was not a startling performer but it was geared low enough to climb any hill— given time. A 12 hp (108×165 mm) engine was used after 1901 and this gave the sturdy, no-nonsense, go-anywhere machine a top speed of about 25 mph.

In 1905 the Company was re-formed as the New Arrol-Johnston Car Co. Ltd with Sir William Beardmore as Chairman. J.S. Napier came as chief engineer and though the original design was continued for another eighteen months he set about producing a conventional up-to-date motor car. Conventional, that is, as far as the chassis, multiplate clutch, shaft drive and so on were concerned, but unconventional in retaining the opposed piston engine, though this was now placed at the front instead of the back. The bore was increased to 121 mm and the peak output was 18 hp. The designer contrived to drive one of these cars into first place in the first Tourist Trophy Race, beating Percy Northey's 'light twenty' Rolls-Royce by a small margin. Had it not been for tyre trouble this triumph would almost certainly have been repeated in 1906.

In 1907 conventional 4-cylinder engines were used for two new models— 108×127 mm, curiously rated at 24/60, and 143×152 mm more reasonably described as a 38/45 hp. Both of these had the i.o.e. valve arrangement. The opposed piston engine made its last bow and the firm continued to race with honour if with no startling successes.

T.C. Pullinger, from Sunbeam, became General Manager in 1909 and under his aegis a new 15·9 hp appeared at that year's Show. This had 4-wheel brakes and a Renault-type dashboard radiator and bonnet. The front wheel brakes were dropped in 1911 when a fine 6-cylinder 25·8 hp came on the market supplemented by a little 11·9 4-cylinder car with the popular dimensions of 69×120 mm. No startling technical innovations were made, though some models were fitted with an anti-roll device of awe-inspiring complexity, and experiments were made with a petrol-electric car which was too heavy to drag itself about. Also, rather curiously, a battery-electric car was produced in 1912; this was not of the obsolete brougham type but a small coupé for the owner-driver.

1902 2-cylinder 12 hp dog cart

1901 10 hp (R.A.C. 14·45) *Engine:* Horizontal, transverse, rear, 2-cylinder, 4-piston $4\frac{1}{4}$ in. bore combined stroke $6\frac{3}{4}$ in., A.I.V., L.T. magneto ignition. *Transmission:* Primary Renold silent chain to cone clutch, 4 speeds and reverse gearbox and single roller chain to live axle.

1905/6 12/15 hp (T.T. Type) (R.A.C. 18·2) *Engine:* As above, but forward mounted. *Transmission:* Multiplate clutch, 4 speeds and reverse, shaft, bevel-geared live axle. (Bore increased by $\frac{1}{2}$ in. and stroke reduced by $\frac{1}{4}$ in.)

1911 11·9 hp (R.A.C. 11·8) *Engine:* 4-cylinder, 69 × 120 mm, S.V., H.T. magneto. *Transmission:* Plate clutch, 4 speeds and reverse, shaft, bevel-geared live axle.

1911 4-cylinder 11.9 hp tourer

1912 11·9 hp (R.A.C. 11·8) *Engine:* 4-cylinder, 69 × 120 mm, H.T. magneto ignition, thermo-syphon cooling. *Transmission:* metal-to- metal flat plate clutch, 4-speed gearbox, propeller shaft to bevel-geared live axle.

1912 23·9 hp (R.A.C. 23·9) *Engine:* 6-cylinder, 80 × 120 mm, otherwise as 4-cylinder models.

Austin

England

The original Austin-designed Wolseleys (qv), with their transverse horizontal engines, were undeniably very good cars within their limitations despite a chronic tendency to lubrication troubles, but as so often happens Herbert Austin let his love of his original design blind him to the merits of others. In 1902 for example, in the course of a lecture on transmission systems, he condemned the now-universal Renault system of jointed propellor-shaft and gear-driven live axle in the strongest terms. When he left Wolseleys and set up in business on his own, however, his business sense enabled him to come to terms with more up-to-date designs than his own.

Austin models from 1906 onwards therefore were unashamedly copied from other sources, and the similarity of, say, a 1907 Austin to a contemporary

Gladiator or Clément is marked. Indeed, for some while English Gladiator cars were made at the Austin factory and many of the models of Austin and Gladiator were identical except for the radiators and nameplates. On his own cars, with the exception of the 15 hp, Austin clung to the practice of using separate cylinders long after most of his contemporaries had abandoned the idea.

In addition to a wide range of touring cars from 10 hp to 50 hp Austin also built a number of racing cars. The 1908 Grand Prix car which survives has,

1910 4-cylinder Town Carriage,
15 hp

like the touring models, a strong flavour of Clément about it—and is none the worse for that.

For the 1910 season Austin took the, apparently, retrograde step of bringing out a single-cylinder runabout; but this was, in fact, a Swift and, following the Gladiator precedent, the 7 hp Swifts and Austins were both built in the Austin factory and indistinguishable except for the radiators and nameplates.

Unlike most manufacturers, Austins did nearly all their own body building, and many extremely practical and striking special bodies were evolved. Herbert Austin himself was responsible for most of these designs and they show that the originality he lacked as an engineer was amply compensated by his artistic sensibility as a coach-builder.

1907 25/30 hp (R.A.C. 32·4)
Engine: 4-cylinder, $4\frac{1}{2} \times 5$ in., S.V., H.T. magneto and coil ignition.

Transmission: Cone clutch, 4 speeds and reverse, bevel-geared countershaft, side chains, dead axle.

1910 15 hp (R.A.C. 19·6) *Engine:* 4-cylinder, $3\frac{1}{2} \times 4\frac{1}{2}$ in., S.V., H.T. magneto and coil ignition.

Transmission: Cone clutch, 4 speeds and reverse, shaft, bevel-geared live axle.

1911 7 hp (R.A.C. 6·85) *Engine:* 1-cylinder, 105×127 mm, S.V., H.T. magneto ignition (with coil

optional extra). *Transmission:* as 15 hp above but 3 speeds.

1912 50 hp (R.A.C. 45) *Engine:* 6-cylinder, 110 × 127 mm, S.V., H.T. magneto and coil ignition.

Transmission: As above, but 4 speeds.

1913 6-cylinder 50 hp enclosed-drive Austin landaulette

Austro-Daimler

Austria

In 1900 an Austrian offshoot of the Daimler Motoren Geselleschaft was set up at Wiener-Neustadt under the direction of Daimler's eldest son Paul.

Some purists insist that the cars were called Austrian Daimlers, not Austro-Daimlers and the cars were certainly sold in England by the Austrian Daimler Co. Ltd, but there is some confusion about nomenclature. Some of the cars were sold as 'Wiener-Neustadts', the name 'Osterreichisches-Mercedes'

1912 27/80 4-cylinder 'Prince Henry' tourer

(usually abbreviated to 'Ost-Mercedes') was also given to some models and for a long while the cars, particularly those exported to America, were simply called 'Maja' this being the name of Mercedes Jellinek's younger sister.

For the first few years the Austrian cars were very little different from those of the parent concern but after 1907, when Paul Daimler returned to Cannstatt and Ferdinand Porsche took over at Wiener-Neustadt, various changes became apparent. This particularly applies to the 'Prince Henry' Austro-Daimlers which were originally chain-driven but which, in shaft-driven form, were sold to the public. These had ohc engines of 105×165 mm, which were described as 27/80 hp, and it is said that this engine, with its inclined 'tulip' valves and hemispherical combustion chambers provided the inspiration for W.O. Bentley's original 3-litre engine.

1913 16/25 hp (Alpine) *Engine:* 4-cylinder, 80×110 mm, S.V., H.T. magneto. *Transmission:* Multidisc clutch, 4 speeds and reverse, shaft, bevel-geared live axle.

1913 20/30 hp (R.A.C. 20) As above, but cylinder dimensions 90×140 mm.

1913 27/80 hp 'Prince Henry' model *Engine:* 4-cylinder, 105×165 mm, O.H.C., dual ignition (2 H.T. magnetos). *Transmission:* As above.

Baker (Electric) America

Apart from a few runabouts imported from America at the beginning of the century, the electric car in England almost invariably took the form of a large closed 'town carriage' with an exposed box-seat for driver and footman. These are now always referred to as electric broughams though, in fact, all but a few were landaulettes.

In America the 'electric' often took the form of a small car designed for the owner-driver; the earliest examples, of which the Baker was one of the best known, closely resembled the contemporary gas- or steam-buggy type of vehicle.

Naturally, they were ideal for women drivers—safe, simple and silent—and in closed coupé form they were still being made in the late 'twenties. For the first few years of the century great things were promised for the new Edison battery which would, it was claimed, entirely overcome the snags of great weight and limited range and so make petrol and steam cars obsolete overnight. Perhaps it is not now too much of a heresy to say that the wizardry of the Wizard of Menlo Park was over-estimated, for the new Edison battery, when it did appear, did not greatly improve matters and the bugbear of limited radius on a charge was not overcome. In fact, the new nickel-iron battery was not much used for private cars.

A range of about fifty to sixty miles with a maximum speed of about 20–25 mph was usually claimed by electric car makers, but it was generally found, after a few months use, that the batteries could only be depended upon for about 25–30 miles, and consequently the electric car never developed beyond the point it had reached quite early.

The Baker Runabout was very well made and the designer clearly paid great attention to keeping weight down and avoiding friction; the typical buggy-type underframe has lancewood reach-bars (lighter even than steel tubes) and ball-bearings were used throughout. In addition to his bread and butter work Charles Baker made a gallant attempt on the land speed record with an electric vehicle of extremely interesting design. Inspired, perhaps, by the fact that the first road vehicle to exceed 60 miles an hour had been Jenatzy's cigar-shaped electric car 'La Jamais Contente', Baker designed and built, towards the end

left 1902 runabout two-seater

right 1900 single-cylinder 4 hp two-seater

of 1902, the first totally enclosed, aerodynamically correct racing 'shell' ever seen. In many ways it was about forty years ahead of its time, and it showed itself capable of well over 85 mph before disaster struck. As so often happens the crowd which had assembled to watch the attempt at the Staten Island track crowded on to the course before the run was over; to avoid ploughing into them Baker jammed on his brakes with such force as to lock the back wheels one of which collapsed under the strain. This, naturally, made nonsense of the official timing of the run.

1902 Runabout *Motor:* Elwell-Parker 1¼ hp (approx.) 4-pole compound/series wound: normally runs as compound wound but a foot switch diverts to series winding to give slight increase of speed on easy going. *Batteries:* Twelve 2-volt Exide cells in series, 70 ampère/-hours. *Controller:* 3-position and reversing switch; i.e. 3 speeds in either direction. 1st, resistance box in series; 2nd, half resistance in series; 3rd, resistance cut out. *Transmission:* Chain to live axle.

Bedford   see Buick

Bégot et Mazurie   France

It appears that Messrs Bégot et Cail were making voiturettes and tricars in 1901 and the Société Cail of Douai was in, or connected with, the motor business from 1904 to 1911. For a short while in 1900 Bégot et Mazurie cars were produced; it is believed that six were built of which, miraculously, one survives. It is one of many rather similar machines built in small batches by small engineering concerns, and it is nasty enough to explain why so few of these ventures prospered. The surviving specimen was known to one loving owner as the 'Bag o' Misery', but even so it is a great deal better than many and

has the rare feature, for that period, of an over-square engine. Even rarer, on so small a car, is a 4-speed gearbox—and one, moreover made of cast bronze tastefully decorated in the Art Nouveau manner with incised arabesquerie, entwined foliage, fleurs-de-lis, doves of peace and other charming incongruities, for the makers were brass founders as well as general engineers and would-be motor manufacturers.

1900 4 hp (R.A.C. 6·2) *Engine:* 1-cylinder, 100 × 95 mm, A.I.V., trembler coil ignition. *Transmission:* Cone clutch, 4 speeds and reverse, bevel-geared countershaft, side chains, dead axle.

Belsize   England

In 1899 Messrs Marshall & Co. of Belsize Works, Manchester, started building an Anglicised Hurtu which was, in its turn, a Gallicised Benz. The mechanical features were not much altered, though sundry details were improved and

Marshalls soon added a radiator to Benz's rather ineffective irrigation system with its primitive annular condenser: they also developed various new patterns of bodywork including, in 1900, a 'Doctor's Coupé' which must have afforded the driver less view of the road than any vehicle before or since.

In 1901 Marshalls began to produce more modern vehicles to which they gave the name Belsize—though the old belt-driven Marshall was not immediately dropped. The 1902, 12 hp shaft-cum-live-axle Belsize soon earned a good reputation; it was propelled by a 2-cylinder Buchet engine of 100 mm bore and stroke with mechanical inlet valves and well planned plumbing. M. Buchet had realised the virtues of unobstructed gas passages and high compression earlier than most of his contemporaries and many an early De Dion motor had been hotted up by the substitution of 'Culasse Buchet' for the original cylinder head.

Marshalls soon developed their own engines from the Buchet design and throughout the Edwardian period they produced notably efficient, fast-running motors which would not have seemed out-of-date in 1930. Most Belsize cars had shaft and live axle transmission but a 20 hp 3-cylinder model of 1903 had enclosed single chain drive to a live axle. This model, incidentally, anticipated Renault by a few months in having the radiator mounted on the dashboard. The 2- and 3-cylinder cars were soon followed by a 4-cylinder 40 hp and a magnificent 6-cylinder 60 hp. Not many of these were made and Belsize were best known for their small to medium cars in the 12 to 16 hp bracket, with their neat and advanced small 4-cylinder engines, shaft drive and, on late examples, worm- or bevel-geared final drive to choice.

An unusual feature, c.1906/7, was the use of a foot-operated pump on the dashboard to draw oil from the base-chamber and return it to the sight-feed lubricator tank—an early form of dry-sump lubrication in fact. Following on the tradition of the Marshall 'Doctor's Car' Belsize cars were much favoured by the medical profession and the firm specialised in those elegant sit-up-and-beg coupés into which the Edwardian practitioner fitted as appropriately as, in its turn, the wooden stethoscope fitted into his top hat.

left 1900 single-cylinder 5 hp 'Doctor's Car'

top right 1914 4-cylinder 10/12 hp two-seater

1899/1901, known as Marshall cars and generally similar to contemporary Benz models.

1902 12 hp (R.A.C. 12·4) *Engine:* Buchet, 2-cylinder, 100 × 100 mm, S.V. (M.O.I.V.), trembler coil ignition. *Transmission:* Cone clutch, 3 speeds and reverse, shaft, bevel-geared live axle.

1909 14/16 hp (R.A.C. 20) *Engine:* 4-cylinder, 90 × 120 mm, S.V., H.T. magneto ignition. *Transmission:* as above.

1912 10/12 hp (R.A.C. 11·8) *Engine:* 4-cylinder, 69 × 130 mm otherwise as for 14/16 above except for worm-geared final drive.

Benz   Germany

As is well known Carl Benz put a slow-running engine, little different from a stationary gas-engine, into a specially designed 3-wheeled chassis in 1885. Benz's car was by no means the first to be driven by an internal combustion engine, and many other people were working on the same lines at the same time, but it is usual to give him the credit for 'inventing' the petrol car, merely because he was the first man to sell workable motor cars, to a set pattern, to the ordinary public.

Until 1890/1 his cars were all 3-wheelers, like the first attempt, but with various improvements. The horizontal engine was placed at the back of a tubular frame with an exposed vertical crankshaft and a vast horizontal flywheel. Power developed was about $2\frac{1}{2}$ hp at 300 rpm, and this demoniacal energy was conveyed by a flat leather belt to a countershaft amidships where fast and loose pulleys acted as a clutch for starting, and a chain-and-sprocket reducing gear provided high or low speed. There was a fully sprung back axle, final drive by side chains, differential gear, mechanical slide inlet-valve, water-cooling from a small tank above the cylinder—(no radiator) and trembler-coil electric ignition. Maximum speed under very favourable conditions was about 12 mph.

The 1891 to 1901 4-wheeled cars were based on the original design and did not change much except in detail. A number of models were listed but all were basically the same: the engine varied from $1\frac{1}{2}$ to 10 hp, the latter being a twin-cylinder first produced in 1897. These engines were now made with smaller flywheels so they could be placed 'right side up' with crankshafts (still not enclosed) horizontal instead of vertical, and they could run up to a dizzy 600 rpm. Two pulleys of different sizes were fixed on the crankshaft and two belts plus two sets of fast-and-loose pulley mechanism looked after the 2-speed gearing.

Though undeniably rather primitive (by comparison with Panhard, Peugeot etc.) and painfully slow, these early Benz cars sold quite well because they were so simple and reliable; they were built under licence (or pirated) by many other firms. But by 1901 sales began to fall and half-hearted attempts were made to modernise the design—at least outwardly—but without much success. In 1902 sales dwindled right away and Julius Ganss (Financial and Sales Director) and Benz were at loggerheads, with Ganss insisting that a modern vertical-engined, shaft-driven live-axle car be built and Benz insisting on continuing with the slow-running engine and belt primary drive. This quarrel resulted in the extraordinary situation of Ganss calling in Marius Barbarou and a team of French engineers to produce a modern design alongside Benz, his sons, and a team of Germans who continued to build the older type.

Unfortunately the Benz-Parsival, as Barbarou's car was called, sold no better than the old type which was now little better than a laughing stock. Indeed, at this point in the story it is usual to point the finger at Carl Benz as an embattled old reactionary, which indeed he was, but he had the courage and good sense to go against his own principles and design an admirable 4-cylinder vertical engine. This was combined with a re-designed version of Barbarou's chassis (Barbarou in the meanwhile having returned to France), and the result was quite a good car which put the Company back on its feet by the end of 1904.

From this point onward the firm prospered, partly because their cars were good, and largely because they pursued an active and successful racing programme. Design lay largely in the hands of a brilliant engineer called Hans Nibel; in addition to a variety of touring and 'sports' models varying from 6 to 100 hp Nibel and his gang designed a series of fine racing cars including the

left 1893 1½ hp single-cylinder 'Velo'

right 1905/6 40 hp 4-cylinder tourer

fabulous 4-cylinder 200 hp 'Blitzen Benz'. Poor Carl Benz had to swallow his strong dislike of these goings on, which certainly brought home the bacon, and as late as 1914 he was often to be seen solemnly puttering about at 12 mph on one of his early horseless carriages.

The Benz range of models, and their list of racing honours, cannot be enumerated here. The later Benz cars were never so well known in England as the Mercedes against whom they so often fought; but they always won high praise in the motoring press, particularly for superb steering and road-holding—much superior to Mercedes said some critics. Unfortunately, in common with many German cars of the time, they were mostly rather ugly.

1888 1½ hp (R.A.C. 8·34) *Engine:* Horizontal, rear-mounted, vertical crankshaft, 1-cylinder, 116 × 160 mm, M.O.I.V. (slide valve), trembler coil ignition. Surface carburettor. *Transmission:* Primary, by leather belt, clutch action by belt on fast-and-loose pulleys, chain and sprocket 2-speed gear, final drive by side chains, dead axle.

1894 'Velo' 1½ hp (R.A.C. 7·5) *Engine:* As above, but crankshaft horizontal, 110 × 110 mm, A.I.V. *Transmission:* Primary drive and 2-speed mechanism by two belts and two sets fast-and-loose pulleys. Final drive as above.

1895/1900. Minor variations, i.e. 1897 onwards 110 × 110 mm engine called 3½ hp. Late 1898 some models fitted with third speed by 'crypto' epicyclic gear. Reverse available some models 1899. 4½ hp model similar to above with 115 × 110 mm engine, etc. Late 1899 onwards 4½ hp model fitted with single belt primary drive and 3-speed gearbox.

1900 10 hp (R.A.C. 17·8) *Engine:* As above but horizontally opposed, 2-cylinder, 120 × 120 mm. *Transmission:* As above, with crypto low speed and reverse.

E.24

1912 15/20 hp (R.A.C. 15·84)
Engine: 4-cylinder, 80 × 120 mm, S.V., dual ignition by H.T.

1914 100 hp *Engine:* 4-cylinder, 130 × 190 mm, O.H.V., dual ignition by H.T. magneto.

magnetos. *Transmission:* Cone clutch, 4 speeds and reverse, shaft, bevel-geared live axle.

Transmission: Cone clutch, 4 speeds and reverse, shaft, bevel-geared live axle.

Brasier   (Georges Richard-Brasier,   France
Richard-Brasier, Unic)

Georges Richard started by making Benz-type cars in 1897, and went on to building 1,000 of the little Belgian Vivinus voiturettes under licence in 1900/1. In 1902 something larger and more up-to-date than the Benz-style cars was demanded and vertical-engined cars on Panhard lines were produced to the designs of Brasier who had been responsible for the extremely successful Mors cars (both touring and racing) from 1899 to 1902. The first productions under the new régime had sliding-pinion gearboxes providing direct drive in top— one of the first recorded examples of the now universal system. They were called Georges Richard-Brasier, then Richard-Brasier and finally just Brasier cars, and they were turned out by the Société Anonyme des Anciens Etablissements Georges Richard which was soon re-named, less cumbrously, the Sté des Autos Brasier. Brasier cars were fine, high-quality machines which continued to distinguish themselves in racing throughout the Edwardian period, winning, amongst other events, the 1904 and 1905 Gordon Bennett Races. Georges Richard himself was more interested in the medium-powered, medium-priced car, and in 1904 Georges Richard et Cie became again a separate entity, which was in turn re-named the Sté Anon. des Autos 'Unic' a few months later when the first Unic cars came on the market. A one-model policy led to this nomenclature, and though the policy did not long survive, the name did. Georges Richard's financial and directorial interest in the Brasier cars continued.

To anyone of middle age or over the name Unic is inseparably connected with London taxis. Although there was a sprinkling of Rationals, Argylls and Napiers on the London streets the French contrived to dominate the taxi trade, and both in London and Paris Unic cabs predominated, with Renaults and Charrons as runners-up. The 12/14 hp Unic taxi, designed expressly to conform to Metropolitan Police regulations, remained in production with little alteration from 1908 to 1928. In contrast to the large 2-cylinder engine found in most Renault cabs it had a neat and advanced (for 1908) small 4-cylinder monobloc unit of 75 × 110 mm.

Private cars, very similar but with higher-geared back axles, were very popular as doctors' cars and were usually furnished with handsome coupé bodies: 10 and 16 hp models were made in addition to the 12/14.

There was nothing startling about the Unic machines—except their longevity which almost equalled that of the contemporary Renaults. Many Unic cabs were still able to pass the annual police inspection after twenty or twenty-five years of constant traffic work.

Brasier was a designer of great versatility and probably had more influence than he is given credit for. His influence certainly crossed the Atlantic, and the highly successful Thomas Flyer was a direct crib from the Richard-Brasier, for although Mr Thomas denied the rumours that he had imported French labour as well as French components he did admit to the use of Brasier parts as patterns.

right Georges Richard 1903 20 hp 4-cylinder Lonsdale Wagonette
right, below Unic 1913, 10/12 hp 4-cylinder Coupé

1900 Georges-Richard (before amalgamation) 3½ hp (R.A.C. 5·6)
Engine: Horizontal, transverse, rear-mounted, 1-cylinder, 95 × 100 mm, A.I.V., trembler coil ignition. *Transmission:* Similar to contemporary Benz.

1900/1 Georges-Richard 9 hp (R.A.C. 12·4) *Engine:* 2-cylinder, 100 × 110 mm, A.I.V., trembler coil ignition. *Transmission:* Cone clutch, 4 speeds and reverse, bevel-geared countershaft, side chains, dead axle.

1908 Brasier (or Richard-Brasier) 10/12 hp (R.A.C. 10) *Engine:* 2-cylinder, 90 × 120 mm, S.V., H.T.

magneto ignition. *Transmission:* Cone clutch, 3 speeds and reverse, shaft, bevel-geared live axle.

1914 Brasier 24 hp (R.A.C. 30·1)
Engine: 6-cylinder, 90 × 140 mm otherwise as above but 4 speeds.

1912 Unic (or Georges Richard-Unic) 12/16 hp (R.A.C. 13·9)
Engine: 4-cylinder, 75 × 120 mm, S.V., H.T. magneto ignition.

Transmission: Cone clutch, 4 speeds and reverse, shaft, bevel-geared live axle.

1912 Unic 10/12 hp 65 × 110 mm
and
Unic 12/14 hp 75 × 110 mm
(Commonly used for taxi chassis)
specification of these, apart from
dimensions of engines, as for 12/16
above. In production 1908 onwards
little altered. Some models 3 speeds
only.

Brooke
England

East Anglia is not generally thought of as an industrial area yet many fine engineering works are established there, and one of the best known, J.W. Brooke and Co. Ltd of Lowestoft, added motor car manufacture to their other activities in 1900.

Three-cylinder engines with mechanical inlet valves were used for the firm's 12/14 hp models of 1902/3, and transmission was via an unusual all-chain gearbox on the principle re-introduced by Maudslays some years later. These early models had transverse horizontal engines, but by 1904 Brookes realised opinion was hardening against such things and brought out new vertical, longitudinal engined 3-cylinder cars with the chain gearboxes refangled to suit the new layout. The 3-cylinder cars were soon supplemented by 15 and 20 hp 4-cylinder models and Brookes were not far behind Napier in producing admirable 6-cylinder machines (indeed, they produced a 6-cylinder boat engine some months before the first 6-cylinder Napier appeared), but as they had no Edge to push them they never became very well known. In any case motor cars were only a side line to the firm's general and marine engineering, output was always small and ceased altogether in 1913.

Brooke cars had very deeply dished steering wheels, Napier fashion, and on their early models the rim and the boss were connected not by spokes but by a sheet metal pressing. This resulted in a sort of basin a-top the steering column which, said the makers, afforded a convenient receptacle for the driver's gloves, tobacco pouch or what-have-you: from contemporary photographs, however, it does look as though Messrs Brooke feared their clients might be overcome with nausea at any moment.

1903 14 hp 3-cylinder limousine

1904 20 hp (R.A.C. 21·4) *Engine:* 4-cylinder, $3\frac{5}{8} \times 4\frac{3}{4}$ in., S.V. (T-head) M.O.I.V., L.T. magneto ignition. *Transmission:* Cone clutch, shaft to bevel-geared cross shaft in gearbox, chain and sprocket 3 speed and reverse mechanism (speeds engaged by dog-clutches) then by spur gears to countershaft, side chains and dead axle.

1913 40 hp (R.A.C. 43·5) *Engine:* 6-cylinder, 108×120 mm, S.V., dual ignition. *Transmission:* Disc clutch, 4 speeds and reverse, shaft, bevel-geared live axle.

Brotherhood   see Sheffield-Simplex

Brush Runabout   America

Like most other aspects of motor car design suspension by coil springs is not particularly new; indeed, it certainly goes back to the middle 'nineties when the belt-driven Cannstatt-Daimlers had coil springs at the back between underframe and body—the rear axle itself being unsprung. Various other early efforts had coil springing, notably the first production Vauxhalls of *c.* 1903. There was also the American-sounding Brushmobile which was very Vauxhall-like in many ways for the excellent reason that many of its components were made by the Vauxhall concern.

There was no connection between the Brushmobile and the cars made by the Brush Runabout Co. of Detroit except that these also had coil springs—but with a difference. On the American Brush the springs were in tension whereas all other makers used them in compression. The argument was that springs generally break on the rebound and that, with them normally in tension, they would merely be passing through a neutral phase on rebound and consequently less likely to break. Even more bizarre was the use of wooden axles. This is not so impossible as it sounds for the Brush Runabout had final drive by side chains and therefore the back axle was dead. Both axles, there-

1910 10 hp single-cylinder two-seater

37

fore, were made of maple spars with suitable metal extremities to carry the steering heads, hubs, sprockets, etc. The arrangement seems to have worked admirably though a modern motor mechanic might be nonplussed by a complaint of furniture beetle in the back axle.

The Brush Runabout also had the faint eccentricity of an anticlockwise engine—single cylinder vertical—with an ingenious counter-rotating balancing device on the lines of the Lanchester harmonic balancer. As with so many American cars of the time performance was sacrificed to ease of driving by the use of a 2-speed epicyclic gear, but if this drawback be disregarded the Brush must be seen as a refreshingly original and wholly successful production.

As an example of the sort of thing that makes the authors reach for the bottle, *The Autocar* buyers' guide and the makers' catalogue disagree about the engine dimensions of the Brush. Assuming that the makers knew best (which is by no means always the case) the specification stands as follows:

1910 10 hp (R.A.C. 6·4) *Engine:* 1-cylinder, 4 × 5 in., S.V., coil ignition. *Transmission:* 2 speeds and reverse epicyclic, all gears actuated by multidisc clutches, bevel-geared countershaft, side chains, dead axle.

B.S.A. England

It is extremely doubtful whether the private car business of the English Daimler Company ever operated at a profit for long enough on end to offset their more usual losses. As, at one time, they listed no fewer than eighteen

1913 13.9 hp 4-cylinder torpedo tourer

models in a single year this is hardly surprising, and during one of the many financial re-organisations the equity was acquired by the Birmingham Small Arms Co. Ltd.

B.S.A. cars, which were made from 1907 to 1926 and again from 1933/36 (4-wheelers that is, the tricars were made by a different offshoot), were virtually scaled-down Daimlers. This particularly applies to the sleeve-valve B.S.A.s of 1911 onwards which were very Daimlerish in all but name, size, shape of radiator and in having transverse back springs. They were also apt to be light and lively where their more costly stable mates were ponderous and slow. The Company began making pressed steel bodies for their cars in 1912 and they were, almost certainly, first in the field with this innovation.

An intriguing ramification of the Daimler-B.S.A. affair was their affiliation with the Stoneleigh concern. In the 'twenties Stoneleigh was known to be a subsidiary of Armstrong-Siddeley and produced a V-twin light car, but the rare and little known Edwardian Stoneleighs are identical with Daimler-B.S.A.s except for radiators and name plates. All this doubtless came about on the well-known big-business principle that if you make a big enough loss you will have no difficulty in borrowing enough extra capital to extend your business so as to make a bigger and better loss.

1910 15/20 (R.A.C. 20) *Engine:* 4-cylinder, 90 × 120 mm, S.V., H.T. magneto ignition. *Transmission:* Cone clutch, 3 speeds and reverse (4 speeds on Colonial Model), shaft, worm-geared live axle.

1912 13·9 hp (R.A.C. 13·9) *Engine:* Daimler-Knight, 4-cylinder, 75 × 114 mm, double-sleeve valves, H.T. magneto ignition. *Transmission:* Cone clutch, shaft to 3 speeds and reverse gearbox integral with worm-geared live axle. (Unusual features: single transverse rear spring, no transmission brake—both hand and foot brakes on rear wheels, pressed steel body.)

Bugatti   France

There are a good many gaps in the early history of Ettore Bugatti, and a great many hotly contested opinions about the inspired genius and/or obstinate perversity of his designs. But there was never anything dull about the man himself or the motor cars he made. As it would be impossible to do justice to his work in the available space it is fortunate for the authors that he belongs more to the 'vintage' period than to the pre-1914 era.

Apart from experimental and one-off efforts made before he was seventeen, Bugatti's first work as a designer was on behalf of the De Dietrich concern (qv). Bugatti-designed De Dietrichs were listed alongside Turcat-Méry De Dietrichs until 1905 in which year Bugatti entered into an agreement with Mathis, then concessionaire for F.I.A.T. cars in France. This collaboration produced the Hermes[1] cars of 40, 90 and 120 hp which displayed several features in embryo which later appeared in the Type 13—the first model to

[1] Not to be confused with the Hermes cars built by the Autocar Construction Co. of Manchester.

be made under Bugatti's own name. Very few Hermes cars were built, but the *marque* won distinction in the Kaiserpreis and other events and was offered on the English market as the 'Burlington'.

In 1906/7 Bugatti designed an advanced ohc 4-cylinder car for the Deutz Motorenfabrik—the successors to the Otto and Langen gas-engine concern for whom Daimler had designed the first commercially successful 4-stroke engine in 1876. Amongst other typical features the Deutz had Bugatti's plate clutch in which the first-intention engagement is by means of a fairly weak spring (giving very light pedal action) and extra pressure to make the clutch hold is provided by centrifugal force as the speed rises. The whole concept of the engine was greatly in advance of its time, and the beautifully neat ohc valve gear, compact magneto and water pump drives, internal manifolding and clean cut architectural appearance were all in marked contrast to most contemporary engines with their exposed valve mechanism, tortuous external piping and untidy chain or belt drives running hither and yon to water pump or lubricator tank. But with all his neatness Bugatti perversely designed his engine so that the lower halves of front and rear main bearings came away with the sump—an indefensible arrangement.

1913 5-litre 25 hp 4-cylinder sports two-seater (Black Bess)

In addition to the Hermes and the Deutz it is apparent that the 1909 Type S.61 Fiat was largely Bugatti's work and his responsibility for the astonishing little 62 × 100 mm 4-cylinder Isotta-Fraschini, which made its bow at the 1908 Grand Prix des Voiturettes, is well known. There is also a belief that the Chalmers Motor Co. of Detroit built to Bugatti's designs, and even after he had started making cars under his own name he sold a new design of light car to Peugeot in 1911. This, the Bébé Peugeot (qv), incidentally gives the lie to the devout Bugattisti who claim that all Ettore's motor cars had impeccable steering and road-holding.

It was not until late 1909 that Bugatti established his own small works at Molsheim and began production under his own name. The first model, the famous Type 13, had a high speed ohc 4-cylinder engine of 1·4 litres capacity in a very light, very rigid chassis and five cars were built in 1910. In 1911 production rose to 75 (one of which took second place in the Grand Prix de France) and in the same year the 2·8 litre straight-eight was produced by the wholly unmechanical but wholly successful expedient of coupling two 4-cylinder engines back to back. This formed the basis for the small, fast revving straight-eights so particularly associated with the name of Bugatti. In addition to these two models (and variations), a few 5-litre, 4-cylinder, chain-driven cars were also produced *c.* 1913/14: these derived from the Hermes and Deutz types of some six or seven years earlier.

As an artist Bugatti left his hall-mark on everything he did: as an inspired but empirical engineer his designs were frequently 'impossible' and confounded his critics by working a great deal better than they had any right to do—rather on the lines of the bumble-bee which has been proved incapable of flight by aerodynamic experts.

1910 Type 13 10 hp (R.A.C. 10·45)
Engine: 4-cylinder, 65 × 100 mm, O.H.C., H.T. magneto ignition.

Transmission: Semi-centrifugal plate clutch, 4 speeds and reverse, shaft-bevel-geared live axle.

1914 1.3 litre 4-cylinder sports three-seater

1913 5-litre (R.A.C. 24·8 hp, maker's rating 25 hp, output 100 hp)
Engine: 4-cylinder, 100 × 160 mm, O.H.C., 2 exhaust valves, 1 inlet per cylinder, H.T. magneto ignition.
Transmission: Clutch as above, 4 speeds and reverse, bevel-geared countershaft, side chains, dead axle. The characteristic reversed quarter-elliptic rear springs appear on the 5-litre model (pre-1913 Type 13s had semi-elliptics).

Buick (Bedford) America

David Buick, of Scottish descent and formerly of Buick and Sherwood, Plumbers' Furnishers, began to make motor cars in 1903, and his first efforts were not unlike most contemporary American horizontal-engined cars except that, like the Winton, they were sturdier than most and powered by very large engines. The first Buick model had a 2-cylinder engine, with overhead valves, rated at 22 hp. In 1904 the Buick concern was re-financed and revitalised to the tune of $1,500,000 by William Durant and an improved 22 hp twin went into series production.

In 1906 David Buick left the firm he had founded and the first 4-cylinder vertical-engine cars were made; this does not seem to have been cause and effect but William Durant was busy building up a large combine—soon to be famous as General Motors—and as is so often the way Buick's face did not fit. The original Model D 4-cylinder had a nearly square engine of $4\frac{1}{4} \times 4\frac{1}{2}$ in. rated at 30 hp, and it was supplemented in 1908 by a 45 hp of 5×5 in. The twin cylinder model was continued until quite late and the firm did not produce a 6-cylinder until 1914.

In 1909/10 General Motors started a subsidiary Company at Bedford Works, Long Acre and Willesden, and assembled there the 15/18 hp and the very popular 18/22 hp model with 4 in. bore and stroke. These English-built cars were sold as Bedfords or Bedford-Buicks.

Both the American and the English Buicks had ohv engines, but though advanced in this one respect, they were otherwise curiously old-fashioned in design with more-than-ordinarily tortuous gas passages and totally exposed push-rod and rocker mechanism lubricated only by oil-can and grease-cup.

The transmission, suspension and brakes conformed to the common American practice with the propellor shaft enclosed in a torque tube, bevel drive to a Hyatt roller bearing live axle and full-elliptic back springs. Most American makers after about 1907 eschewed the European-style transmission foot-brake, and Buicks conformed to this wise custom by having the foot brake working by internal expanding shoes inside the rear-wheel drums whilst the hand lever controlled contracting band brakes acting outside the drums. This system certainly relieved the universal joints and final drive gear of stress but had the failing, again shared by many other American makes, that the drums were so thin that it was necessary to use both hand and foot brakes simultaneously to avoid distortion.

1911 Bedford 18/22 25 hp
4-cylinder tourer

1906 Model F. 22 hp (R.A.C. 16·1)
Engine: Horizontally opposed, transverse, centrally mounted, 2-cylinder, $4\frac{1}{2} \times 5$ in., M.O.I.V., coil ignition. *Transmission:* 2 speeds and reverse epicyclic gear. Clutch action for low speed and reverse by contracting brakes on epicyclic gear drums, for high speed by disc clutch, single chain to live axle.

1909 15/20 hp (R.A.C. 22·4)
Engine: 4-cylinder, 95×95 mm, O.H.V., H.T. magneto and coil ignition. *Transmission:* Pedal controlled, 2 speeds and reverse epicyclic. Clutches: for low speed and reverse, by contracting bands on epicyclic gear drums, high speed by cone. Shaft, bevel-geared live axle.

1911 Bedford 18/22 (R.A.C. 25·8)
Engine: 4-cylinder, 102×102 mm, pump cooled, magneto and H.T., coil ignition. *Transmission:* Leather cone clutch, 3-speed gearbox, shaft-driven bevel-gear rear axle.

1913 15/18 hp (R.A.C. 22·4)
(English assembled 'Bedford' model) *Engine:* As above but only magneto ignition. *Transmission:* Cone clutch, 3 speeds and reverse, shaft, bevel-geared live axle.

Cadillac
America

Henry M. Leland started his engineering career as a toolmaker with Brown & Sharpe, and by the beginning of this century he was in partnership with Falconer doing general machining work. Amongst other things they were employed to make engines for Ransom E. Olds to use in his Oldsmobiles; these were so satisfactory that Leland decided to make complete motor cars. The prototype was built in 1902 but the new Cadillac Motor Car Co. was not really under way until 1903.

The first model was based on the Oldsmobile—the archtype of the early American gas-buggy—except that the full length springs were not used, and the Oldsmobile's convex curved dash and tiller steering were replaced by wheel steering, and a concave dash with the radiator built into it. Otherwise the formula was much the same and included a horizontal slow-running engine (1-cylinder, 5×5 in., $6\frac{1}{2}$ hp) mounted amidships, epicyclic low-speed and reverse, direct-drive on 'high', final drive by central chain to a divided live axle. As with all similar cars driving was very simple. The lever to tighten the band brake to start the car from rest on the low speed also controlled the direct drive clutch and no co-ordination of clutch pedal and gear lever was needed. Top-speed was about 25 mph and the low gear gave about 5 mph.

From 1904 onwards Cadillacs were fitted with dummy bonnets and bigger engines, but no major alterations were made and nobody could pretend they were notably fine examples of the engineer's art. The engines were inefficient, in terms of specific output, and the 2-speed gear restricted performance, but the cars had one great virtue which is too easily overlooked. They worked, and went on working. They were furnished with generously dimensioned engines and kept as light as possible, so that they could do most of their running on the high gear. In this, as with so many of their compatriots, the example of the Yankee mass-production clock and watch industry was followed; the famous Waterbury watch for example had a main-spring eight feet long and therefore had no option but to go.

Cadillacs brought out their first 4-cylinder car in 1905. This was on conventional European lines with a distinctive feature in that it had separately cast cylinders with spun copper water jackets. The single cylinder model was still being made in 1908 and the Cadillac Company won the Dewar Trophy in that year when the English concessionaire, F.S. Bennett, entered three 10 hp cars for a standardisation test under R.A.C. observation. The test consisted in having the cars completely dismantled, the parts 'scrambled', and the cars were then rebuilt from the assorted bits and given a 500 mile non-stop run on Brooklands track.

In 1912 the firm fitted electric starting and lighting sets as standard equipment—the first concern in the world to do so. Their next venture was a V-eight engined car in 1915, which is often claimed to be the first V-eight to be marketed, though this seems a little hard on De Dion Bouton, Rolls-Royce and a few more. But another innovation of two years earlier had not been done before and passed relatively unnoticed. This was an electrically-controlled overdrive in the form of a 2-speed back axle giving ratios of 2·5:1 or 3·66:1 at will. This was fitted to the standard 20/30 hp car which was also equipped with an electric heater for warming the carburettor on cold mornings. At £472 for the fully equipped 5-seater this car was good value.

1906 9/10 hp single-cylinder two-seater

1903 6½ hp (R.A.C. 10) *Engine:* Leland & Falconer, horizontal, transverse, amidships, 1-cylinder, 5 × 5 in., M.O.I.V., trembler coil ignition. *Transmission:* 2 speeds and reverse epicyclic. Clutches: for low and reverse by contracting bands on epicyclic gear drums, high speed by single plate clutch, single chain, live axle.

1912 20/30 hp (R.A.C. 32·4) *Engine:* 4-cylinder, 4½ × 4½ in., S.V., coil ignition. *Transmission:* Cone clutch, 3 speeds and reverse, shaft, bevel-geared live axle.
1913 as 1912 but with 2-speed rear axle making six forward speeds.

Cannstatt-Daimler   see Daimler

C.G.V.   (Charron, Alda)   France

Fernand Charron was a well-known French bicycle racing champion who became one of the world's first racing car drivers. From 1895 he and Giradot (also a former bicyclist) drove for Panhard et Levassor in most of the principal events. They opened an agency for Panhard cars in 1897 and made a lot of money, then, in 1900, with financial help from Emile Voigt, also a Panhard racing driver, they set up a factory at Puteaux and started building motor cars.

The first C.G.V. appeared in 1901; it was a 15 hp 4-cylinder car with an unusually low centre of gravity by 1901 standards. A 20 hp model soon followed with separate steel cylinders and sheet brass water jackets; an arrangement which remained a C.G.V. characteristic for some years. The chassis was of steel, reinforced with wood, in contradistinction to the more

1905 C.G.V. 25 hp 4-cylinder tourer

usual wood frame reinforced with steel. Various other models were made later on including a very sound 8 hp 2-cylinder live axle car—the larger models had chain drive.

In 1902 C.G.V. embarked upon that *ignis fatuus* of the early motoring scene —a gearless car. Their effort took the form of a straight-eight-cylinder model rated at 40 hp. This was the first real straight-eight in the world; that is, it was designed as such and did not consist, as other early efforts did, of two 4-cylinder engines coupled. It was a T-head engine with mechanical inlet valves, and the cranks were angled at 45°. Drive was direct from expanding clutch to bevel-geared countershaft and then by the usual side chains. The car was not a success, largely because 1902 carburation and ignition systems could not cope with an 8-cylinder engine, but it was a stout effort.

In 1905 the partnership broke up and Charron sold manufacturing rights to a new English company, Charron Ltd, which produced cars and taxi-cabs for the English market. These ranged from the 8 hp twin up to 75/90 racing cars—the latter were most probably imported complete from France where the original company, now re-constituted, also made Charron cars. The Renault type of dashboard radiator was adopted and both French- and English-built Charrons were practically indistinguishable from Renaults at first glance. As late as 1936 a few pre-Kaiser-War Charron taxis were still running on the London streets though, in their last years, they were outwardly modernised by new bonnets and dummy forward-mounted radiators. Except that a few of the 1912 cars were fitted with the Lentz automatic-hydraulic transmission (of a type that has just been re-invented for the umpteenth time), there was nothing startling about the Edwardian Charrons; indeed they were rather old-fashioned in many ways, but they were pleasant to drive and very reliable. A 1912 15 hp coupé was used daily by half the authors between 1947 and 1953.

For a short while after selling out of C.G.V., Fernand Charron managed the Clément-Bayard works for his father-in-law, Adolphe Clément, but this did not last long. In 1913 he started a new works at Courbevoie where cars called Aldas were built until 1928. These were very similar to the contemporary Charrons except for a peculiar arrangement of double transverse rear springs which was said to provide the ability to corner fast without rolling.

1906 C.G.V. 20 hp (R.A.C. 30 hp)
Engine: 4-cylinder, 110 × 130 mm, S.V. (T-head), H.T. magneto and coil ignition. *Transmission:* Cone clutch, 4 speeds and reverse, bevel-geared countershaft, side chains, dead-axle.

1910 Charron 50 hp (R.A.C. 48·6)
As above but engine 140 × 160 mm.

1912 Charron 15 hp (R.A.C. 15·8)
Engine: 4-cylinder, 80 × 120 mm,
S.V. (L-head), H.T. magneto
ignition. *Transmission:* Cone clutch,
3 speeds and reverse, shaft, bevel-
geared live axle.
(The above chassis used in great
numbers for taxi work in London
and Paris. Available with 4-speed
gearbox for £20 extra.)

1912 Charron 15.8 hp 4-cylinder
drophead coupé

1914 Alda 15/38 hp (R.A.C. 17·9)
Specification identical with 15 hp
Charron and many parts
interchangeable, but engine
dimensions 85 × 140 mm and rear-
suspension Alda double transverse.

Chadwick   America

Gottlieb Daimler's first design of 'high-speed' petrol engine specified a valve
in the piston crown the object of which was to allow the air compressed in the
crankcase to pass into the cylinder at the end of the firing stroke to help with
scavenging the exhaust gases. This arrangement, which was probably never
actually used anyway, has often been referred to as a form of supercharging
—which it was not. It has also been said that some of Renault's racing engines
of *c.* 1903 were supercharged—which they were not. This statement originates
from the translation of a biography of Louis Renault by a translator who
seems to have had little knowledge of French and less still of motor engines.

In all probability the first motor designer to use a supercharger was Lee
Chadwick in 1907. This was done as a desperate measure to improve the
performance of a new 6-cylinder engine, the porting and manifolding of which
were so bad that the engine's output was less than that of its 4-cylinder predecessor of similar dimensions. The engine was soon re-designed so as to
perform well without boosting and although not very many Chadwick cars
were made and none, apparently, were exported, the Chadwick soon became
one of the finest of America's pre-1914 makes. The Company was founded in
1905, according to Doyle, though Lee Chadwick may have made a few 'one
off' motors before then. Four-cylinder cars of 24 and 40 hp were made up to
1906/7, and were then superseded by the Great Chadwick Six, which was a
4-speed, chain-driven car made to the very highest standards regardless of
expense—$5,500 was the basic price. Though great in both senses, the car was

said to be far lighter to handle than most large machines of the period. A sporting version, capable of 100 mph, came out in 1908.

Unfortunately, as so often happens with perfectionists, Chadwick's cars were unprofitable. Though they were undeniably good value for money the sort of customer ready to spend between $5,000 and $9,000 on a motor car was apt to buy an imported European or English one for snob-value. Chadwick's insistence on doing most of his foundry work and component manufacture himself (instead of 'buying out' as most American manufacturers did) ensured a fine product but made it difficult, on such small scale production, to reduce costs and the Company went into liquidation in 1914 though production did not cease until 1916.

1907 60 hp 6-cylinder tourer

1906 45/50 hp (R.A.C. 39·9)
Engine: 4-cylinder, 5 × 6 in., S.V. (T-head), H.T. magneto ignition with coil stand-by. *Transmission:*

Cone clutch, Mors-type gearbox with two pairs of bevel gears to countershaft, side chains, dead axle.

1907 60 hp (R.A.C. 59·9) *Engine:* 6-cylinder, 5 × 6 in., S.V. (T-head), H.T. magneto and coil ignition.

Transmission: Cone clutch, 4 speeds and reverse, bevel-geared countershaft, side chains, dead axle.

Charron   see C.G.V.

Chenard et Walcker   France

Although Messrs Chenard et Walcker began dabbling in the motor business in 1897, chiefly with the production of engines and components, their cars were not very well known until after the turn of the century. Apart from their better-than-average workmanship and finish their unique final drive system, to which they remained faithful for many years, makes them of interest.

The Chenard and Walcker arrangement comprised a normal propellor shaft and a cranked 'dead' back axle on which was mounted an aluminium housing containing the bevel gears and differential: these gave motion to a pair of half shafts which carried at their extremities small pinions meshing with internally toothed drums (which served also as brake drums) on the back wheels. The merit of the system was that the final drive reduction was divided into two stages, therefore the bevel gears could be more nearly equal in size than is usually the case (to the benefit of longevity and silence), and the driving shafts were relieved of much torsional strain. It is for this reason that a variant of the arrangement, with geared-down wheel hubs, has recently been adopted for some heavy duty goods vehicles.

Apart from their final drive, which the firm saw no reason to alter in sub-

1903 14 hp 2-cylinder tonneau

stance for some thirty years, the early Chenard cars were fairly conventional, though the system of throttling used in the early days was interesting and scientifically sound. Mechanical inlet valves were used in a T-head and c. 1901/4 they were furnished with ingenious mechanisms which allowed the duration of opening to be varied (to control engine speed) but left the *degree* of opening unaltered. This worked well, but was found to be unnecessary with the improved automatic carburettors which became available later on.

Chenard et Walcker were chiefly concerned with medium sized cars—2- and 4-cylinder mostly—though a single cylinder 9 hp (100 × 120 mm) model was still listed in 1911 and a 6-cylinder was offered in 1913/14. They did not figure much in racing until after the war, but many credits and successes were scored in reliability runs, hill-climbs, and fuel consumption trials.

1902/3 14 hp (R.A.C. 12·4) *Engine:* 2-cylinder, 100 × 120 mm, S.V. (T-head, variable-duration M.O.I.V.), trembler coil ignition. *Transmission:* Double cone clutch, 4 speeds and reverse, shaft, bevel gear, dead axle, final drive spur gears to internally toothed drums. (The rear conical face of the clutch also served as a transmission foot brake by being brought against a fixed conical brake ring.)

1913 16/20 hp (R.A.C. 15·9)
Engine: 4-cylinder, 80 × 150 mm,
S.V., dual ignition from H.T.

magneto. *Transmission:* As above,
but normal cone clutch and
separate transmission brake.

Clément (Clément-Bayard, Clément-Gladiator, Clément-Panhard, Clément-Talbot) France

Any hope that the ramifications of Adolphe Clément's connections with the automobile industry can be dealt with in 300 words, without at least one major boob, is a vain one indeed.

He started making bicycles in a tiny workshop in Paris in 1878 and did well. In the 'nineties he acquired the French patent rights in the Dunlop tyre and did even better. With part of his fortune he bought a large holding in the Gladiator concern, which was an Anglo-French company formed to develop and expand Alexandre Darracq's 'Gladiator' bicycle-building business (in which Clément had originally had a part anyway). Before 1900, this firm started making motor-tricycles, quadricycles and voiturettes under the name of Gladiator or Clément-Gladiator, and most of these were propelled by Aster engines supplied by another concern in which M. Clément had a large interest. He was also responsible, between December 1899 and 1903, for building under licence from Panhard et Levassor a rear-engined voiturette called the Clément-Panhard, except in England where it was named the Stirling, Stirling-Panhard or Clément-Stirling. It was, incidentally, designed by Commandant Krebs, a director of Panhard et Levassor, who took the curiously retrograde step of using a centrally pivoted front axle.

Towards the end of 1901 Clément began producing conventional front-engined Panhard-type cars (probably designed by Marius Barbarou, who was afterwards with Benz and Delaunay-Belleville), which were most successful. Racing Clément cars took part in the Paris–Vienna, the Paris–Madrid and other events. Gladiator cars, also front-engined now, were also selling well

1903 Clément 9/11 hp 2-cylinder tonneau

and an offshoot of the business was started in England.

The English concessionaire for Clément cars was D.M. Weigel who organised a syndicate, financed by the Earl of Shrewsbury and Talbot, which set up a magnificent factory at Ladbroke Grove to build Clément cars for the English market. This happened in 1903 and at first the cars were practically identical with French-built Cléments and were called Clément-Talbots. Thereafter the 'Clément' was gradually dropped from the name and Talbot cars developed along slightly different lines.

1903 Clément-Talbot 18 hp
4-cylinder tonneau

Another British concern called the Clement Motor Co. Ltd was formed to buy the manufacturing rights of the French Clément cars, and a factory was in operation by 1907 in Coventry, building British Clément cars. This company claimed, incidentally, to have sold their entire year's output at the 1909 Motor Show.

By 1909 the English Gladiator cars were being built in the Austin Company's factory at Birmingham (in which old man Clément appears to have had an interest), and apart from the radiators the 15 hp, 18/24 hp, 40 hp and 60 hp English Gladiators were identical with Austin models of similar rating. Both the Gladiators and the Austins differed only from French-built Clément-Gladiators in being slightly more expensive.

Having sold manufacturing rights in so many different quarters Adolphe Clément undertook not to build motor cars under his own name and consequently he set up yet another business and the cars produced were called Bayards or Bayard-Cléments or Clément-Bayards (the last being the commonest form in England). The later examples were easily distinguished from Clément-Gladiators, British Cléments, and so on because they had Renault type bonnets and radiators.

All of these makes earned good reputations, and it will not surprise the poor long-suffering reader to learn that M. Clément was never short of the price of coffee. Fortunately the Clément-Rochelle need not concern us as it did not appear until 1927, but was not there an early tricar called a Clément-Garrard ...? And what about the Diatto-Clément or Clediaber?

1899 Clément-Panhard 3½ hp (R.A.C. 5)   *Engine:* Transverse, inclined, rear, 1-cylinder, 90 × 120 mm, A.I.V. (i.o.e.), hot-tube ignition. *Transmission:* Cone clutch, 3 speeds, no reverse, constant mesh gears engaged by sliding keys, spur gears to countershaft, side chains, dead axle. (Reverse gear fitted 1900.)

1903 Clément 9 hp (R.A.C. 8·96) *Engine:* 2-cylinder, 85 × 120 mm, S.V., L.T. magneto ignition with o/head camshaft for igniter operation. *Transmission:* Expanding clutch, 3 speeds and reverse, shaft, bevel-geared live axle.

1903 Clément-Talbot (or Talbot, nomenclature varied) 27 hp (R.A.C. 30) *Engine:* 4-cylinder, 110 × 130 mm, M.O.I.V. (i.o.e.), L.T. magneto. *Transmission:* Coil clutch, 4 speeds and reverse, bevel-geared countershaft, side chains, dead axle. (The coil clutch was used only on early models: later examples had cone clutches.)

1911 Clément-Bayard 15 hp (R.A.C. 18·2)   *Engine:* 6-cylinder, 70 × 110 mm, S.V., H.T. magneto ignition. *Transmission:* Cone clutch, 3 speeds and reverse, shaft, bevel-geared live axle.

1913 Clément-Bayard 8 hp
4-cylinder two-seater

Clyde   England

The Clyde Motor Co. of Leicester (1899/1930) was one of that large band of small-production, workaday concerns who had nothing to do with racing, whose advertisements were few and modest, who never became widely known but whose customers remained loyal to them for the best of reasons—they were given value for money.

Transverse engines with silent chain primary drive to the gearbox, which was integral with the live back axle, formed the basis of the Clyde design. De Dion or Aster single- and twin-cylinder units were used at first, and Clydes remained faithful to transverse engines and chain transmission throughout the pre-war period. The very short and squat White and Poppe engines of *c.* 1906 onwards, were very well suited to the Clyde layout and made it possible to provide plenty of passenger space on a short wheel-base. White and Poppe-powered models which continued unchanged for some years included an

8/10 hp twin, 12/14 hp 3-cylinder and 16/20 hp 4-cylinder: all three had the same bore and stroke.

The founder of the firm, G.H. Wait, still drove an early model Clyde quite frequently when he was nearer ninety than eighty, and the car was well past the half-century mark.

1907 12/14 hp (R.A.C. 11·68)
Engine: White & Poppe, vertical, transverse, 3-cylinder, 80 × 90 mm, S.V. (T-head), coil ignition.
Transmission: Silent chain to cone clutch and 3 speeds and reverse constant mesh gear integral with live back axle. Gear engagement by dog clutches. Final drive by spur gear from layshaft to differential.

1907 12/14 hp 3-cylinder tourer

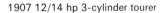

Coventry-Daimler   see Daimler

Crossley   England

It was very right and proper that Crossleys of Manchester should go into the motor car business—for they were one of the oldest exponents of internal combustion engines in this country and the first English company to build the new-fangled 4-stroke engine under licence from Otto & Langen of Deutz. Gottlieb Daimler himself worked at Crossleys for a short time during his sojourn in England in 1862, and acted as consultant later on when they began making engines to his design.

J.S. Critchley, who had been with Daimlers during the early Lawson period, went to Crossley as car designer in 1902 and his first model, a 22 hp 4-cylinder, came out late in 1903; apart from the engine this model was largely composed of imported parts, and it was soon supplemented by a similar 28 hp car. By 1906 a 40 hp had been added to the range, and though this was clearly derived from the contemporary F.I.A.T. the construction was English throughout. The engine was a conventional T-headed affair of 121 × 150 mm and great things were claimed for the suspension—the rear springs were no less than four feet long.

Messrs Charles Jarrott and Letts looked after the sale sides of Crossley's motor business, and Jarrot himself became to Crossleys much as Edge became to Napiers. He had, indeed, started his motor career under Lawson's rather murky shade, as Edge did, and had shared many early motoring adventures with his more notorious contemporary. However, he soon found the Edge-Ducros set-up distasteful and broke away to become concessionaire, first for De Dietrich and Oldsmobile cars then, with Letts, for Crossleys; consequently he found himself in opposition to his former playmate. As the Crossley Company never made anything but 4-cylinder cars until 1925 Jarrott, on their behalf, became hotly embroiled in Edge's six versus four controversy.

From 1906 to 1910 the 20 hp and 40 hp models were the firm's mainstay, but thereafter the 20 was re-vamped into the extremely popular 20/25, the 40 hp was dropped and new 12 and 15 hp models were introduced.

The 15 hp, though primarily designed as an owner-driver's touring car (beautifully planned, as all Crossleys were for easy maintenance and adjustment), soon showed itself to be an above-average performer. In mildly hotted-up form it achieved fame as the Shelsley Crossley following success in the Shelsley Walsh Hill Climb. The L-head sv engine of 80×130 mm (against the 120 mm stroke of the standard 15 hp), was given high-lift cams and matched with an excellent 4-speed gearbox to make one of the pleasantest sports-touring cars of the pre-war era. This model, and the 25 hp, formed the basis for the famous R.F.C. tenders which did such stout work during the Kaiser's war—and for long afterwards, too, for one of them was still hard at work as a greengrocer's hack in Derby as late as 1954.

1909 40 hp (R.A.C. 36·3) *Engine:* 4-cylinder, $4\frac{3}{4} \times 6$ in., S.V. (T-head), L.T. magneto ignition (or coil and/or H.T. magneto optional). *Transmission:* Expanding clutch, 4 speeds and reverse, shaft, bevel-geared live axle.

(Cone clutch instead of expanding on late 1909 and subsequent models: two transmission foot brakes were fitted to 40 hp Crossley 1906/9 and could be fitted for water cooling if desired.)

1914 20/25 4-cylinder R.F.C. tourer

**1914 15 hp 'Shelsley Crossley'
(R.A.C. 15·84)**   *Engine:* 4-cylinder,
80 × 130 mm, S.V., H.T. magneto
ignition (dual ignition optional).

1914 20/25 (R.A.C. 25·8)   *Engine:*
4-cylinder, 102 × 140 mm, S.V. 4½
litres, H.T. magneto, Smiths
carburettor, pressure fed, thermo-
syphon cooling (pump added to

Transmission: Cone clutch, 4 speeds
and reverse, shaft, bevel-geared live
axle.

R.F.C. cars), forced lubrication.
Transmission: cone clutch, 4-speed
gearbox with reverse, bevel-drive
live axle.

Daimler   (Cannstatt-Daimler)   Germany

The 4-stroke engine was first brought to commercial success by Gottlieb
Daimler in 1876 when he was Technical Director of the Otto and Langen Gas
Engine Works. The modern car engine is the direct offspring of Daimler's
'high speed' liquid-fuel engine which he patented in 1885; yet the first Daimler
cars to be sold to the public were the work of one Max Schrödter who became
chief engineer of the Daimler Motoren Gesellschaft (founded 1890), when
internal dissensions caused Daimler and Maybach, his right hand man, to
resign from the company soon after it was founded. Schrödter's design was
based upon one of Daimler's experimental carriages of 1889.

This vehicle was a serviceable but uninspired horseless carriage, with an
archaic centre-pivoted front axle, and belt-and-pulley 4-speed transmission
from a rear-mounted 2-cylinder engine. With certain improvements, but no
fundamental change, this type remained in production until 1899; it sold quite
well as it was reliable and quiet though lamentably slow. Being frightened by
French competition the Directors swallowed their pride and recalled Daimler
and Maybach late in 1894, and during the next six years a number of much
improved cars were designed and produced under Daimler's supervision. Most
of the detail work was done by Wilhelm Maybach.

1895 4 hp 2-cylinder Victoria

The new models included a $5\frac{1}{2}$ hp front-engined 'Victoria' in 1897/8, with wheel-controlled Ackermann steering, and transmission on Panhard-Levassor lines. This model had hot-tube ignition (an early Daimler patent) and a selective or 'gate' gear control on the lines previously used by Daimler on his early belt-driven carriages. A greatly improved 8/9 hp model followed the $5\frac{1}{2}$ hp and one of the innovations was the Simms low-tension magneto ignition, though hot-tubes were still fitted as standby. The famous 'honeycomb' radiator, which, like the 'gate' gear control, was hailed as something new on the Mercedes of 1901, was used on the 1898 models and had, indeed, appeared on at least one car in 1894, if the evidence of an exhibit in the Daimler-Benz museum at Untertürkheim is to be believed.

A number of different sizes and types of motor vehicles, varying from 4 to 10 hp were made in 1898—including the old belt-driven model. Daimler's sons and Maybach talked him out of his dislike of racing, and a specially-built 6 hp 'racing' car did well in the Austrian Trials in 1899. Paul Daimler was chiefly responsible for this effort, and also for a new model, the P.D., which had a transverse forward-mounted 6 hp engine in unit with the gearbox, an inclined steering column and a very respectable performance.

The last car to be designed during Daimler's lifetime (he died in March 1900) was the famous 24 hp 4-cylinder model produced late in 1899 and intended to beat the French manufacturers at their own game. This car had the largest engine used up to that time. The 5,515 cc 'Phoenix' unit had cylinders of 106×156 mm, automatic inlet valves and low-tension ignition. It developed about 28 bhp at its governed speed of 800 rpm at which pace the car was geared to run at 46 mph. With the governor cut out a maximum of about 53 mph could be attained by a sufficiently brave man. For the car was tricky to handle (though half the authors has found it far less dangerous than it was made out to be) and on Emile Jellinek's urging the need for something equally fast but less cumbersome Maybach redesigned it.

The result was the Mercedes which surely deserves a separate entry!

1899/1900 24 hp 4-cylinder two-seater

1894/9 Cannstatt-Daimler 4 hp (R.A.C. 10)   *Engine:* Vertical transverse, rear-mounted, 2-cylinder, 90 × 120 mm, A.I.V. overhead exhaust valves rocker operated, hot-tube ignition. *Transmission:* 4 speeds, no reverse, by four pairs of pulleys and leather belts to countershaft. Clutch action by jockey pulleys, final drive from countershaft by spur pinions to internally toothed gear rings on back wheels. Rear axle unsprung, centre-pivot steering.
(Some later models had 90 × 130 mm engines.)

1899 Cannstatt-Daimler 24 hp (R.A.C. 27·9)   *Engine:* 4-cylinder, 106 × 156 mm, A.I.V., L.T. magneto ignition. *Transmission:* Cone clutch, 4 speeds and reverse, bevel-geared countershaft, side chains, dead axle. (The first selective or 'gate' change speed control system was used on the Cannstatt-Daimler belt-driven cars and was perpetuated on the later gear-driven models. The 'honeycomb' or marine condenser type of radiator also first appeared on the belt-driven models of *c.* 1898.)

Daimler   (Coventry-Daimler)   England

That remarkable financial adventurer, Harry J. Lawson, floated the English Daimler Motor Co. in January 1896. It was intended to be the foundation stone for his projected 'Empire' to control the whole motor industry in England. The Company shared with his other concerns many financial crises.

Pre-1914 Daimler cars fall, broadly, into three categories. Those of the Lawsonian era were fairly straightforward copies of the contemporary nineteenth century Panhard-Levassors; very well made but of much greater weight and lesser performance than the French originals. The engines were Cannstatt-Daimler types and many of the first Coventry cars were almost certainly fitted with German-built engines. Twin-cylinder 4 hp models (later called 6 hp) were built from early 1897 onwards and a 12 hp 4-cylinder model appeared in 1899. Critchley was the engineer chiefly responsible for production, and Gottlieb Daimler himself was made a Director but took no part in the concern.

Sales declined during 1900/2, largely because performance of the cars would not stand comparison with those of other makes, and the Company was embroiled, anyway, in the disintegration of Lawson's schemes. The Company was re-formed in 1903, Percy Martin, an American, became Managing Director, and a variety of 4- and 6-cylinder chain-driven cars were produced under the auspices of an almost equally great variety of designers of whom, perhaps, George Iden was the most notable. During this period the famous finned radiator became the Daimler hall-mark. The cars of this period were lively performers and did well in numerous trials, hill-climbs, etc., but they were not particularly refined in the manner of their going. Frederick Lanchester was called in as Consulting Engineer, primarily to solve the problem of crankshaft failures on the 6-cylinder models (a failing which he cured by inventing the Lanchester crankshaft vibration-damper now so widely used), and he induced the Company to adopt live-axle transmission, using the Lanchester worm-gear, in place of the noisy side chains.

right 1898 4 hp 2-cylinder wagonette

below 1907 60 hp 4-cylinder tourer

The next era was that of sleeve-valvery—Daimlers being the first of many firms to succumb to that once fashionable disease. Lanchester was primarily responsible for making the ingenious Knight double-sleeve-valve engine a practical success though he never approved of it himself. After 1909 Daimlers produced only sleeve-valve cars and a bewildering variety of models—too many to enumerate—were made.

Many of the later Daimler models—*c.* 1912 onwards—had the change-speed mechanism built into the back axles. This practice became quite fashionable and was adopted by many firms who, like Daimler, had squawked loudly only a few years earlier about the undesirable unsprung weight of the live axle. Daimlers were often fitted with lofty and heavy closed bodies which contrived always to look older-fashioned than they were; they were extremely refined, quiet, smoke-belching, costly, complicated and slow. They secured a virtual monopoly of the 'Dowager Trade' and as the cars never wore out, many were sold out of private service into the undertaking business. The majority of people who rode in Daimlers, therefore, only did so after they were dead.

1897 Coventry-Daimler 4 hp (R.A.C. 10) (The 'Coventry' was generally dropped from the name from 1900 when the Cannstatt-Daimlers became known as 'Mercedes'.) *Engine:* Phoenix Daimler type. Probably imported from Germany, possibly made in England. 2-cylinder, 90 × 120 mm, A.I.V., hot-tube ignition. *Transmission:* Cone clutch, 4 speeds forward, 4 speeds reverse (reversing gear on countershaft), bevel-geared countershaft, side chains, dead axle. Tiller steering.

1905 30 hp (R.A.C. 38·75) *Engine:* 4-cylinder, 125 × 150 mm, S.V., trembler coil ignition. *Transmission:* Cone clutch, 4 speeds and reverse, bevel-geared countershaft, side chains, dead axle.

1913 30 hp (R.A.C. 30) *Engine:* Knight type, 6-cylinder, 90 × 130 mm, double sleeve valve, H.T. magneto and coil ignition. *Transmission:* Cone clutch, 4 speeds and reverse, shaft, worm-geared live axle.

1910 38 hp 4-cylinder sleeve-valve tourer

Darracq

France

Alexandre Darracq sold out of his bicycle business in 1896 with a nice fortune which he invested partly in the bicycle-component industry, and partly in developing horseless carriages. After rather tentative and unsuccessful ventures with electric vehicles and a motor bicycle with a 5-cylinder radial engine in the back wheel he began production, in 1898, of a 5-speed, horizontal-engined, belt-driven car designed by Léon Bollée.

This, like most Bollée designs, was quite an effective machine, but by the end of 1899 Darracq realised that the future lay with the vertical-engined gear-driven car and late 1900 saw the first 6½ hp single cylinder shaft-driven Darracq, which was soon followed by 8 and 9 hp singles, 9 and 12 hp twins and, in 1902, a 4-cylinder 20 hp model. This had a pressed steel frame—the earlier, smaller cars having had either tubular or reinforced wooden chassis. By 1903 one of Darracq's most talked-of innovations had appeared. This was a most remarkable piece of presswork and comprised a complete chassis (all but the rearmost cross-member), of deep-section side girders, upswept over the rear axle, complete with transverse struts and a deep under-shield-cum-engine-bearer all pressed from one piece. In varying dimensions this served for a range of models. Other distinguishing features of pre-1905 Darracqs were mechanical inlet valves, L-head engines, steering-column gear levers and well-designed live axles with tubular torque rods.

The 12 hp twin and the 4-cylinder 'Flying Fifteen' were particularly sought after, and the Darracq flair was not confined to touring cars. In their racing machines, Darracqs cut the weight-to-engine-capacity ratio to very fine limits: the 1905 *Circuit des Ardennes* cars, for example, came within the 750 kilos limit but sported 150×140 mm 4-cylinder engines rated at 80 hp, whilst the 200 hp V-8 Darracq with which Hémery captured the Land Speed Record of 109·65 mph later in 1905 weighed only 32 cwt.

1903 12 hp 2-cylinder double phaeton

Throughout the Edwardian period Darracq design was as up to date as any, and in 1912/13, when the sleeve-valve fever was at its height, 15, 16 and 20 hp 'valveless' cars were made under Henriod's patents. These had a rotary 'distributor', or multiple cylindrical plug valve (something like that of a Corliss steam engine) rotating horizontally at combustion chamber level. A feature of the design was that the rotating valve was arranged to be masked by the piston at the moment of combustion: this avoided overheating the valve and its bearings but, as critics pointed out, this delayed the start of induction until the piston had travelled some way down the cylinder. However, the arrangement seems to have worked well, but like most rotary valve engines it was not in production very long and it is probable that the advantages of silence were bought at the expense of high maintenance costs. Some of the rotary valve Darracqs had Renault-style dashboard radiators and all had worm-gear final drive.

1899 5 hp (R.A.C. 5·02) *Engine:* Léon Bollée, horizontal, transverse, air-cooled, forward-mounted, 1-cylinder, 90 × 148 mm,[1] A.I.V., hot-tube ignition. (Trembler coil on late models.) *Transmission:* 5 speeds by single belt and stepped pulleys on engine-shaft and countershaft, then by cone clutch and spur gears to live rear axle. Epicyclic reversing gear in flywheel.

1904 15 hp (R.A.C. 20) *Engine:* 4-cylinder, 90 × 120 mm, S.V., trembler coil ignition. *Transmission:* Cone clutch, 3 speeds and reverse, shaft, bevel-geared live axle.

1912 20 hp (R.A.C. 22·4) *Engine:* 4-cylinder, 95 × 140 mm, Rotary valve, H.T. magneto ignition. *Transmission:* Cone clutch, 4 speeds and reverse, shaft, worm-geared live axle.

1911 15 hp 4-cylinder tourer

1914 16 hp (R.A.C. 17·9) *Engine:* 4-cylinder, 85 × 130 mm, S.V., H.T. magneto ignition. *Transmission:* As for rotary valve model above.

Deasy   see Wolseley

Decauville   France

A 1902 10 hp 2-cylinder Decauville car owned by F.H. Royce did not satisfy him and he set about making something better. Hence the Rolls-Royce, and hence also the assertions of most Rolls-Royce historians that all cars of the

[1] Engine dimensions not definitely verified but conjectured from contemporary reports; De Saunier gives 108 × 140 mm for 5 hp model.

time were horrible, coarse, noisy, unreliable contraptions, that the Decauville was amongst the worst and that Royce's Decauville gave him a lot of trouble. All of which is a little unfair, because perfection itself was scarcely good enough for Royce, and much of the 'trouble' with his car arose when he was experimenting with different carburation and ignition systems. The first Royce cars were very Decauville-like, and is there not something about imitation being the sincerest form of flattery . . .?

The Société .Decauville, locomotive engineers, started making light voiturettes in 1898. Only they called them 'voiturelles' in deference to Léon Bollée who,at that time, claimed proprietory rights in the name 'voiturette'. They were very light tubular-framed machines with rear-mounted 2-cylinder air-cooled engines—virtually two $1\frac{3}{4}$ hp De Dion tricycle engines coupled—driving by cone clutch to an exposed 2-speed gear mechanism and then by exposed crown wheel and pinion on the unsprung rear axle. All of which sounds pretty crude but which worked far better than it had any right to; the exposed gearing gave no trouble. As if to make up for the unsprung back axle, the Decauville had independent front wheel suspension of the sliding pillar and transverse spring variety. It was the first production car to have this refinement, the merits of which passed entirely unnoticed at that time. These little cars did quite well in trials. A 5 hp water-cooled version of the 'voiturelle', came out in 1899 and towards the end of 1900, 8 hp front-engined shaft-driven cars were produced as well; one of these covered 1,000 miles without engine stoppage at the Crystal Palace. For 1902 the rear-engined model was discontinued and a 10 hp twin cylinder substituted; it was on this type that the Royce was modelled.

A Decauville innovation which was copied by Royce and, soon after, by many leading firms was the 'fully floating' axle in which the driving wheel bearings are carried on the axle casing and the driving shafts take none of the weight.

A 30 hp 4-cylinder Decauville did well in the Paris–Madrid and averaged 53·9 mph, but after that time less was heard of the make in competition. Thereafter the firm made a variety of straight-forward, well-engineered cars until 1911.

1901/2 10 hp 2-cylinder tonneau

1898 3½ hp (R.A.C. 5·4) *Engine:* Vertical, air-cooled, rear-mounted, own make but possibly some De Dion Bouton components. 2-cylinder, 66 × 76 mm, A.I.V., trembler coil ignition. *Transmission:* Cone clutch, 2 speeds, no reverse, exposed change speed gears, final drive by exposed bevel gears on unsprung live axle. Independent front suspension.

1901/2 10 hp (R.A.C. 15) *Engine:* 2-cylinder, 110 × 110 mm, S.V., A.I.V., trembler coil ignition. *Transmission:* Cone clutch, 4 speeds and reverse, shaft, bevel-geared live axle.

De Dietrich (Lorraine-Dietrich) Franco/German

That great industrial organisation the Société Lorraine des Anciens Etablissements de Dietrich et Cie. turned their attention to the motor business in 1897 when the Baron Adrian de Turckheim bought the right to build to the designs of Amédée Bollée *fils*.

The Amédée Bollée machines were rather heavy but quite effective twin cylinder (horizontal, transverse) affairs with primary belt drive to a Panhard-type gearbox and final drive from a transverse counter-shaft by two longitudinal jointed propeller shafts with spiral-bevel gears at either end. This eccentric arrangement (which is of interest as being the first recorded example of spiral bevels for motor car work) allowed for the use of dished wheels, on canted axle-ends, in carriage fashion, but the frictional losses must have been prodigious and normal side-chain transmission soon supplanted the side-shafts. The De Dietrich-Bollée cars sold quite well and the designer's boat-shaped racing *torpilleurs* caused great excitement; a wonderfully elaborate closed carriage was built for the Empress of Russia in 1899, in which year an advanced machine was designed and built both at the Bollée works and by De Dietrich. This had an extremely rigid steel chassis, underslung below the rear axle, independent front suspension and a monobloc 4-cylinder horizontal engine with two carburettors.

1902 16 hp 4-cylinder two-seater
(De Dietrich/Turcat Méry)

Late in 1899 the firm started building belt-driven voiturettes under licence from Vivinus of Brussels, and shortly afterwards they added to their range front-engined cars designed by Turcat-Méry of Marseilles. These were of fairly conventional form (except that the early models had 5-speed gearboxes), having been born, as it were, by Peugeot out of Panhard-Levassor.

De Dietrich cars began to be well known in England in 1902, by which time the Bollée design had been dropped, when Charles Jarrot and Letts became concessionaires following the successful, though not spectacular, participation of a new 16 hp model in the Paris–Vienna race. This type, a Turcat-Méry design, sold well as a touring car—for which, indeed, it was designed; apart from L.T. magneto ignition it was very similar to the contemporary Panhard-Levassor. Both in touring and racing-car classes the firm took part in racing for many years.

1909 Lorraine-Dietrich 40 hp 4-cylinder tourer

De Dietrich cars were listed in 1903/4 to the designs of both Turcat-Méry and Bugatti; the former being of 16 and 24 hp, and the latter 24/28 and 30/35 hp. Unfortunately little is known of the Bugatti De Dietrichs, but a letter to *The Autocar* from a satisfied user gives a valuable clue by remarking upon the excellent performance and economy but the unnecessary complication of dismantling for adjustment—the Patron was running true to form even then.

For the middle period De Dietrich cars remained much as Turcat-Méry and Bugatti had left them; that is they were fast, reliable and slightly old-fashioned chain-driven cars. Shaft-drive was not adopted until 1909 and then only on the smaller models, but a system of compressed-air starting was available on some from 1907.

By 1912 the name had been changed to Lorraine-Dietrich and a new 21 hp model was subjected in that year to an R.A.C. observed 7,000 miles test, during which its average speed was kept down to the legal 20 mph and its consumption was 19·95 mpg which worked out at a commendable 37·14 ton-miles-per-gallon. But its consumption of ten pints of gear and axle oil might occasion a little eye-brow raising today.

1902 De Dietrich (Turcat-Méry system) 16 hp (R.A.C. 26·85)
Engine: 4-cylinder, 104 × 120 mm (A.I.V.), L.T. magneto ignition.

Transmission: Cone clutch, 4 speeds and reverse, bevel-geared countershaft, side chains, dead axle.

1909 Lorraine-Dietrich 20 hp (R.A.C. 30) *Engine:* 4-cylinder, 110 × 130 mm, S.V. (T-head), L.T.

magneto ignition. *Transmission:* Multidisc clutch, 4 speeds and reverse, shaft, bevel-geared live axle.

1914 Lorraine-Dietrich 40/75 hp (R.A.C. 38·8) *Engine:* 4-cylinder, 125 × 170 mm, S.V., H.T. magneto

and coil ignition. *Transmission:* Cone clutch, 4 speeds and reverse, shaft, bevel-geared live axle.

De Dion Bouton   France

That vast, aristocratic, picturesque and rumbustious ornament of Parisian Society, the Count de Dion, employed Messrs Bouton and Trépardoux (brothers-in-law and jobbing engineers in a small way of business) in 1882 to work full time on his project of building light steam carriages. Later on a partnership was formed and for a dozen years a bewildering variety of practical and efficient steamers was produced. The first vehicle home in the first real motoring event in the world—The Paris–Rouen Trial in 1894—was a De Dion high-speed steam tractor drawing a landau. Before this, however, de Dion had decided that the petrol engine was more suited than steam for light pleasure vehicles and he and Georges Bouton began experiments in 1891. M. Trépardoux was horrified and predicted bankruptcy. By 1895 the first $\frac{1}{2}$ hp engines were in production followed soon after by more powerful types. M. Trépardoux would have none of it and left the firm.

De Dion Steamer, Count De Dion Driving (1888)

1900/1 $4\frac{1}{2}$ hp single-cylinder voiturette

The significance of de Dion and Bouton's early work is that they carried Daimler's principle a logical step forward by making the first really high-speed engines, which ran at 1,500 rpm normal speed, and were capable of 3,000 rpm without bursting, against the 700–900 rpm of the Daimler. To achieve this entailed much lighter reciprocating parts, machining to fine limits and the invention of a new form of electric ignition able to function at high speed. The result was that by 1896 De Dion engines were developing 7 hp per litre which was more than twice the output of the contemporary Daimler and nearly four times greater than the Benz. De Dion and Bouton immediately began producing motor tricycles (which soon became all the rage) and supplying engines in quantity to other firms. Between about 1898 and 1908 more than 100 different makes of bicycle, tricycle, quadricycle, tricar, fore-car and light car proper in Europe, England and America were powered by De Dion Bouton engines.

The first 4-wheeled De Dion voiturette came on the market in 1899, and was a neat 2¾ hp 3-seater *vis-à-vis* with the engine at the back (air-cooled barrel and water-cooled head) driving via an ingenious 2-speed gear to an unsprung back axle. Not many of these were made and in a few months a vastly improved 3½ hp (fully water-cooled) version came out with the famous 'De Dion axle' (used ten years before on the steamers and probably designed by Trépardoux), in which the final drive and differential unit is rigidly attached to the chassis and drive is transmitted by independent, universally-jointed half shafts; the wheels being carried on a light tubular 'dead' axle mounted on springs in the usual way. The clever 2-speed gear was retained: the gears were always in mesh and each pair was brought into action as wanted by expanding clutches —one for each speed—controlled by a steering-column gear lever without the

1910 14 hp 4-cylinder tourer

need for a separate foot operated clutch. A faster 4½ hp model soon appeared and a 6 hp in 1902. These admirable machines sold like hot cakes, and many survive to refute the wiseacres who said the high-speed De Dion Bouton engines could not possibly last.

An 8 hp front-engined car came out for the 1902 season, then a 6 hp, and the rear-engined voiturettes were discontinued in 1903. The 8 hp model was given a 3-speed version of the 'easy change' gearbox and could climb any gradient on which the wheels would grip. A 10 hp 2-cylinder was introduced for 1904 and this had the important innovation of pressure lubrication. In 1906 a new 8 hp single appeared with a pressed steel chassis, sliding-pinion 3-speed gears, plate clutch and mechanical inlet valve in place of the original automatic valve. For this car a new pattern radiator and bonnet was evolved, but the older type, tubular-framed, expanding-clutch car remained in production until 1909. Four-cylinder models were made from 1904 onwards, in various sizes and they were as good and popular as the singles and twins. From about 1909 the firm gradually gave up their final drive system (thinking it rather old-fashioned) in favour of normal live axles which they made of quite unnecessary weight. In 1910 they brought out three sizes of V-eight engines for their larger cars. Many writers have said these were bad engines (though without saying why), but one half of the pair of present writers says they were very good engines; he bases his assertion on experience of a much-neglected 25-year-old specimen used in a large motor boat.

The firm did not participate much in racing officially after 1900, though they did enter two 3-litre 4-cylinder cars in the Paris–Madrid, but they built many special engines for other firms to use. To the great regret of many no more single-cylinder De Dions were made after 1912. Many thousands of motorists the world over owe thanks to the ingenuity of Georges Bouton and the shrewdness of Count de Dion (Marquis after 1901) for their first taste of cheap and reliable road transport.

1899/1900 3½ hp (R.A.C. 3·96)
Engine: Vertical, transverse, rear-mounted, 1-cylinder, 80 × 80 mm, A.I.V., coil ignition. *Transmission:* 2 speeds, no reverse, constant mesh gears, brought into action by separate expanding clutches. Final drive by spur gear to differential carrier thence by independent cardan shafts to rear wheels carried on tubular dead axle.
(The rear-engined De Dions were continued until 1903 being fitted with 4½ and finally 6 hp engines. Reverse gear optional on later models.)

1904 8 hp (R.A.C. 6·2) *Engine:* 1-cylinder, 100 × 120 mm, A.I.V., coil ignition. *Transmission:* Shaft to 3 speeds and reverse constant mesh gear, with two expanding clutches as above. Final drive by bevel gears to differential carrier then by 'De Dion axle' as above.

1911 14 hp (R.A.C. 13·9) *Engine:* 4-cylinder, 75 × 120 mm, S.V., H.T. magneto ignition. *Transmission:* Single plate clutch, 4 speeds and reverse, shaft, bevel-geared live axle. (Some models *c*. 1911 still fitted with the 'De Dion rear axle'.)

1913 50 hp (R.A.C. 44) *Engine:* 8-cylinder, V-type, 94 × 140 mm, S.V., H.T. magneto ignition. *Transmission:* As 14 hp above.

Delage France

Like the brothers Sizaire, Louis Delage entered his cars for sporting events in the *voiturette* and *voiture légère* classes consistently from 1907 onwards. The successes won by these specially built and prepared machines boosted sales of his bread-and-butter cars to such effect that his payroll rose from two men in 1906 to 350 in 1912, by which time production was running at about 1,000 cars a year.

The first Delages appeared late in 1906 and were powered by De Dion

engines; 4½ hp or 9 hp singles being available to choice in the one chassis model. By 1908 Delage was coaxing something over 30 bhp from an engine derived from the standard 100 mm bore De Dion single—very much modified of course, with new cylinder head, larger valves, increased compression and no fewer than four sparking plugs to the one cylinder; with a Delage of this sort Guyot won the Grand Prix des Voiturettes at an average speed of nearly 50 mph having put up practically the most consistent series of lap-times recorded in racing history. In 1909 the singles were dropped in favour of 4-cylinder models with De Dion or Ballot engines, but Louis Delage soon developed his own designs of 4-cylinder side valve engines which were as well made as they were conventional.

Conventional, that is, as far as the touring cars were concerned, for Delage continued for many years to produce extremely interesting and original machinery for his racing cars. For example the 1911 3-litre cars for the *Coupe de l'Auto* (won by Bablot's Delage) had daringly thin steel pistons, delicate tubular connecting rods, a massive built-up crankshaft running in extraordinarily large ball bearings and horizontal overhead valves. A 5-speed gearbox was used with direct drive on fourth and overdrive top gear; although these *Coupe de l'Auto* cars were not spectacularly fast they were consistently reliable, handled beautifully and were very light on tyres. These virtues were also to be found on the firm's production cars.

1910 10 hp (R.A.C. 9·5) *Engine:* 4-cylinder, 62 × 110 mm, S.V., H.T. magneto ignition. *Transmission:* Cone clutch, 3 speeds and reverse, shaft, bevel-geared live axle.

1914 15 hp (R.A.C. 15·7) *Engine:* 6-cylinder, 65 × 130 mm, S.V., H.T. magneto ignition. *Transmission:* as above but 4 speeds. (4-cylinder 12 hp (65 × 110 mm) and 14 hp (75 × 120 mm) available 1910/13; stroke of 14 hp increased to 130 mm in 1914. Multiplate clutch on first 6-cylinder models 1911/12.)

above 1911 16 hp 4-cylinder Coupé de l'Auto, racing two-seater
above left 1910 10 hp 4-cylinder tonneau

Delahaye   France

This was one of the many makes which started life (in 1896) as a free-hand copy of the Benz, with single-cylinder slow-running engine, flat leather belts, fast-and-loose pulleys and all. A 2-cylinder 9 hp model on this plan came out in 1898 and soon earned a good reputation as a reliable, comfortable and (comparatively) fast machine. Three speeds and reverse were provided by an ingenious combination of belts, fast-and-loose pulleys and a train of gear wheels, and an unusual feature of the big horizontal engine was that the belt pulleys on the crankshaft were made to serve as a flywheel, and it was not fitted with the large curly-spoked affair found on most Benz-type cars.

After 1902 the horizontal-engined chassis were made only for carrying light van bodies, and a variety of up-to-date front-engined cars were produced: 15 hp 2-cylinder and 8 hp singles were the first models, but by the end of 1903 a new 12 hp twin and a 24 hp 4-cylinder car had been added. One of these was timed over the flying kilo in 1904 at 61·75 mph. By 1903 most manufacturers were breaking away from the detachable cylinder heads which had been so frequent a source of trouble on the earliest cars, and the new technique of casting cylinder body and head in one piece was thought to be a great improvement. Delahaye, however, never made fixed-head engines and never, apparently, had trouble with their detachable heads. H.T. magneto ignition was used from 1905 onwards and the then-common steering-column lever looked after the gear change. Final drive by side chains was found on all models up to 1907.

In addition to private cars, Delahayes had a large business in light vans and trucks, and when the White company finally gave up the unequal struggle and stopped building steam cars they adopted a Delahaye design as the basis for their extremely fine petrol cars: indeed throughout the pre-war period Whites had a noticeably Delahaye flavour.

Although largish 2-cylinder models were continued up to 1914, Delahayes were early in the field with relatively high-speed, small-bore monobloc 4-cylinder engines, and their 12 hp 65 × 120 mm model was one of the first to make use of those popular dimensions.

Delahaye innovations included water-jacketing of the exhaust manifolds and exceptionally rigid deep-section chassis girders at a time when so many chassis were about as rigid as a filleted blancmange. In 1909 Delahaye cars came on the English market, the concessionaire being H.M. Hobson of Claudel-Hobson carburettor fame, and in 1911 a 13·9 hp Delahaye was one of the first cars to be fitted with the Parry Thomas electric gearbox: it came through an R.A.C.-observed 1,000 miles test with flying colours.

1899/1900 10 hp (R.A.C. 12·84)
Engine: Horizontal, transverse, rear-mounted, 2-cylinder, 100 × 140 mm, A.I.V., trembler coil ignition, surface carburettor. *Transmission:* Belt and spur gear, 3 speeds and reverse. Clutch action by belt on fast and loose pulleys. Side chains, dead axle. Contemporary records differ and De Saunier records engine of 110 × 160 mm for this model.

1897 4½ hp single-cylinder Victoria

1903 12 hp (R.A.C. 12·84) *Engine:* 2-cylinder, 100 × 140 mm, S.V. (M.O.I.V.), trembler coil ignition. *Transmission:* Cone clutch, 3 speeds and reverse, bevel-geared

countershaft, side chains, dead axle. 24 hp as above but with 4 cylinders.

1912 8/12 hp (R.A.C. 10·45)
Engine: 4-cylinder, 65 × 120 mm,
S.V., H.T. magneto ignition.

Transmission: Cone clutch, 3 speeds
and reverse, shaft, bevel-geared live
axle, 4 speeds optional extra.

Delaunay-Belleville

France

Delaunay-Belleville was a name to conjure with before, and for some time after, the Hohenzollern nuisance, partly because the cars always looked as imposing as the name sounded but largely for the simple and excellent reason that they were jolly good. The S.A. des Autos Delaunay-Belleville was founded in 1903 as an offshoot of an old-established marine-engineering and boiler-making concern, but it seems that the motor business was not really under way until 1904.

Marius Barbarou joined the firm as designer after his abortive sojourn *chez* Benz, and the excellence of D.-B. cars suggests that Barbarou's departure from the Benz works was due more to the squabbles raging there than to the alleged shortcomings of the Benz-Parsival car he designed.

Fairly large and luxurious 4- and 6-cylinder cars were the mainstay of the Delaunay-Belleville business, and though no particular innovations came from them their cars, especially the 6-cylinder ones, were remarkably quiet and vibrationless. They used crankshafts much stouter, shorter and more rigid than most of their contemporaries, consequently they avoided the torsional vibration and crankshaft failures which bedevilled the early Napier and

1908 15 hp 4-cylinder tourer

Daimler 6-cylinder cars. The large diameter bearings called for good lubrication and, after Lanchester, D.-B. were one of the first to standardise a full pressure system, which they provided for by an oscillating oil pump similar to

71

that used on their marine steam-engines. The firm used mechanical inlet valves from their beginnings and their cylinders were L-headed and cast in pairs.

Being fairly expensive, and intended for the 'carriage trade', D.-B. cars were usually furnished with imposing closed coachwork by the leading makers: Messrs d'Ieteren made many special bodies for D.-B. chassis and these were superb indeed. Exceptionally long springs were fitted and the firm retained the old 'platform' suspension throughout the period: that is, the two back half-elliptic springs were not shackled to the chassis at their rearward ends but to a third inverted transverse spring. Many of their larger models were equipped with two foot brake pedals each working on a separate drum on the transmission. This was a fairly common Edwardian practice and was not done to provide particularly spectacular stopping (for, after all, it was still a back-wheels-only system), but to avoid overheating the brakes by using them alternately. Both shaft- and chain-driven models were offered at first and the Delaunay-Belleville fully-floating live axle was famous for silence and durability.

Circular bonnets and radiators were D.-B. features for many years; it is said they were used to underline the firm's boiler-making activities, but this piece of picturesque fiction does not explain why so many other makes also had round radiators. The finish of all the mechanical parts was in the best tradition of fine marine engineering, and French opinion put the Delaunay-Belleville on a level with Rolls-Royce.

1912 37 hp (R.A.C. 37·2) *Engine:* 6-cylinder, 100 × 140 mm, S.V., H.T. magneto. *Transmission:* Cone clutch, 4 speeds and reverse, shaft, bevel-geared live axle.

Dennis   England

Like many comparatively obscure car-producing firms, Dennis produced no less than 24 models in the comparatively short space of 14 years before 1914 when car production ceased.

Unlike most firms who undertook such a varied production, they ceased manufacture voluntarily, due to the pressure of work on the fire engine and commercial vehicle side of their business. They survived, and one presumes profitably, due to their policy of buying out engines from such firms as De Dion, Aster, and White & Pope. Only a few cars survive as examples of the Veteran period, and it is evident that, despite the usual exploration of the big-six field with a car of nearly 10 litres capacity produced in 1910/11, the more mundane cars of under 3 litres sold best.

Dual ignition was featured on the 1908 20 hp 4-cylinder car, and in 1912 a colonial version was available of the 18 hp, with extra ground clearance. Also in 1912 chain drive gearboxes were available as an optional extra. Essentially the indirect gear pairs were coupled by inverted tooth chains, which gave silent running in these gears.

Except for overslung worm axles featured from 1904 onwards, Dennis cars were not technically exciting, but from the evidence of contemporary literature they were reliable.

1902 8 hp single-cylinder rear-entrance tonneau

1902 8 hp (R.A.C. 6 hp) Single-cylinder, 100×110 mm, De Dion water-cooled engine, drip feed lubrication, coil ignition.

Transmission: leather-faced clutch, 3-speed gearbox, bevel-gear rear axle.

1912 18 hp (R.A.C. 20·9 hp) *Engine:* 4-cylinder, 90×130 mm, thermo-syphon cooled, pump lubrication, Bosch magneto

ignition. *Transmission:* Leather-faced cone clutch, 4-speed gearbox, worm-drive back axle. Chain drive gearbox optional.

D.F.P. France

Though the Dickensian-sounding Doriet, Flandrin & Parant Co. (which then had only two owners, Messers Doriet & Flandrin) had set up production of single-cylinder cars in 1906, no foothold was gained in the British market until 1910, when 4-cylinder 10/12 and 12/16 cars were imported together with a 14/20 model, again of 4-cylinders.

A variety of models were available in the period 1910 to 1914. A 10/12 hp of 65×120 mm, supplemented by a 10/14 for 1911 only, together with an 80×120 mm car (which was called both a 12/16 and a 14/20, and were each of 15·9 R.A.C. hp) were available for the years 1911 and 1912 respectively. The 10/12 continued to 1914 and the confused 12/16/14/20 became the 16/22 of the same R.A.C. hp as before for 1913. The brief appearance of a 6-cylinder car, called the 20/25, occurred in 1911, which was a version of the 14/20 of that year. The engines were made by Chapuis Dorner until 1912, when D.F.P. manufactured their own.

From 1912 onwards, W.O. Bentley imported D.F.P. cars in chassis form, and he wrote of them 'D.F.P.'s were excellent, reliable vehicles, possessing the indefinable quality which makes certain cars a pleasure to drive, and always feel just right. The steering and roadholding were first class and they were ruggedly built.'

Also in 1912 the 12/15 hp appeared. It had a bore and stroke of 70×130 mm, and was R.A.C. rated as 12·1 hp. This model was developed by Bentley by fitting aluminium pistons and increasing the compression ratio. Together with other modifications the model became the 12/40, and was successfully raced in this form. With a saloon body, the 12/40 was capable of 60 mph. A standard body was available from J.H. Easter of New Street Mews, or could be built to customer specification. All bodies were made with meticulous care, and this was reflected in the 1914 price of a 12/40 sports model of £410.

1910 10/12 hp (R.A.C. 10·4)
Engine: 4-cylinder, 65×120 mm, thermo-syphon cooling, H.T. magneto. *Transmission:* Leather

cone clutch, 3-speed gearbox, shaft transmission to bevel-geared live axle.

1912 12/15 hp (R.A.C. 12·1)
Engine: 4-cylinder, 70×130 mm,

other details as above except 4-speed gearbox fitted.

Duryea

America

The Duryea story is rather a sad one, for this pioneer American concern, which produced some designs of great ingenuity in the early days, never had the success it deserved and it did not survive after 1917.

The Duryea brothers fell out in later life and each claimed to have been primarily responsible for their first cars. On balance, it seems that the first efforts were developed by Charles from Frank's hazy and impractical ideas in 1893/4. Their first motorised horse-buggy was followed by a much improved machine which was altered and rebuilt several times until it ran to Charles's satisfaction: whereupon the Duryea Motor Wagon Company was founded—almost certainly the first American company expressly formed to build petrol cars.

On Thanksgiving Day 1895 Frank Duryea 'won' the first American road race—the *Times-Herald* affair from Chicago to Evanston. This was not all that of a triumph for the entries comprised only the Duryea, two electric runabouts which dropped out early, and three imported Benz cars only one of which struggled over the whole fifty-four miles, which even the Duryea took more than nine hours to cover. However, the Company went ahead and produced a first production run of thirteen similar cars, with horizontal engines, belt-and-jockey-pulley 3-speed transmission and dynamo-powered low-tension ignition. Two of these took part in the London-to-Brighton 'Emancipation' run in 1896 and many years later Frank Duryea claimed to have been first in at Brighton. The official list makes no mention of this—but then Lawson's list of finishers is highly suspect and probably mentioned only those makes in which he had a financial interest.

1901 8 hp 3-cylinder Motor Surrey

After this promising start the Company languished and nothing much was done for two years, after which a re-formed company went ahead, first with a horizontally opposed twin, and then with Charles's new design of 3-cylinder car which formed the basis for the standard Duryea model of the next few years. This not only had one of the first 3-cylinder in-line engines but it is the first known example of the *désaxé* crankshaft—that is, the shaft is set to one side of the longitudinal centre line of the cylinders with the object of reducing the side thrust of the pistons during the power strokes. *Désaxé* engines became quite the thing about ten years later. Duryea's 3-cylinder was smooth running and quiet but not markedly efficient; 4 in. bore × 6 in. stroke developing only 10 bhp at 600 rpm. The dimensions were soon altered to $4\frac{1}{2} \times 4\frac{1}{2}$ in.

The engine was inclined and set transversely amidships, and transmission, in what soon became the most usual fashion in America, was direct from crankshaft to back axle by central chain: an epicyclic gear, carried in a 'power drum' beside the flywheel, provided one low speed and reverse. Steering was by tiller via a series of connections which looked terrifyingly tenuous to English eyes: in fact they were not so frightening as they seemed as the system was designed to have all the rods in tension and the king-pins were steeply inclined to bring the point of suspension in line with the point of contact between tyre and road. Much ingenuity was displayed in making all the controls of the steering, low gear and high-speed clutch operation, engine speed, and brake operate from one lever. Other features were overhead valve gear (automatic inlets at first, but an unusual form of mechanical valve was used later), L.T. magneto ignition from 1902 onwards, and distinctive sweeping body lines. Much of this ingenuity, which has been compared to the contemporary Lanchester, was stultified by rather poor finish, inadequate cooling and excessive oil-throwing which resulted in heat and smells making the occupants feel they were riding in a mobile fish fryer. A tricar version of the Duryea Power Carriage was also made but did not have very much success.

A British Duryea Company was in existence for about four years from late 1903. It was headed by Henry Sturmey, first editor of *The Autocar*, and the weaknesses of the design, particularly the heat and stink problem, were soon overcome. Components for the English cars were made by Willans and Robinson, pioneers of the high-speed steam engine. Probably because it was unorthodox the Duryea did not have the success it deserved. The English Duryea Co. was wound up in 1907 whilst in America production was taken over by the Stevens Arms and Tool Co.

1900 Duryea 8 hp (R.A.C. 16·5)
Engine: Inclined transverse, rear-mounted, 3-cylinder, $4\frac{1}{2} \times 4\frac{1}{2}$ in., Variable lift A.I.V., dynamo and battery electric ignition by incandescent wire and slide valve.

Transmission: 2 speeds and reverse epicyclic gear. Clutches: for low and reverse by band brakes on epicyclic gear drums, for high speed by metal cone; single chain drive to live axle.

1910 Stevens-Duryea 30/35 hp (R.A.C. 36·1) *Engine:* 4-cylinder, $4\frac{3}{4} \times 4\frac{1}{2}$ in., S.V., H.T. magneto.

Transmission: Cone clutch, 3 speeds and reverse, shaft, bevel-geared live axle.

English Mechanic   England

It was natural enough in the early days of motoring for engineers both amateur and professional, to build their own motor cars, and a few manufacturers, principally in America, supplied do-it-yourself kits for home assembly. The *English Mechanic* magazine commissioned an eminent consulting engineer, T. Hyler-White, to write a series of articles giving instructions which, if followed carefully, resulted in a workable home-made car. Parts were not supplied, but advice was given on how and where to buy the engines and other components which were beyond the constructional ability of the average backyard mechanic.

The confection differed little from the contemporary belt-driven Benz: indeed, readers were advised to buy standard Benz (or Benz-type) engines. At the time, 1900, the original Benz designs had almost passed its heyday but it possessed the great merit of simplicity which must, at least, have saved Mr White a deal of trouble in the compilation of his articles.

Later articles in the journal gave instructions for making single- and twin-cylinder vertical-engined shaft-driven cars, and a light steamer. These, too, were fairly obviously cribbed from existing makes.

1900 3 hp (R.A.C. 6·4)   *Engine:* Horizontal, transverse, rear-mounted, 1-cylinder, 4 × 5 in., M.O.I.V., trembler coil ignition. *Transmission:* Similar to contemporary Benz (q.v.).

1899 3½ hp single-cylinder dog cart

F.I.A.T.

Italy

The Fabbrica Italiana Automobili of Turin[1] was founded in 1899; the moving spirits being Cavaliere Agnelli, Count Biscaretti di Ruffia and Count Brichesario who had the Turin Bank behind him. Although Italy came into the motor business rather later than France and Germany two national characteristics soon became apparent—wholehearted appreciation of the sporting side of motoring and that combination of artistry with engineering which seems inherent in Italian design.

The F.I.A.T. concern started by taking over the Ceirano business which had been making 'Welleyes' bicycles and a few voiturettes powered by De Dion engines; this provided a nucleus of about fifty skilled workmen and the services of Signor Faccioli who designed the first production F.I.A.T.s. These had 2-cylinder 6 hp horizontal engines mounted at the back, and with one of them the firm scored their first bull's-eye by making fastest time in the Padua Circuit Race in 1900 at an average speed of 30 mph, though not actually winning, having been disqualified for receiving manual assistance on a hill.

Agnelli was in favour of the 'new' layout of front-mounted vertical engine, but Faccioli would have none of it and resigned. He was replaced by Enrico who produced, for 1902, the first 4-cylinder model which was clearly based upon the Mercedes and which was soon followed by new models, each with some distinctive and advanced feature. For example: in 1903 came a pressure lubrication system, 1904, friction shock-absorbers and multiplate clutch, 1905, overhead valves, 1906 enclosed torque tube transmission and compressed-air starting.

[1] F.I.A.T. became Fiat in 1906.

F.I.A.T. racing cars were very much in the 'monster' tradition and remained so until comparatively late, reaching, in 1912, the awe-inspiring 200 hp *Grand Prix* car with a 4-cylinder engine of 150 mm bore × 200 mm stroke: this, like its 120 hp predecessor of 1911 had a shaft-driven overhead camshaft. By contrast the 1914 *Grand Prix* car had a relatively small engine of 100 × 143 mm rated at 80 hp. Until 1908 the racing cars had low-tension magneto ignition although H.T. magnetos were available on many of the touring models rather earlier.

left 1913 12/15 (Tipo Zero) 4-cylinder tourer

below 1913 20/30 4-cylinder landaulette

About eighteen models of passenger cars were offered between 1903 and 1914. The 24 hp 4-cylinder model of *c.* 1904/7 was one of the best known of the early types, and a large number of the later 20 hp were particularly favoured as town cars and carried those towering and impressive closed bodies which appear capable of accommodating half a parish. But the 'man of modest means', as the period phrase had it, was not neglected for the 12 hp models were economical and long-lived, whilst at the far end of the scale the wealthy and great rolled in splendour and state in the sporting 70s of 1907/8 or the ohc 90s of 1909/11.

Amongst the other assets taken over from the Ceirano concern were two apprentices, Vincenzo Lancia and Felice Nazarro both of whom soon became as famous in racing affairs as René de Knyff, Jenatzy, Hémery *et al.* Lancia did not leave Fiat to set up in business on his own until 1908.

1899 3 hp (R.A.C. 8·5)   Engine: Horizontal, transverse, rear-mounted, 2-cylinder, 83 × 100 mm, A.I.V., trembler coil ignition.

Transmission: Cone clutch, 3 speeds, no reverse, spur gears to countershaft, side chains, dead axle.

1909 40 hp (R.A.C. 41·9)   *Engine:* 4-cylinder, 130 × 140 mm, S.V., H.T. magneto ignition.

Transmission: Disc clutch, 4 speeds and reverse, bevel-geared countershaft, side chains, dead axle.

1913 12/15 hp (R.A.C. 12·1) *Engine:* 4-cylinder, 70 × 120 mm, S.V., H.T. magneto ignition.

Transmission: Multiplate clutch, 4 speeds and reverse, shaft, bevel-geared live axle.

1913 20/30 (R.A.C. 24·8)   *Engine:* 4-cylinder, 100 × 140 mm, other details as for 12/15.

Ford
America

Henry Ford's contribution to motoring is, of course, the Model T which has become as deep-rooted a part of American folk-lore as the cowboy—but long before the first flivver trundled out of the works Ford cars had made their mark.

Ford's first satisfactory experimental belt-driven car was built in 1896 as the outcome of spare-time efforts spread over some years: in 1901 he became superintendent of the Detroit Automobile Co. which folded up after making only thirty horizontal-engined gas-buggys. He then built a large sprint car for publicity purposes, succeeded in getting financial backing and started the Ford Motor Co. in November 1903. In conjunction with Tom Cooper two more extremely crude but effective sprint cars were built—the Arrow and the famous 999 which must be one of the first American ohc machines on record. With the publicity these earned as a booster, Ford settled down to get a firm grip on the cheap car market, as he was convinced the future lay there rather than with expensive cars for the 'carriage folk'.

Model A came out in 1903; this was a 2-cylinder horizontal-engined car rather on the lines of the single-cylinder Oldsmobile—then the best seller in its class. For many years the Ford Company 'bought out' most of their components and most of their machining was done by the Dodge Brothers. A vertical 4-cylinder $2,000 Model B followed in 1904, together with Models C and F, which were improved versions of Model A. Two more new cars came out in 1906—K and N. The former was Ford's only 'luxury' car, produced at his partners' insistence and a commercial failure. It had a remarkably smooth-running and flexible 6-cylinder engine, with the odd firing order of 1-2-3-6-5-4, a 2-speed epicyclic gearbox (like all the other Ford cars), and a bevel-geared live axle, in which the crown-wheel and pinion were often found inadequate to take the torque of the big engine. Model N was the direct ancestor of the T and had a 4-cylinder engine with the flywheel in front balanced by the rotating masses of the epicyclic gearbox aft, on the lines of the 1905 20 hp Lanchester (one of which the Ford Co. bought for examination). Model N sold very well and reinforced Ford's ambition to build one model only, and to continue with it year after year so as to bring prices down to a level his competitors could not touch.

With Model T, he felt strong enough to do this and, to Cassandra-like cries from his associates, he announced his one-model policy in 1908: this succeeded beyond all expectation as the world knows. As a result it is usually said that Ford was an engineering genius and the 'inventor' of mass production. He was neither; mass production was already established in other trades, notably the

1904 10 hp 2-cylinder Model C tonneau

cheap clock industry, and Ford's genius lay much less in design work than in producing the right thing at the right moment.

Model T had a 4-cylinder full-monobloc engine of 2·9 litres, for which the R.A.C. rating was 22·4 hp, but which probably developed no more than the 20 hp claimed by the makers. It had very small valves and gas-passages and a detachable cylinder head—often said to be the first in the world but this was just not true. Transmission was still by 2-speed and reverse epicyclic gears, now arranged to be controlled by the feet, which made the cars exceptionally easy to drive. Ignition was by flywheel magneto generator and four trembler coils which, if not kept at concert pitch, often made starting very uncertain in cold weather. The Model T undoubtedly broke more wrists than any other make—but it did have the advantage of numbers. The chassis looked frail but was in fact very tough, and suspension was by transverse leaf springs fore and aft. Riding comfort was extremely good at moderate speeds, but over 30 mph a good deal of side-sway and bounce set in which made the car wander. Rough roads or cross-country pounding held no terrors for the Ford. Pre-war models had a handsome brass-bound radiator which leaked on the slightest provocation and boiled vigorously on no provocation at all.

Within a short while the Model T outstripped all its rivals in its class; not because it was a particularly good car in the engineering sense, but simply because it was cheaper, and better value, than anything of comparable specification. Although it was not very long-lived unless treated with more care than it usually got, it achieved the effect of longevity because spare parts could be cheaply bought and fitted by unskilled labour. The car was very light —13½ cwt for a 5-seat tourer—so the absence of an intermediate gear was not too grave a disadvantage though, if forced off its high gear, progress on 'low' was middling tedious. Up to about 28 mph the engine was fairly smooth and quiet, but at anything faster it became rather rough, and the shortcomings of steering and suspension became apparent. But despite its little peccadilloes it was a great achievement.

1903 10 hp (R.A.C. 12·9) *Engine:* Horizontally opposed, transverse, centrally mounted, 2-cylinder, 4 × 4 in., S.V. (M.O.I.V.), coil ignition. *Transmission:* 2 speeds and reverse epicyclic gear. Clutches: for low speed and reverse by contracting brakes on epicyclic gear drums, high speed by forcing friction-facing of low speed drum in contact with flywheel, single chain, live axle.

1906 (Model N) 15 hp (R.A.C. 15·7) *Engine:* 4-cylinder, 3⅝ × 3¼ in., S.V., coil ignition. *Transmission:* As above, but multiplate clutch for high speed and final drive by shaft to bevel-geared live axle.

1910 (Model T) 20 hp (R.A.C. 22·4 hp) *Engine:* 4-cylinder, 3¾ × 4 in., S.V., L.T. flywheel magneto, L.T. distributor and H.T. trembler coils. *Transmission:* As for Model N above, but with pedal control of the change-speed gear.

1912 20 hp 4-cylinder Model T limousine

Gardner-Serpollet France

The theory that the steam car was 'killed' by the vested interests of the petrol car trade has been stated so often that it is now accepted as fact. But it is just not true, for despite the theoretical advantages of steam power for road locomotion the steam car could not compete in the end merely because it was more troublesome and expensive to run than a comparable petrol car. The matter was summed up very simply by a writer to *The Autocar* in 1907— himself a steam engineer and therefore biased in favour of steam—who sent comparative data on the running of a 45 hp Napier and a 20 hp White steamer over 15,000 miles: his conclusion was that though he preferred the steamer, his workshop records showed that for every hour of maintenance and repair work devoted to keeping the Napier in apple pie order, *seven* hours were spent on the steamer.

Léon Serpollet's contribution to the steam car was his re-invention, in a practical form, of the 'flash boiler' or instantaneous steam generator which he patented in 1888. In the following year he and Armand Peugeot collaborated in building a large 3-wheeled 4-seated carriage powered by a Serpollet generator and engine. Unfortunately for Serpollet, Peugeot then turned his attention to petrol engines and for the next few years most of Serpollet's time was spent on his bread-and-butter work of making steam power plants for tramway work and so on—though he did turn out about a dozen experimental light steam cars. By 1896 it was quite apparent that coke-fired boilers would be unacceptable to the public and Serpollet began grappling with the vagaries of vaporising paraffin burners; a little later he developed a 4-cylinder single-

1904 18 hp 4-cylinder Tulip Phaeton

acting engine with trunk pistons and poppet valves which was better suited to the high temperature superheated steam from the Serpollet generator than the conventional slide-valve engine. What it lost in efficiency by not being double-acting, as most steam engines were, it gained in reliability as it did not deposit a lot of oil in the condenser and had no troublesome stuffing-boxes to keep free from leaks.

By 1899 Serpollet was being financed by the rich American Frank Gardner, and very soon Gardner-Serpollet touring cars were in regular production, and racing steamers were doing well both in sprints and long-distance events. In March 1901, for example, a 10 hp (nominal) Gardner-Serpollet decisively beat the Baron Henri de Rothschild's 35 hp Mercedes over the flying kilometre and the flying mile at the Nice Speed Trials. Two years later a Gardner-Serpollet demonstrated its ability to cope with long-distance events when Le Blon covered the first stage of 342 miles in the Paris–Madrid at an average speed of 50·7 mph.

Apart from continual improvement of the details, particularly by the addition of a donkey engine to feed water to the generator and fuel to the furnace to avoid hand-pumping when the car was standing, the recipe did not alter: flash boiler and burner in a 'boot' at the back, flat-four horizontally opposed engine sometimes under floor and sometimes under a bonnet, condenser in front like a petrol car's radiator to conserve water from the exhaust, and water tanks under the seats.

When all was well the Gardner-Serpollet provided delightfully effortless motoring, but it was all too apparent that the reliability of a steamer depended largely upon rigorous maintenance and skilful handling, and after the death of Léon Serpollet in 1907 the firm did not last long.

1900 5 hp (R.A.C. 6·7) *Engine:* Horizontally opposed, transverse, single acting, simple 4-cylinder, 52 × 60 mm, poppet valves. *Boiler:* Serpollet 'flash' generator. Average working pressure 300 lb sq in. superheated. *Transmission:* Single chain to live axle.

1904 18 hp (R.A.C. 15·04) *Engine:* As above, but forward-mounted and longitudinal. 4-cylinder, 78 × 78 mm. *Boiler:* As above, but with donkey engine for feed and average pressure 500 lb sq in. *Transmission:* Shaft, bevel-geared live axle.

Georges Richard

(and Georges Richard-Brasier) see Brasier

Germain   Belgium

That the Germain started life as the Daimler-Belge says all that needs to be said about the engine design of the earliest models, but chassis and transmission details obviously owed more to Panhard-Levassor than to the Daimler Motoren Geselleschaft. By 1903 distinctive Germain features began to appear, such as spun-brass water jackets shrunk on to separate steel cylinders and an ingenious system of valve-lift control.

Early models had wood and flitch plate chassis and the pressed-steel frame was not used until 1906. The later Germain chassis were of notably deep section and more rigid than most. With the new steel chassis came a patented design of forged steel, fully floating, live axle, though chain or shaft drive could be had to choice on the 28 hp 4-cylinder models. The engines of *c.* 1904/6 were L-headed with variable lift mechanical inlet valves, and the first 6-cylinder model, which appeared at the Paris Show in 1906, had a built-up crankshaft running in very large ball bearings. Cylinder dimensions of this fine car were 120 × 130 mm.

By 1909, though the brass water jackets were still in use, most of the new Germain models had T-head engines. Full pressure lubrication and automatic advance/retard mechanism were fitted at a time when such refinements were still rare. Transmission on the new 28 hp model was via an expanding clutch to a gearbox which would be considered commendably short and compact today. The lay-shaft was arranged to be out of mesh when the direct drive top gear was in use, but an ingenious little turbine affair, worked by the lubricating oil, kept it spinning gently and this had the effect of a primitive synchromesh when changing down and a clutch stop helped with upward changes. Quite a wide range of models was made, the smallest being a 4-cylinder 14 hp of 92×110 mm and the largest the 100 hp *Grand Prix* type 4-cylinder 155×165 mm. Six-cylinder cars of 20, 30, 40 and 60 hp were listed.

The Germain business in England was in the hands of Capt. Theo Masui who competed regularly in sporting events and who also designed many special bodies of outstanding elegance for Germain chassis. For 1913 Germain began using the double sleeve-valve engine for many of their models, without in any way suffering the 'auntification' which overtook so many of those who succumbed to Knight's disease.

1905 14 hp (R.A.C. 22·4) *Engine:* 4-cylinder, 95×110 mm, S.V. (Variable lift M.O.I.V.), coil ignition. *Transmission:* Cone clutch, 3 speeds and reverse, shaft, bevel geared live axle.

1909 28 hp (R.A.C. 35·7) *Engine:* 4-cylinder, 120×130 mm, S.V., H.T. magneto ignition with coil optional extra. *Transmission:* Expanding clutch, 4 speeds and reverse, shaft, bevel geared live axle.

1908 28 hp 4-cylinder tourer

Gladiator   see Clément

Gobron-Brillié   France

Arrol-Johnston were not the only enthusiasts for the opposed-piston engine, and the Société Gobron-Brillié of Boulogne built opposed-piston engines for their cars (and for other purposes) from 1898 to 1916: after the war they used normal engines made by Chapuis-Dornier.

The Gobron engines differed from the Arrol-Johnston in being vertical instead of horizontal and in doing without the rocking-lever linkage. Cylinders were cast in pairs with valve chests and combustion spaces midway, and each pair contained four pistons: the lower pair were direct-coupled by normal connecting rods to a common crank-pin in the usual way, and the upper pair were coupled to a cross-head from each end of which long, flimsy tubular connecting rods (on which the stresses were always in tension), gave motion to crank-throws opposed at 180° from those actuated by the lower pistons. 4- and 6-cylinder engines were made by coupling the twin-cylinder blocks on a common crankcase. The owner of one 4-cylinder Gobron-Brillié is apt to baffle enquirers, by remarking that his car has two cylinder blocks, four cylinders, eight pistons and a six-throw crankshaft. Imagination boggles at the Gobron Brillié aero engine which had thirty-two pistons working in sixteen cylinders arranged in an X formation.

The arrangement gave smooth running, relieved the main bearings of stress and made possible the advantages of long-stroke working without the dis-advantage of excessive piston speed. The first Gobron-Brillié model of 1898 had a 2-cylinder, 4-piston engine mounted transversely at the back, a curious variable-ratio steering gear and an ingenious carburation device which fore-shadowed the direct-injection principle in a primitive way.

Vertical front-engined cars, with 2, 4 and ultimately 6 cylinders, were pro-duced from 1901 onwards, and apart from their engines they were perfectly conventional machines with pressed-steel chassis, double cone clutches, drip-feed lubrication and final drive by side chains: shaft drive was not adopted until very late.

One of the firm's chief claims to a niche in motoring history is that a Gobron-Brillié was the first to crack the 100 mph mark. This was done by a 1903 110 hp 4-cylinder car which Rigolly drove over the flying kilometre at 103·56 mph early in 1904—a record which stood until November 1905 when Macdonald on a Napier raised it to 104·65.

1899 6 hp (R.A.C. 7·9) *Engine:* Vertical, transverse, rear-mounted, 2-cylinder, 4 pistons, bore 80 mm, combined stroke 160 mm (equal stroke upper and lower), A.I.V., trembler coil ignition. Positive petrol feed device in lieu of normal carburettor. *Transmission:* by spur gears to cone clutch, 3 speeds and reverse to countershaft, side chains, dead axle.

1908 40/60 hp 4-cylinder Limousine de Luxe

1907 40/60 (R.A.C. 30) *Engine:* 4-cylinder, 8 pistons, bore 110 mm, combined stroke 200 mm (upper pistons 90 mm, lower 110 mm), S.V., H.T. magneto ignition. *Transmission:* Double cone clutch, 4 speeds and reverse, bevel-geared countershaft, side chains, dead axle. (Smaller models had shaft and live axle transmission after 1910; 40/50 hp chain driven, 1913; bevel-axle, 1914; worm-drive 1915.)

Grenville

England

The Grenville steam carriage was built in 1875, and has the distinction of being the oldest surviving road-going passenger carrying vehicle in Britain.

It was designed by Robert Kneville Grenville of Butleigh Court Somerset and George Jackson Churchward (a gentleman engineer, later to be the chief mechanical engineer of the G.W.R.).

The carriage was built at Newton Abbot and was designed to carry six passengers. The vertical boiler supplies steam at 120 psi to a twin-cylinder engine of bore and stroke 5 × 6 in. (though the carriage at one time had a single cylinder). A simple 2-speed epicyclic gearbox is fitted and drives the rear

The Grenville six-seater steam carriage

wheels by means of a differential gear acting through the right-hand wheel to propel the carriage along. The rear axle is fitted with 4-ft diameter wheels, and the assembly is connected to the body of the carriage by 4 ft half elliptic springs. A single wheel of 2 ft 6 in. diameter supports the front. All the wheels are built of teak segments.

The driver, seated at the front, controls the speed and direction of the vehicle, aided by a brakesman, though normal braking is by means of engine reversing, the crude wood brake blocks being rather ineffective. A fireman is placed at the rear of the vehicle and is responsible for stoking and, surprisingly, changing gear. The carriage is capable of 18 mph, and can take 1:10 hills in top gear.

Little is known about the working life of the vehicle, which ended in 1897 when it was converted to drive a cider press in Glastonbury. It was rediscovered in 1932 by Commander J.D.R. Davies at Butleigh Court and was restored to working order. Before it vanished into the storerooms of the Bristol Museum in 1947, it recorded a run of 40 miles in 4 hours 4 minutes running time, together with some $3\frac{1}{4}$ hours spent watering, oiling and coaling. During this run it consumed $4\frac{1}{2}$ cwt of coalite, and 180 gallons of water.

G.W.K. England

Variable-ratio friction-disc transmission is of respectable antiquity, for the Tenting cars of 1894 were driven by this system. In theory it is a splendid idea — a disc is rotated by the engine to drive another disc at right angles to it, and the latter is arranged to slide on its shaft across the face of the driver (poor chap! No. No—the face of the first-motion disc of course) so that, the nearer it approaches the circumference, the faster it revolves. On being moved towards the centre the 'gear ratio' becomes lower and if moved past the centre the direction of rotation is reversed.

Unfortunately there are quite a few snags which cannot be gone into here, but none the less a great many attempts were made, particularly in America, to produce a satisfactory friction-disc car. The G.W.K. was the only English example to be wholly successful. Messrs Grice, Wood and Keiler built their first car in 1910/11: it was a 'bitza' with a Coventry-Climax boat engine, a pair of old-type De Dion Bouton tubular radiators, a Chater-Lea front axle and so on, but it worked admirably and late in 1911 a Company was formed, with factory at Datchet, to produce an improved version of the prototype. These were fitted with vertical 2-cylinder Coventry-Simplex engines of 86×92 mm and they were made without much alteration until 1915, when a 4-cylinder model was embarked upon. This did not reach the public until after the war.

The first experimental car earned Wood a place among the nine competitors to finish the tough Scottish six-day trial, two gold medals were won in the London–Edinburgh Reliability Run and Keiler collected a third medal in the six-day trial in 1912. Soon after, a mildly tuned and stripped touring car won a 5-lap race at Brooklands and further successes followed in 1913/14.

Private owners found the car good value at £150, and the performance was much better than that of most cheap, light cars of the time; top speed was not far short of 55 mph and petrol consumption was 45 mpg. Given reasonable care the friction disc transmission gave little trouble, though if allowed too much slip when starting from rest the friction lining on the rim of the driven disc developed flat spots which produced a characteristic 'wunk-wunk-wunk' noise as the car went along. However, it was not a difficult matter to renew the lining.

1914 8 hp (R.A.C. 9·16) *Engine:* Coventry-Simplex, transverse, central/rear, 2-cylinder, 86 × 92 mm, S.V., H.T. magneto ignition. *Transmission:* By friction discs, theoretically progressively variable from neutral to maximum, but arranged for 4 speeds forward and reverse; short shaft, bevel live axle.

Hispano-Suiza

Spain/France

Although the country of origin of this make is Spain both Switzerland and France come into the picture, for Swiss design and finance were behind the concern at first, and the Sté Français Hispano-Suiza S.A. was set up in 1911 with works at Bois-Colombes. According to Doyle the Barcelona firm was founded in 1904 but it does not appear that any cars were produced until the end of 1906 when two models, a 20/24 hp and a 40 hp, were exhibited at the Paris Salon.

These were beautifully made cars with well-braced pressed-steel chassis, T-head engines with H.T. magneto ignition and exceptionally large rear-wheel brake drums. An unusual feature was that the foot-brake (on the transmission as usual) was water-cooled by means of hollow-cast shoes connected to the bottom tank of the radiator: previous water-cooled brakes, *à la* Mercedes, had merely relied upon a crude arrangement to dribble water into the brake drum from a tank on the dash.

1912 15.9 hp 4-cylinder sports two-seater

In 1910 the *Coupe de l'Auto* race was won by a 4-cylinder Hispano-Suiza, and the death-knell of the big single and twin cylinder units for light cars and voiturettes grew decisively louder. Marc Birkigt, Hispano's designer, produced for the occasion a machine of such admirable handling qualities that the winning car of the team of three had no difficulty in stealing the race from potentially faster rivals. The car was powered by a T-head engine of 65 mm bore (the largest allowed by the regulations) and 200 mm stroke. With very little alteration beyond enlarging the bore to 80 mm and reducing the stroke to 180 mm the *Coupe de l'Auto* type was developed into the famous 'Alfonso' model as supplied to, and named after, King Alfonso XIII.

There are those who say that the 'Alfonso' Hispano was the first true 'sports car', but as similar claims are made for a great many other makes and models, and as no one has yet satisfactorily defined a sports car anyway, we prefer to pass to safer ground by saying that the car had all the qualities one could wish for either in 1912 or 1962. It was handsome to look at, excellently finished reliable, economical and capable of a safe 70 to 75 mph in standard form.

In addition to the 'Alfonso' two smaller 4-cylinder models were made (80 × 110 mm and 80 × 130 mm), and an ohv version of the latter came out for 1914, together with two ohv 6-cylinder models.

1912 'Alfonso' 45 hp (R.A.C. 15·9) *Engine:* 4-cylinder, 80 × 180 mm, S.V. (T-head), H.T. magneto ignition. *Transmission:* Multidisc clutch, 3 speeds and reverse, shaft, bevel-geared live axle. 4-speed gearbox after 1913.

Humber

England

Thomas Humber's bicycle building firm became part of Lawson's gallimaufry in 1896, and was at first intended to produce machines to the designs of the mountebank Pennington and a copy of Léon Bollée's tricar. These projects

1903 5 hp single-cylinder two-seater Humberette

misfired, almost literally, for Pennington's designs were soon found to be worthless, and a disastrous fire destroyed the Bollée tricar and drawings before production was under way. A re-formed Humber Company cut away from Lawson in 1900 and several models of single-cylinder light cars were put on the market. The first of these to be made in largish numbers was the Humberette which appeared in 1903. It was a tubular-framed voiturette, very light, propelled by a 5 hp engine which was practically identical with the contemporary De Dion except that it was constructed to run anti-clockwise. It was not really a very good car and in particular it was bedevilled by a wide-ratio 2-speed gearbox. A greatly improved $6\frac{1}{2}$ hp 3-speed version came out in 1904 and was deservedly popular, though the 2-speed 5 hp model was continued.

Production was divided between Coventry and Beeston, Notts. and, at one time, those who owned Beeston Humbers thought they were one up on those who only had Coventry Humbers. Louis Coatalen joined the firm in 1901 and designed an excellent 4-cylinder, 4-speed, 12 hp car which was very good value at £300. During the next four years production included the Humberettes (made both at Coventry and Beeston), and available with single-cylinder engines of 5 or $6\frac{1}{2}$ hp plus 2-cylinder cars of $7\frac{1}{2}$ hp and 10 hp. Coventry also turned out 4-cylinder models of 10/12 hp, whilst Beeston made 16/20 hp cars. There was also a brief flirtation with a 9 hp 3-cylinder Beeston car in 1903/4: this had low-tension magneto ignition.

1904 $8\frac{1}{2}$ hp 2-cylinder tourer

The Humberette was dropped in 1905 together with the 2-cylinder car and the range reduced to two basic types—a 10/12 hp 4-cylinder, 3-speed, tubular chassis car from Coventry and the 16/20 hp Beeston Humber which had a pressed-steel chassis and 4-speed box. A 15 hp Coventry Humber was added in 1907, but despite their excellent reputation the firm did not prosper; consequently the Beeston factory was closed and production concentrated in new, larger, premises at Coventry.

Gradually the number of models increased again and the firm re-entered the light car market in 1908 with an 8 hp 2-cylinder. This was a refined and superior little car, but it was too expensive to compete with others in its class and it was dropped in 1910. It had the peculiarity that, although the engine ran clockwise, it was arranged to be cranked anti-clockwise—a feat which most people find very difficult but which, allegedly, reduced the risk of a broken wrist in the event of a back-fire. The Humberette was revived for 1913 in the form of a sprightly 8 hp V-twin air-cooled model which weighed less than 7 cwt and was consequently classed as a cycle car, although specification, performance and durability were much superior to most of the breed. It was good value at £125, completely equipped, and over 2,000 were on the roads by mid-1914 by which time they had become water-cooled.

The pre-war Humber story ends with the first and only team of Humbers to be specially built for racing. F.T. Burgess was responsible, and the Humber team of three cars for the 1914 Tourist Trophy had 4-cylinder engines of 82 × 156 mm from which an impressive 100 hp was developed at 3,200 rpm. They were still suffering from teething troubles at the time of the race, and the war stopped further development of their advanced twin ohc engines.

1903 'Humberette'. 5 hp (R.A.C. 5·25) *Engine:* 1-cylinder, $3\frac{5}{8} \times 3\frac{5}{8}$ in., A.I.V., trembler coil ignition.

Transmission: Cone clutch, 2 speeds and reverse, shaft, bevel-geared live axle.

1914 28 hp 4-cylinder 'Tourist Trophy' racing two-seater

1904 10/12 hp (R.A.C. 12·8) *Engine:* 2-cylinder, $4 \times 4\frac{1}{8}$ in., S.V. (M.O.I.V.), coil ignition.

Transmission: Cone clutch, 3 speeds and reverse, bevel-geared live axle.

1914 28 hp (R.A.C. 27·3) *Engine:* 4-cylinder, 105 × 140 mm, S.V., H.T. magneto and coil ignition.

Transmission: As above, but 4 speeds.

Hupmobile America

The horizontal-engined gas-buggy type of vehicle, so typical of the early American scene, was dying out by 1906/7 and the arrival of Henry Ford's admirable Model T was the final nail in its coffin. Ford showed that a 'proper' full-scale 4-cylinder car could be put on the low-priced market and the other manufacturers interested in that profitable field (and a host of newcomers) had to follow suit or go under. Consequently from about 1908 onwards a great crop of low-priced 4-cylinder cars came on the market: most of them could not hold a candle to Model T and only a relatively few survived. Most of those which did not long survive really were both cheap and nasty, unlike the Ford and the best of its contemporaries, which contrived to be cheap without being all that nasty. Inaccessibility, rough finish of machined parts, skimpy springing, unhardened roller bearings and axle-shafts were fairly common complaints, whilst all but a few makers disguised the inherent roughness of their engines by the simple expedient of keeping output low by the use of very small valves and inadequate gas passages.

The Hupmobile was one of the better ones: true, their first 15 hp models of 1908/11 were marred by a disastrously wide ratio 2-speed gear without the flexibility of engine of the Ford to compensate for its nastiness, but the improved 18 hp car, with a 3-speed box, was much better and with it the Hupp Motor Co. managed to get quite a slice of the export trade. This was one of the first cars apart from the very earliest Renaults, to be made with a central gear-lever, and in 1913 the Company brought out what was claimed to be the first all-steel body, though it is probable that B.S.A. were about a year ahead of them. Electric lights and starter were fitted in 1913.

The flywheel-fed splash lubrication was a fairly obvious crib from Model T and the only peculiarity of design was that the timing chain was at the back of the engine so that the magneto took up an Unnatural Posture on top of the flywheel housing. Like most of its kind the Hupmobile was not a brilliant performer considering the size of engine. Half the authors still remembers the excitement when the family Hupp attained a clamorous 42 mph, and he also recalls the poorly designed steering arrangements jamming on full lock in Tunbridge Wells—which was not, in 1921, the sort of place to appreciate such goings-on.

1913 15/18 hp 4-cylinder tourer

1911 12/16 hp (R.A.C. 17·1)
Engine: 4-cylinder, 80 × 86 mm, S.V., H.T. magneto ignition.

Transmission: Multidisc clutch, 2 speeds and reverse, shaft, bevel-geared live axle.

1914 15/18 hp (R.A.C. 17·1)
Engine: As above but dimensions

83 × 140 mm. *Transmission:* As
above but 3 speeds.

Hurtu France

Needless to say the more waggish anti-motorists of the 'nineties exercised their wits on the name of the Hurtu, the makers of which had started in the sewing-machine business and then taken up cycle building about 1885. Young Alexandre Darracq worked for them at one time, but that was before they took to making motor cars in 1896. Like so many others they started by building Benz cars (whether under licence or just plagiarizing is not clear). They made a few improvements of their own as time went on, chief of which were a brass cover to keep the dust off the crank shaft and a less primitive means of lubricating the big-end bearing than 'Papa' Benz's grease-cup. By 1899 they had made arrangements with the Marshall Engineering Co. (who later made the Belsize, qv), to construct the Hurtu-Benz under licence in England, and for a few years business was quite good. For the 1901 season, a vertical-engined shaft-driven car was put on the market. It will occasion no surprise to learn that the engine was by De Dion Bouton, and it seems that a few of these little cars were sold by Gamages under their name.

Thereafter the Hurtu company seem to have pursued a blameless course confecting sound but uninspired small-to-medium cars largely from proprietary bits. The Renault type of dashboard radiator was adopted in 1907, and for some years the main product was a light car, rated at 10 hp, with a small monobloc 4-cylinder engine. This was quite a popular car, comfortable and quiet with a top speed of 45 mpg. The English Agents, Ariel & General Repairs Ltd, guaranteed 30 mph and ability to stop and re-start on the 1 in 4 test hill at Brooklands with a full load. Slightly larger versions with 70 × 110 mm 12 hp, or 75 × 120 mm 14 hp engines came out in 1912.

1899 3½ hp (R.A.C. 9·69) *Engine:* Horizontal, transverse, rear-mounted, 1-cylinder, 125 × 135 mm, A.I.V., trembler coil ignition. *Transmission:* Primary drive, clutch action and 2 speeds (no reverse) by two belts and two sets of fast and loose pulleys on countershaft. Side chains, dead axle.

1901 3½ hp single-cylinder tonneau

1913 10 hp (R.A.C. 12·1) *Engine:* 4-cylinder, 70 × 100 mm, S.V., H.T. magneto ignition. *Transmission:*

Cone clutch, 3 speeds and reverse, shaft, bevel-geared live axle.

Hutton England

J.E. Hutton was in business importing cars from France in 1900 and, as the practice then was, some of these were anonymous 'assembled' voiturettes which he sold as Huttons. By 1903 he was London agent for Brooke cars (famous in their day and, with Sunbeam and Napier, one of the first makes to standardise a 6-cylinder engine), he had an interest in the Ariel-Simplex and he was also making 4-cylinder Hutton cars which were recognisably derived from the contemporary Berliet.

In 1904 the Hutton Company produced an extremely advanced machine with automatic transmission and hydraulic brakes. The standard pattern was a 4-cylinder 20 hp, but three 100 hp, 6-cylinder cars, with the automatic transmission, were entered for the eliminating trials for the Gordon Bennett race; unfortunately they were not ready in time.

1908 26 hp 4-cylinder Tourist Trophy racing two-seater

The engine of the 20 hp car was quite conventional and had L.T. magneto ignition, mechanical inlet-over-exhaust valves and exposed timing gears in the fashion of the time, but the transmission was distinctly unusual. The basis of it was the Barber progressively-variable gear which is too complex to describe without drawings. Briefly, the Barber gear depended upon the oscillating action of an eccentric sheave, the eccentricity of which could be varied according to load or engine speed. It was an old idea, but the distinctive feature of the Barber device was the system of pawls which gripped by tilting rollers to give a wedging action upon a smooth annulus, thereby avoiding the jerky motion of a conventional pawl-and-ratchet system. The automatic variation of the gear ratios to suit load and speed was done hydraulically by an engine-driven pump, which also furnished power for one of two sets of brakes on the back wheels. These brakes, and the over-riding control of the gear mechanism, were worked by small levers mounted on the steering wheel.

It is usually said that the Barber gear made a clutch and differential unnecessary. This is not quite correct but arises from a mistake in the original report in *The Autocar* which has been repeated ever since. Differential action was provided for in the arrangement of two sets of bevels which coupled the Barber gear to the two halves of the countershaft (final drive was by chains), and there *was* a clutch between engine and gearbox though, theoretically, it could have been dispensed with. This clutch was of a new, patented, expanding variety, and similar expanding mechanism was used for the brakes. Perhaps the automatic transmission was before its time, probably it was too expensive, for although it gave satisfactory results it was dropped after two years in favour of an ordinary gearbox.

Hutton cars were not built after 1910 and one of the most famous Huttons is, in fact, a Napier. This came about because the regulations for the 1908 T.T. —the 'four-inch' race—favoured large bore 4-cylinder engines, and as S.F. Edge had beaten the 6-cylinder drum so hard on Napier's behalf, and decried the big 4-cylinder engine so scathingly, it would have seemed inconsistent to make big 4-cylinder Napiers as such. Consequently three suitable cars were built and called Huttons—and very fine cars they were too, as will be agreed by those who have seen the surviving example (the actual T.T. winner) in action at the hands of the braver half of the authors.

1904 20 hp (R.A.C. 24·8) *Engine:* 4-cylinder, 100 × 130 mm, mechanical variable lift inlet valves, (I.o.E.), L.T. magneto ignition. *Transmission:* Barber expanding clutch, Barber progressively variable hydraulically controlled gear, bevel-geared countershaft, side chains, dead axle. Also offered with 90 × 120 mm engine (R.A.C. rating 20·1 hp).

1908 26 hp (R.A.C. 25·6) *Engine:* Napier, 4-cylinder, 4 × 7 in., S.V., H.T. magneto and coil ignition. *Transmission:* Cone clutch, 4 speeds and reverse, shaft, bevel-geared live axle.

International   see Roger

Iris   England

The Iris car was advertised as entirely British, but its parentage was at least part French, for the makers were Legros & Knowles of Willesden and Aylesbury, and René Legros was also concerned with an interesting 3-cylinder

2-stroke car called *La Plus Simple* which was built at Fécamp from 1900 to 1912.

Iris cars were first produced in 1905 and throughout the Edwardian period they were perfectly straightforward machines, neither particularly advanced nor particularly old-fashioned. The company concentrated on 4-cylinder models from 15 to 35 hp, which, from the first, had mechanically operated inlet valves, H.T. magneto ignition, shaft transmission and a distinctive diamond-shaped radiator with a steeply 'roofed' bonnet. The name Iris derived from their early slogan—'It Runs In Silence', and though the cars were far from noisy this claim was, perhaps, short of the literal truth. A 6-cylinder 40 hp model was also made.

1912 15 hp 4-cylinder tourer

In common with so many other makers the Iris Car Company brought out a 'Colonial' model in 1911. This had the standard 15·8 hp 80 × 114 mm engine, a strengthened chassis, lower-geared-than-normal final drive and oversize tyres. One of these models was encountered carrying a dilapidated 16-seater 'bus body with unabated vigour in Nairobi during the late war. The Company also did general engineering work, and were given the job of making a horizontally opposed 4-cylinder engine for Geoffrey de Havilland's first aeroplane.

1906 25/30 hp (R.A.C. 28·9)
Engine: 4-cylinder, 108 × 133 mm, S.V., trembler coil ignition with dynamo. *Transmission:* Multiplate clutch, 3 speeds and reverse, shaft, bevel-geared live axle.

1909 40 hp (R.A.C. 43·4)
Specification and dimensions as above, but 6-cylinder and H.T. magneto.

1913 15 hp (R.A.C. 15·8) *Engine:* 4-cylinder, 80 × 114 mm, S.V., H.T. magneto ignition. *Transmission:* As above but cone clutch.

Itala   Italy

To most enthusiasts in England the name Itala is inseparably connected with the famous 1908 12-litre *Grand Prix* car which, more than any other vehicle, was instrumental in fostering interest in the 'Edwardian' period motor cars some twenty-five years ago when, as a class, such cars were thought of insignificant historical interest by comparison with the pre-1905 'Brighton Bangers'. Recently an even more splendid Itala, the $14\frac{1}{2}$-litre *Grand Prix* car of 1907, has been restored to activity and the sight of these two monsters (but Oh! such thoroughbred monsters) disporting themselves at Prescott or Silverstone is not readily forgotten. Like most of the early racing cars (particularly French and Italian) these racing Italas were directly derived from, and similar to, the firm's production models—or vice versa as the reader may prefer.

Itala cars came on the market in 1904, when the standard 24 hp model already displayed features which the firm had no reason to abandon for many years. The design was obviously inspired by the Mercedes, and included a pressed-steel chassis, honeycomb radiator and selective gear change but did not include the chain final-drive which the German firm favoured until relatively late. All Italas, even the largest racing cars, were built with shaft and live axle transmission from the word go, and the firm successfully demonstrated that the gear-driven live axle could be made as suitable for large cars as for small ones, and for rough roads as for smooth, despite the dogmatic assertions to the contrary of several latter-day Lardners. Conclusive proof of the point came in 1907 when Prince Borghese's Itala 'won' the Pekin to Paris Race despite the croakings of the know-alls who prophesied collapse of the live axle before the car left Chinese territory.

Like the Mercedes, Itala engines were furnished with low-tension magneto ignition, but with the movable contact pieces inside the cylinder heads much more readily removable and adjustable than those on the Mercedes plan (which was more generally copied). On the Itala, the contacts were mounted upon circular plates (which served also as valve-caps and were held in place by bridge pieces), and operated by horizontal cams mounted on vertical shafts, one to each pair of cylinders, which were in turn driven by skew gears from the inlet camshaft. This system worked so well that the firm continued with it until 1908/9. A commendably smooth multidisc clutch was also an Itala feature for many years.

An innovation which appeared in time for the 1912 models was a rotary valve engine. Like so many of their contemporaries Italas felt they must join the anti-poppet-valve movement, and their answer to the innumerable new patents for double sleeve valves, single sleeve valves, cuff valves, piston valves, split-ring valves and such was a new form of vertical rotary distributor revolving at one quarter engine speed, and with only one port to each cylinder serving for both inlet and exhaust in the manner of the first Lanchester engines. Advantages claimed were complete silence and absence of wear owing to the slow speed of rotation; criticism levelled was that this slow rotation of the distributor made rapid opening or closing of the port impossible. Therefore, it was said, the rotary valve Italas would be sluggish and inflexible: in practice, as test figures show, this opinion seems to have been unfounded, but in common with most similar devices the Itala rotary valve was not in production long and no rotary valve Italas are known to survive.

Just as the many-headed usually read LANCHESTER as LANCASTER, so ITALA is almost invariably rendered as ITALIA—and appears so throughout in a splendid new American book on the Savannah Races of 1908/11. 'As I was driving my Italia down Constitutional Hill I turned left to go under Admiralty Arch instead of keeping straight on to Westminster.' Oh! dear. . . .

1907 40 hp 4-cylinder tourer

1907 'Coppa Della Velocita' 120 hp (R.A.C. 76) *Engine:* 4-cylinder, 175 × 150 mm, S.V., L.T. magneto ignition. *Transmission:* Multidisc clutch, 4 speeds and reverse, shaft, bevel-geared live axle.

1911 15 hp (R.A.C. 13·9) *Engine:* 4-cylinder, 75 × 110 mm, S.V., H.T. magneto ignition. *Transmission:* As above.

1911 80 hp (R.A.C. 72·9) As 15 hp but 6-cylinder, 140 × 140 mm.

1914 50/70 hp (R.A.C. 41·9) *Engine:* 4 cylinder, 130 × 160 mm, rotary valves—otherwise as above.

James and Browne   (Vertex)   England

Following the success of the Panhard and Mercedes 'systems' the tiny motoring world of 1901 made it clear, on the whole, that it wanted a vertical engine mounted in front of the car and covered by a 'bonnet'—the name originally given to the projecting curve of the Regency sun-blind. A fairly vocal minority in England, however, deplored the waste of space and the 'ugly motor bonnet', consequently some English manufacturers refused to follow Continental practice and made horizontal-engined cars of one sort or another. Many of these were excellent, but their makers were sooner or later obliged to bow to public opinion and fall in line with the majority, or, at least, to fit their cars with bonnets even if these only concealed a water tank, a tool box or the chauffeur's sandwiches.

James & Browne Ltd of Hammersmith put the first of their models on the market in 1901. These had the horizontal cylinders mounted side by side with the 'breeches' (cylinder heads to you) forward, low down between the side members of a sturdy steel chassis. Twin cylinder 9 hp or 4-cylinder 18 hp models were made and in either case the flywheel was in the middle, with one cylinder or one pair of cylinders, on either side of it. Power was transmitted by spur gears to a patent toggle-action metal cone clutch, a 4-speed and reverse gear (1st and 2nd speeds being housed on one side of the clutch, the remaining gears being separately housed on the other), and final drive by side chains. Other features of the design included admirably powerful expanding brakes, rack-and-pinion steering, aluminium water jackets (claimed as a Napier innovation a year later) and an advanced automatic carburettor designed, like the rest of the car, by F. Leigh Martineau.

Like the N.E.C. and a few other unorthodox makes, the design lent itself particularly well to carrying stately, enclosed, bonnetless town-carriages which were by no means as slow as their altitude suggested (and the firm's open cars were quite sporting), and it was a great blow to J. & B. when motors were prohibited from using Hyde Park between 4 and 7 pm. Two vertical-engined models were introduced in 1906. They both had cylinder dimensions of 4×5 in.; one was a 4-cylinder 20 hp, and the other a veryfine 30/40 hp 6-cylinder. Both were quite conventional, with T-head engines and chain or shaft transmission.

The older type of car was made side by side with the new 'Vertex' and for a short while a light 8 hp model was produced with a horizontally opposed twin-

1904 9 hp 2-cylinder tonneau

cylinder engine, and single-chain drive to a live axle. But it appears that the Company fell between two stools; public opinion had really hardened against horizontal engines by 1907 and the new Vertex models were too late to compete with established makes. Production stopped in 1910.

1902 James and Browne 9 hp (R.A.C. 12·8) *Engine:* Horizontal, transverse, forward-mounted, 2-cylinder, 4 × 6 in., A.I.V., trembler coil ignition. *Transmission:* By 'Buffoline' spur gears to metal cone clutch on 1st motion shaft of 4 speeds and reverse gear. Then spur gear to countershaft, side chains, dead axle.

1907 J. & B. Vertex 30/40 hp (R.A.C. 38·7) *Engine:* 6-cylinder, 4 × 5 in., S.V. (T-head), coil *or* H.T. magneto. *Transmission:* Metal cone clutch, 4 speeds and reverse, bevel-geared countershaft, side chains, dead axle, *or* shaft and bevel-geared live axle.

Jowett England

The Jowett brothers, Benjamin and William, were Yorkshiremen and the light car which bore their name had the Yorkshire virtues of hard-working toughness, with an un-Yorkshire reticence about too much display of brass.

The first light car of 1910 was preceded by various experimental machines, and they in their turn sprang from the brothers' experience of engine building which went back to 1901 when they produced a V-twin affair designed as a replacement for the contemporary 6 hp De Dion or Aster units. This was followed by a 950 cc 3-cylinder-in-line engine which had an overhead camshaft and an arrangement whereby the valve and ignition timing could be quickly altered to allow the engine to run in either direction. The early Scott motor bicycles were powered by Scott-Jowett water-cooled 2-stroke engines.

1910/11 8 hp 2-cylinder two-seater Jowett

Their first few cars had tiller steering and the famous flat-twin engine which remained fundamentally unaltered (though specific output steadily improved) until the machinations of Big Business forced the company out of business in 1954.

Various improvements and refinements—such as wheel steering in place of the side tiller—were made between 1910 and 1916 (production only started in earnest late in 1912), but the little Jowett never put on too much weight or too many airs. Despite some rather homely constructional details, such as a clutch cone wound with asbestos string, and a very knife-and-fork-looking 2-star differential, the Jowett cars were extraordinarily durable and their willing performance fully justified the maker's slogan 'The Little Engine with the Big Pull'.

1910/11 8 hp (R.A.C. 6·4) *Engine:* Horizontally opposed, 2-cylinder, 72 × 102 mm, S.V., H.T. magneto ignition. *Transmission:* Cone clutch, 3 speeds and reverse, shaft, bevel-geared live axle. Side tiller steering. Subsequent models, similar specification but wheel steering.

Knight England

The Knight two-seater is a curiosity which dates the early manufacture of automobiles in Britain to 1895. Built in Farnham, Surrey, by a Mr J.H. Knight, who had for some years been associated with the development of oil engines, it first emerged as a three-wheeled vehicle. Some attempt was made to run the car on oil by using a vaporizer, but it was not a success.

By 1896 the car had been fitted with four wheels, with a type of independent front suspension being used. In this form, the car appeared in the 1896 'Motor Show' at Crystal Palace, London. This show was the second of its type to be

1896 single-cylinder two-seater Knight

organised by the Self-Propelled Traffic Association, of which Knight was a member of council. However, the show was a flop, and was little reported, as preference was given to the rival display of the notorious Lawson and his Motor Car Club at the Imperial Institute, London.

The car was used up until 1898, and was then stored in Farnham. It was known to exist in the 1930s, and was eventually resurrected in the 1950s; it has now ended its days in a museum.

There has always been a controversy as to which was the first all-British car to be made in England, to run under its own power. For the four-wheeled vehicle this distinction must go the Lanchester, which was altogether a more refined car, and was better engineered than the Knight.

Knox America

At the beginning of this century the English motoring world accepted the dicta of certain self-appointed experts to the effect that direct air-cooling was impractical for any but the smallest engines. This quaint belief was still current when the British motor industry was given, and rejected, the opportunity of taking over production of the Volkswagen. . . . The Americans suffered rather less from experts and some of their manufacturers were consequently able to sell full-scale air-cooled cars without difficulty. Amongst the best known were the Franklin, which was in production longest, the Frayer-Miller and the Knox Waterless.

The Knox engines were not furnished with the usual sort of radiating flanges but with a great quantity of stout copper pins screwed into the cylinder walls and heads which thus took on a porcupinish appearance. The company started with a little 3-wheeler, like an overgrown bath-chair; this had 2-speed epicyclic transmission and rear-mounted single cylinder engine rated at 4 hp which was then thought (by some) to be about the limit for air-cooled cylinders.

1904 16 hp 2-cylinder detachable tonneau

The tricar was said to be not only Waterless but Vibrationless and Odorless, and a larger 4-wheeled runabout on similar lines was produced in 1902/4. These were followed by conventional 4-wheeled, 4-cylinder cars (4¾ in. bore × 5½ in. stroke), with sliding-pinion gearboxes, shaft drive and magneto ignition. They were conventional, that is except for the cooling which, unabashed by expert opinion, remained waterless until 1908 when the Knox company tried to cash in on the English market in which air-cooled cars were unsaleable.

Both air- and water-cooled Knox cars were regular participants in Stock-Car events, and the former made some pretty impressive long distance trials to demonstrate that the waterless engines could cope with difficult conditions without over-heating.

1906 35/40 hp (R.A.C. 36·3)
Engine: Air-cooled, 4-cylinder, 4¾ × 5½ in., O.H.V., H.T. magneto and coil ignition. *Transmission:*

Metal cone clutch, 4 speeds and reverse, bevel-geared countershaft, side chains, dead axle.

Lagonda England

It seems a far cry from Lagonda Creek, on the Great Lakes of America, to a small workshop at Staines in Middlesex, but it was there in 1904 that Wilbur Gunn, having given up his project of becoming an opera singer, began building a series of twin-cylinder tricars which he named after his childhood's playground. Gunn was a perfectionist (Wilbur Gunn is half done?) and apart from a Longuemare carburettor all the parts, including nuts and bolts, were made under his supervision in the Staines workshop: the Lagonda tricars soon began winning reliability and hill climbing trials up and down the country.

The last tricars were built in 1907 and the first 4-wheeled cars came out in the same year. Four-cylinder 20 hp, and 6-cylinder 30 hp models were made,

1914 11.1 hp 4-cylinder tourer

and cylinder blocks (cast in pairs), pistons and connecting rods were common to both. The rear suspension followed Lanchester practice, with parallel-motion radius links and great tyre economy was, with justice, claimed. For the first few years of production all but a handful of these fine cars were sold direct to Russia and none were available in England until 1912.

Late in 1913 an extremely advanced light car appeared. This had a monobloc 1,100 cc 4-cylinder engine with overhead inlet and side exhaust valves, together with integral construction of body and chassis—this being, it must be admitted, more in the interests of economy than rigidity. It was not, perhaps, a very pretty little car but a genuine 50 mph maximum speed at 50 mpg average consumption is not to be despised then or now—particularly at £135 for a well-equipped 2-seater cabriolet.

1912 20 hp (R.A.C. 20·1) *Engine:* 4-cylinder, 90 × 120 mm, S.V., dual ignition by H.T. magneto. *Transmission:* Cone clutch, 3 speeds and reverse, shaft, bevel-geared live axle.

30 hp as above but 6-cylinder engine.

1914 11 hp (R.A.C. 11·12) *Engine:* 4-cylinder, 67 × 78 mm, I.o.E. valves, H.T. magneto ignition. *Transmission:* Cone clutch, 3 speeds and reverse, shaft, worm-geared live axle.

Lanchester   England

Before 1900 most motor cars, naturally, were composed of elements borrowed and adapted from various sources such as the carriage and bicycle trades, the stationary engine business, and the then common workshop practice of power-transmission by belt and pulley. Since 1900, increasingly with each year that passes, motor design has become a matter of compromise which, for financial reasons, is based upon the use of stereotyped components. The first production model Lanchesters of 1901 to 1905 were unique in owing nothing to any other source, in borrowing nothing from the horse-drawn vehicle and in being designed throughout from first principles as complete mechanical entities.

Frederick Lanchester built his first car (the first English 4-wheeled petrol vehicle) in 1895 and an improved version followed in 1897. This was awarded a special gold medal in the Automobile Club's Trials of 1899 and the car, together with a replica, took part in the 1,000 Miles Trial of 1900. Both of these early Lanchesters had the vibrationless engines and worm-geared live axles which found a place in the production models, the first six of which were produced towards the end of 1900. Lanchester realised, as few designers did, that easy riding and good road-holding depend upon the combination of 'soft' suspension with the utmost rigidity of chassis. Consequently the production cars were designed with integral construction of the lower part of the bodies with the chassis—which were exceptionally deep and rigid. Every part of the mechanism was designed to support and be supported by every adjacent part, and practically every component was so arranged that it added strength and stiffness to the main structure. Even the petrol tank, for example, acted as a transverse brace and also gave torsional strength to the frame.

The engine was amidships and had two cylinders, of $5\frac{1}{4}$ in. bore $\times 5\frac{11}{16}$ in. stroke horizontally opposed, with two counter-rotating crankshafts superimposed between them and linked to the two pistons by a sort of lazy-tongs arrangement of six connecting rods. This apparently complex, but extremely successful, arrangement gave complete freedom from the appalling vibration

above left 1903 12 hp 2-cylinder tonneau
above right 1910 20 hp 4-cylinder torpedo phaeton

so typical of most early engines, and counterbalanced the 'impulse kick', to use the language of the day, and also relieved the pistons of side thrust. There was a large flywheel on each of the two crankshafts which were connected by helical gears, whilst a third helical gear gave motion to a countershaft below the engine. At the forward end this countershaft carried Lanchester's patented compound epicyclic gear system whilst the rear end, which carried the direct-drive clutch for top-gear and the main brake, was coupled by a short propellor shaft to the live axle which contained the famous Lanchester 'hour-glass' high efficiency worm gear.

Other Lanchester features were an apparently old-fashioned, but very efficient, wick carburettor which was retained until 1914; a new form of low-tension ignition with the magneto built into one of the flywheels; an ingenious arrangement to defeat the then prevalent exhaust valve troubles, by having only one valve in the combustion chamber and a mechanical desmodromic 'feed' valve which put the main valve in communication as necessary with inlet or exhaust tracts; automatic lubrication of engine and gearbox; pre-selector control of the low and intermediate gears; cantilever springs front and back with parallel-motion radius links; roller bearings in gearbox and back axle; splined instead of squared driving shafts; and a great many other ingenious details all expressly designed for the car.

The first models had ducted forced draught air cooling, powered by centrifugal blowers, but 'expert' opinion was then so hostile to air cooling for large engines that after 1902 air- or water-cooled models were available to choice; these were rated at 10 hp for the former and 12 hp for the latter. Slightly larger, and faster, models with the cylinder bores increased to $5\frac{3}{4}$ in. were made in 1904/5; these were also air- or water-cooled and rated at 16 or 18 hp, but not very many of these were made, and towards the end of 1904 the first 4-cylinder vertical-engined 20 hp model was produced. Thereafter the big twins were gradually discontinued though they remained available to special order until 1908.

The new cars were arranged with the engine between dashboard and front seat, as on many modern commercial vehicles, so that even with a fairly short chassis all seating was within the wheelbase. The new engines were less unconventional than the old, but still distinctive with horizontal overhead valves, closed by cantilevered blade springs, full-pressure lubrication and square or oversquare bore/stroke dimensions. The epicyclic 3-speed gears, cantilever suspension, worm drive and self-centering tiller steering remained much as before. The 4-cylinder 20 hp was supplemented in 1906 by a 6-cylinder 28 hp; these, like the original models, were designed by Dr Frederick Lanchester, but from 1905 onwards design and production passed more and more into the hands of his younger brother and assistant George. Thus, the next two models, a 25 hp 4-cylinder and a 38 hp six, which came out in 1910/11, were designed jointly by the two brothers and the last of the pre-war models (and the first Lanchester to have a conventional bonnet), the rare side-valve 'Sporting Forty', was the work of George Lanchester.

left 1913 38 hp 6-cylinder torpedo tourer

right 1915 40 hp 6-cylinder sports tourer

The *système* Panhard had already gained so strong a foothold by the time the Lanchester came on the market that many of the firm's excellent features had to be discarded to satisfy public opinion. For example the 2-cylinder cars had the main and emergency brakes, the change speed and clutch operation all looked after by two main control levers and there was only one pedal (for the accelerator). The first 4- and 6-cylinder cars were even more ingenious with preselector control for all gears worked by twisting the grip of the one main control lever, which, again, also looked after the main brake; the emergency brake was foot operated so there were now two pedals, but after 1909 this beautifully easy-to-drive system had to be disguised to work like the normal three pedal and gear lever arrangement which is only now just being discarded again in favour of a return to a two-pedal control.

Demand for ever heavier bodywork made it necessary to substitute wheel steering for the delightful side tiller of the first ten years, but despite this outward conformity Lanchester cars remained highly ingenious and individual. Many of the basic principles of present-day motor engineering may be traced back to the early work of the Lanchester brothers.

1901/5 10 hp (R.A.C. 22·3)
Engine: Horizontally opposed, air-cooled with two counter-rotating crankshafts, centrally mounted, 2-cylinder, $5\frac{1}{4} \times 5\frac{11}{16}$ in., valves: mechanical dual purpose main valve serving both inlet and exhaust in conjunction with desmodromic 'feed' valve, L.T. ignition from flywheel magneto, wick carburettor. *Transmission:* By helical gear to countershaft, 3 speeds and reverse epicyclic. Clutches: for 1st, 2nd and reverse by contracting crab brakes on epicyclic gear drums, high speed direct by metal cone clutch; shaft to worm-geared live axle. Tiller steering, pre-selector control for low gears.

12 hp as above but water-cooled.

16 hp, as 10 hp but cylinder bores $5\frac{3}{4}$ in. (air-cooled).

18 hp as 16 hp but water-cooled.

28 hp (1906 onwards) As for 20 hp but 6-cylinder engine, H.T. magneto ignition. Tiller or wheel steering, 1909/10. Wheen steering only 1912 onwards.

1905 et seq. 20 hp *Engine:* 4-cylinder, 4×3 in., horizontal, O.H.V., L.T. flywheel magneto ignition, wick carburettor. (H.T. ignition after 1906.) *Transmission:* 3 speeds and reverse epicyclic; clutches, as above for low speeds but multidisc for direct drive high speed. Shaft, worm-geared live axle, pre-selector control on all gears.

1911 et seq. 25 hp (R.A.C. 25·6)
Engine: 4-cylinder, 4 × 4 in.,
horizontal, O.H.V., H.T. magneto
and coil ignition, wick carburettor.
Transmission: As for 20 and 28 hp,
but no pre-selector control.

1910 et seq. 38 hp (R.A.C. 38·4)
As 25 hp above but 6-cylinder.
Electric starting and lighting 1913.

**1914 'Sporting Forty' 40 hp (R.A.C.
38·4)** *Engine:* 6-cylinder, 4 × 4½ in.,
S.V., otherwise as 38 hp above, but
this was the first Lanchester car
without the wick carburettor and
with a normal bonnet, and the only
side valve Lanchester to go into
production.

Lancia

Italy

Vincenzio Lancia was the son of a wealthy soup manufacturer, and became
one of the pre-eminent car manufacturers of our time. After an early appren-
ticeship with Ceirano, which was subsequently taken over by F.I.A.T. (where
he became chief inspector), Lancia motor-raced for F.I.A.T. in the distinguished company of Nazzaro. Lancia raced for about 10 years, from 1900 to
1910, finally in a car of his own design and manufacture. His first attempt at
manufacture nearly ended in disaster when his factory caught fire in 1907, but
the prototype appeared in September of that year.

1913 4-cylinder 35 hp 'Theta' cabriolet

The Alpha was a 4-cylinder 15 hp car of R.A.C. 20·1 rating, producing 28
bhp at 1,800 rpm. The car was shaft-driven to the rear end via a 4-speed box
and multi-disc clutch. The first of 108 cars was sold in 1908. A Di-Alpha
6-cylinder car of the same bore and stroke, and of 3·8 litres, was also briefly

produced at this time. It is worth noting that the top speed of the Alpha was 50 mph.

A monobloc in line four, the 3·1 litre Beta followed in 1909, and this became the larger 3·5 litre Gamma of 1910. In 1911 the 4·1 Delta and Di-Delta appeared, followed in sequence by a 4-litre Epsilon, a 5-litre Delta and a 4·1-litre Eta. In 1913 the famous Theta appeared, which had full electrical equipment fitted as standard. About 1,600 cars were manufactured; some cars were optionally fitted with a foot-operated starter and foot-operated exhaust cut out, giving rise to 5 foot pedals, almost the first development of a petrol-powered organ. Powered by a 5-litre 4-cylinder engine of 110 × 130 mm bore and stroke, this car developed 70 bhp at 2,200 rpm, and was capable of over 70 mph.

1913 35 hp (R.A.C. 30) *Engine:* 4-cylinder 110 × 130 mm, pump cooled. *Transmission:* disc clutch, 4-speed gearbox, shaft-driven bevel-geared rear axle.

Lea-Francis   see Singer

Le Zèbre   see Zebra

Léon Bollée   France

Amédée Bollée, senior, and his three sons, Amédée *fils*, Léon and (to a lesser extent) Camille made an impressive number of contributions to the development of mechanical transport between 1870 and 1920.

Léon's first petrol-engined vehicle (patented December 1895) scored instant success and he sold the English manufacturing rights to the egregious Mr Lawson for £20,000. The machine was an unsprung tubular-framed tandem tricar with an air-cooled tube-ignition engine which developed about 2 hp slung horizontally on the left hand side of the frame. An overhanging crank was placed at one end of a long crankshaft and a big flywheel at the other, with three pinions, of different diameters, in the middle. These three pinions were engaged selectively with sliding gear wheels on the second-motion shaft; obviously as there was no way of disengaging the engine from the first motion pinions the transmission gears soon got pretty scuffed and on English-built Bollées the gears were in constant mesh with their respective pinions and the latter were coupled to, or released from, the sleeve carrying the final-drive pulley by a sliding 'feather' device. These rather barbarous arrangements worked a great deal better than they had any right to do. Final drive was by flat leather belt to a belt-rim on the single back wheel, which could be slid backwards in its forks to tighten the belt (in lieu of a clutch), or slid forward to bring the belt-rim in contact with a wooden brake block fixed to the frame.

The tricar was noisy, temperamental, notoriously prone to skidding and the brake power varied from feeble to nil according to the weather, *but*, when all was well, it went like the clappers—the simile is, perhaps, justified for once as the Bollée factory at Le Mans was originally a bell-foundry. A 2-cylinder racing version, with one cylinder each side of the frame was produced, 1897/9, but not very much is known about it.

In 1898 Léon Bollée also designed a 4-wheeled, 5-speed belt-driven light car for Alexandre Darracq. Amédée, *fils*, also designed a light car which was built by the De Dietrich combine.

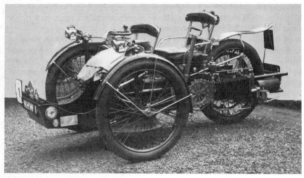

1896 2 hp single-cylinder voiturette

After 1901 Léon Bollée, perhaps ashamed of the Gatling gun noisiness of his tricar, concentrated on producing conventional 4-cylinder cars of the greatest possible silence and refinement. Sixteen and 20 hp models were made at first and other 4- and 6-cylinder cars followed; some of the 20 and 24 hp

1910 24/30 hp 4-cylinder
landaulette

types had hydraulically operated valve tappets on the system designed by his brother. A very fast 40/50 hp chain-driven model was also built, to special order only, between 1906 and 1911. Léon died in 1913 and his widow carried on the business until 1924 when it was bought up by W.R. Morris (Lord Nuffield).

1896 Voiturette (tricar) 2 hp (R.A.C. 3·48) *Engine:* Horizontal, transverse, air-cooled, rear-mounted, 1-cylinder, 75 × 145 mm, A.I.V., hot-tube ignition. *Transmission:* 3 speeds and reverse, pinions on crankshaft meshing with sliding gear wheels on second-motion shaft. Final drive from there to back wheel by belt and pulley. Clutch action by sliding wheel in forks to slacken or tighten belt.

(Model in production approximately four years. 2½ hp 78 × 145 mm engine, 3 hp 85 × 145 mm. Not all models had reverse gear: some late ones may have had electric ignition.)

1905 24/30 hp (R.A.C. 27·9) *Engine:* 4-cylinder, 105 × 130 mm, S.V. (T-head), L.T. magneto ignition, plus H.T. coil. *Transmission:* Cone clutch, 4 speeds and reverse, bevel-geared countershaft, side chains, dead axle.

1912 20 hp (R.A.C. 25·6) *Engine:* 6-cylinder, 83 × 110 mm, S.V., H.T. magneto ignition. *Transmission:* Cone clutch, 4 speeds and reverse, shaft, bevel-geared live axle.

Locomobile (Stanley) America

Were it not for the exigencies of the alphabet Stanley should come before Locomobile, for the twin brothers F.O. and F.E. Stanley were the first successful practitioners of the art of building very light steam buggies which were, for a time, extremely popular on both sides of the Atlantic. These were in limited production by the end of 1897 and two years later the Stanley brothers sold their business to the newly formed Locomobile Company for $250,000. This company did well at first, and an English subsidiary was formed to import and assemble Locomobiles for the European market; but difficulties overtook them—largely because the public discovered in time that the little Stanley/Locomobiles were as troublesome as they were entrancing. In 1902 the Stanley brothers bought back the steam-car business, at a bargain price, brought out improved designs, and went from strength to strength, whilst a re-organised Locomobile Company produced 'gas-buggies' designed by Overman who had formerly been building steam and petrol cars on his own account at Chicopee Falls. Their 9 hp 2-cylinder horizontal-engined runabouts were supplemented in 1903 by a well made 4-cylinder 'European style' car designed by E.L. Riker. The first model was rated at 20 hp (4 × 5 in.) and had the I.o.E. valve arrangement. This soon grew up into an admirable, fast, 45 hp Model F from which was developed the famous No 7, which had a bore and stroke of 7¼ in. and was the first American car to win the Vanderbilt Cup Race: this was in 1908, though the car was built in 1906.

1901 5 hp 2-cylinder phaeton, (the late Richard Shuttleworth driving)

The original Stanley, or Locomobile, steamer was widely copied, and the general arrangement was used for steam, gas or electric propulsion. That is, the vehicle had an unsprung tubular 'reach-bar' underframe, transmission by central chain (scarcely bigger than a bicycle's) to a divided live axle, and all the machinery, boiler and tanks were carried on or in the simple wooden body mounted on full elliptic springs above the reach-bars. A vertical fire-tube boiler went under the seat, just behind the little 2-cylinder 'simple' engine which had its cranks, connecting rods and cross-heads entirely unprotected from dust and mud. A horseshoe-shaped 15-gallon water tank fitted partly round the boiler. The vaporising burner burnt petrol, and the vaporiser was heated for starting the fire by a singularly diabolical contrivance called the 'torch' or 'firing-iron' which had to be made red-hot on the kitchen stove before use. When all was well these little steamers were quite charming—noiseless, vibrationless and good on hills, but they were very frail and really

left 1906 90 hp Vanderbilt Cup 'Old 16' Petrol Locomobile (16 was its number in the 1908 race)

right 1907 2-cylinder 20 hp Stanley 'Gentleman's Speedy Roadster'

only suitable for short runs on smooth city streets. Unless constantly tinkered and adjusted by someone who really understood them they soon became unreliable and dangerous. And at their best their range on a tank of water was only 20 miles, petrol consumption was high and the engine could only be lubricated by squirting vaguely at the bearings with an oil can. By 1903 their early popularity had vanished.

The re-designed Stanley steamers of 1904 onwards were much bigger and sturdier. Unlike their competitors the Stanley brothers avoided the complications of flash-boilers, condensers, compound engines and other refinements. With their simple non-condensing engines, and pot boilers, they were theoretically less efficient but in practice much more suited to the inexpert owner-driver. The recipe remained basically unchanged up to the war and comprised a wooden chassis, full elliptic springs, boiler under the bonnet in front and the engine placed horizontally amidships driving direct on to the back axle by spur-gears. Ten and 20 hp models were made, and the 20 hp 'Gentleman's Speedy Roadster' was particularly popular and a delightful car to drive.

Stanley's onslaught on the World's Speed Record in 1906 culminated in Fred Marriot's famous drive at Ormond Beach in a streamlined car, made from the standard 10 hp chassis with a 20 hp boiler specially constructed to work at greater-than-normal pressures: the car was timed over the flying mile at 121·66 mph. In the following year Marriott tried to beat his own record, but met with disaster in a new car which could work up to 1,300 lb sq in. pressure —a sobering thought. He had reached an estimated 190 mph when the car hit a bumpy patch, turned over and flew to pieces. Miraculously the driver survived, but the Stanley brothers (to the great relief of their internal-combustion rivals) would take no further part in such enterprises though they continued to make steam-cars until 1927.

1899/1900 Locomobile (Stanley-type) Steam-car 5½ hp *Engine:* Mason, vertical, transverse, centrally mounted, double-acting, simple, 2-cylinder, 2½ × 3½ in., slide valves, Stephenson link motion. *Boiler:* Vertical fire-tube, average working pressure 140 lb sq in. *Transmission:* Single chain to live axle. Model also described as 3½, 4 or 4½ hp in contemporary reports.

1904 Locomobile (Petrol car) 20 hp (R.A.C. 25·8) *Engine:* 4-cylinder, 4 × 5 in., Mechanical I.o.E. valves, coil ignition. *Transmission:* Cone clutch, 3 speeds and reverse, bevel-geared countershaft, side chains, dead axle.

1906 Locomobile (Petrol car) 15/20 hp (R.A.C. 22·8) *Engine:* 4-cylinder, $3\frac{3}{4} \times 4\frac{1}{2}$ in., S.V., L.T. magneto ignition. *Transmission:* Cone clutch, 3 speeds and reverse, bevel-geared countershaft, side chains, dead axle.

1911 Stanley (Steam) 10 hp (R.A.C. 8·45) *Engine:* Horizontal, transverse, centrally mounted, double-acting, simple, 2-cylinder, $3\frac{1}{4} \times 4\frac{1}{4}$ in., slide valves, Stephenson link motion. *Boiler:* Vertical fire tube, average working pressure 450 lb sq in. *Transmission:* From crankshaft by spur gears direct to live axle.

Lorraine-Dietrich   see De Dietrich

Lucas and Lucas Valveless   see Valveless

Lutzmann   (Opel)   Germany

The first model of Lutzmann was a knife-and-fork copy of the Benz, though on a rather larger scale, and production started about 1894. Unlike the Benz, the first Lutzmanns had the front wheels in pivoted forks, like the front forks of a bicycle, and as there was no rake or castor-angle to the steering-heads, which were in any case connected to the steering column by a rather vague chain and sprocket system in place of a drag-link, it is hardly surprising that the steering was of an imprecision to make fear.

The horizontal single-cylinder engine (2-litres capacity, 4 hp at 300 rpm), and 2-speed belt-and-pulley transmission were similar to those of the contemporary Benz, except that the countershaft pulleys were of wood and there was no differential gear. The necessary effect was obtained by free-wheel mechanism in the final-drive chain sprockets: this deprived the carriage of any engine-braking effect, but the large external-contracting brakes on the back-wheels hubs were remarkably effective by the standards of the time. A delightful minor feature, perhaps not intended by Herr Lutzmann, is that the countershaft may be observed to bend slightly in time to each resolute 'toonk' from the slow-running engine.

Sales of these belt-driven cars were not very good, and despite improvements and modifications the firm declined. In April 1899 it became part of the Opel bicycle concern which acquired the right to make Darracq cars under licence, though a modernised pneumatic-tyred version of the belt-driven carriage was still advertised late in 1900. Fritz and Adam Opel evolved their own designs out of the Darracq and a variety of conventional 4- and 6-cylinder cars were sold. They had some success in racing and produced some impressive machines in the 'monster' class. Their 1908 *Grand Prix* cars, for example, had 4-cylinder engines of 155 × 185 mm which gave them a capacity of 13,963 cc. One of the 1914 *Grand Prix* Opels survives in England, but this is a much smaller car with a 4-cylinder ohv engine of 4·4 litres.

1895 Lutzmann 4 hp (R.A.C. 12·15)
Engine: Horizontal, transverse, rear-mounted, 1-cylinder, 140 × 154 mm, A.I.V., trembler coil ignition, surface carburettor. *Transmission:* As for contemporary Benz, but no differential gear in countershaft and free wheel mechanism in final drive sprockets.

1896 4 hp single-cylinder Victoria

1900/5 Opel   Similar to Darracq and sometimes called 'Opel-Darracq'.

1909 Opel 8/14 hp (R.A.C. 12·9)
Engine: 2-cylinder, 105 × 120 mm, S.V., L.T. magneto ignition.

Transmission: Cone clutch, 3 speeds and reverse, shaft, bevel-geared live axle.

1914 Opel 40/100 hp (R.A.C. 48·6)
Engine: 4-cylinder, 140 × 165 mm, S.V., H.T. magneto and coil

ignition. *Transmission:* As 1909 but 4 speeds.

Marshall   see Belsize

Maudslay   England

The Maudslay Motor Company, founded in 1902, was an offshoot of the engineering concern whose products, marine engines in particular, had already been famous for nearly a century. Amongst other things they had been responsible for the paddle-engine of the *Great Eastern*, which was probably the largest marine engine ever made with its four oscillating cylinders of 6 ft 4 in. bore × 14 ft stroke.

In the motor engineering field Maudslays are famous for being the first firm to standardise the overhead-camshaft arrangement which appeared on their very first car engines. This was done more in the interests of accessibility than to allow for hemispherical combustion chambers—Maudslay engines were flat headed—also, on the first models, the inlet valves were atmospheric, but it was so easy to add the necessary extra cams to work the inlet valves mechanically that this was soon done. The camshaft was enclosed in a neat housing secured by hinges on one side of the cylinder block and clamp bolts on the other; universal joints in the vertical shaft which drove the camshaft, by skew and bevel gearing, allowed the whole camshaft assembly to be tilted aside if the valves needed attention. This system was used on all the firm's engines irrespective of size and number of cylinders.

Apart from this feature Maudslay engines were conventional, very well made and efficient. Although the combustion chambers may not have been in the best modern fashion they were at least free from the odd protuberances and pockets usually found at the time. The chassis were, at first, of square section tubes filled with ash, and the specification c. 1905 included ignition by H.T. magneto and coil, pressure lubrication, metal-to-metal brakes and 3-speed sliding pinion gearboxes with final drive by side chains.

1910 17 hp 4-cylinder tourer

By 1911 Maudslays had introduced another new feature on their 17 hp 4-cylinder and 27 hp 6-cylinder cars (both 90 × 130 mm), though it had been in use on their 'bus and lorry chassis for some time. This was a silent chain gearbox in which all speeds were indirect, and primary and secondary gear wheels were connected by Renold silent chains, those on the secondary shaft being coupled to it as required by dog clutches. This gearbox, equally silent on all four speeds, was used in conjunction with a Lanchester worm-geared back axle and the result was an exceptionally quiet running car.

Both 17 hp and 27 hp models were offered in 1914 with ordinary poppet valve engines, or a new variety of cuff valve to choice. The latter were built under Reno patents and seem to have had a very good press but it is doubtful if many reached private owners before the war stopped development.

1903 25 hp (R.A.C. 30) *Engine:* 3-cylinder, 5 × 3½ in., O.H.C., trembler coil and/or L.T. magneto,

Transmission: Cone clutch, 4 speeds and reverse, bevel-geared countershaft, side chains, dead axle.

1904 40 hp (R.A.C. 60) As above but with 6-cylinder engine.

1912 17 hp (R.A.C. 20·1) *Engine:* 4-cylinder, 90 × 130 mm, O.H.C., H.T. magneto ignition *or* dual.

Transmission: Cone clutch, 4 speeds and reverse silent chain gearbox, shaft, worm-geared live axle.

1912 26 hp (R.A.C. 30·1) As for 17 hp but 6-cylinder engine.

1913/15 17 and 26 hp models as above but sliding pinion gearboxes

and bevel-geared live axles except to special order.

Mercedes

Germany

Such an aura has grown up around certain makes, particularly Mercedes, that it is a little difficult now to decide just what it was that made them outstanding. That the earliest Mercedes cars *were* remarkable is undeniable, but viewed in cold light were they all that wonderful? The answer probably is—'not quite' —but a combination of mechanical features never previously seen in association (though not new in themselves), together with admirable workmanship, lavish finance and a vigorous racing policy all contributed to their fame.

As is well known the first Mercedes of 1901 (35 hp 4-cylinder 116 × 140 mm), was developed by Wilhelm Maybach, just after Daimler's death, to meet

bottom left 1903 60 hp 4-cylinder Gordon Bennett racing two-seater (Jenatzy driving)
bottom right 1903 18 hp 4-cylinder limousine

Emile Jellinek's complaint that the 1899/1900 24 hp Cannstatt-Daimler was unwieldy and dangerous. Seen with hindsight it may well be that much of this reputation for unwieldiness arose more from overmuch *bravura* on the part of the drivers than from any inherent shortcoming, but the new model was unquestionably a great improvement on the old. The name Mercedes (after Jellinek's daughter) was given to it, and to all subsequent German Daimler products, as a sop to French hatred of the Germans.

The features which distinguished it from its predecessor were its relatively low-slung pressed steel chassis, its 'gate', or selective gear change, its neat honeycomb radiator, and the use of mechanical inlet valves in place of the atmospheric variety then usual. The car also had L.T. magneto ignition; this and the honeycomb radiator and selective gear change had been used on previous Daimler models without exciting much remark. Mechanical inlet valves were not new either, but the combination of all these things, together with excellent brakes and good road holding certainly added up to something which made all other cars seem old-fashioned. In particular the mechanical inlet-valves, electric ignition and an efficient carburettor made it possible to control engine speed, over a wide range, by means of a throttle in the modern fashion. The resultant flexibility was a revelation and rich enthusiasts everywhere queued up to buy.

1908 75 hp 6-cylinder tourer

Almost at once, Panhard, Mors, Peugeot and the rest found their racing laurels being torn from them; the long list of Mercedes successes would take far too much space to detail here. What is more to the point is that perfectly standard touring cars, suitably bodied, could compete successfully in full-scale racing events as the 1903 Gordon Bennett proved.

Mercedes immediately became, and remains, a name to conjure with, and the innovations of the first model influenced designers everywhere. The Company made great progress in the technical, constructional and metallurgical fields though comparatively few 'new' features of car design emanated from them. This does not mean that Mercedes design lagged behind (though the retention of chain drive on the larger models up to 1914 was a little old-fashioned), merely that they did not repeat their great leap forward of 1901. Mercedes gearboxes were, almost without exception, delightful to handle, steering, perhaps, not so brilliant (particularly on some models *c.* 1903 which had three-quarter-elliptic front springs), and brakes well above average for the time. Mercedes pioneered the use of two separate brake pedals working two separate transmission brakes—which were water-cooled on some early models. They also experimented with pneumatic front-wheel brakes, petrol-electric propulsion (the Mercedes Mixte), and produced four models of sleeve-valve car, *c.* 1910 onwards.

Production falls into two 'régimes' in the early period—that of Wilhelm Maybach from 1901 to 1907, after which Paul Daimler took over design. Under the former at least twenty-two different models (both touring and racing) were made ranging from 8/11 hp to 120 hp, and under Paul Daimler, up to 1916, eighteen types were listed including the four sleeve-valvers.

1902 40 hp (R.A.C. 34·5) *Engine:* 4-cylinder, 118 × 150 mm, S.V. (T-head), L.T. magneto ignition. *Transmission:* Cone clutch, 4 speeds and reverse, bevel-geared countershaft, side chains, dead axle. Two footbrakes on transmission, water-cooled.

1903 18/22 hp (R.A.C. 20·1) *Engine:* 4-cylinder, 90 × 120 mm, valves, mechanical I.o.E. otherwise as above, but brakes not water cooled.

1903 60 hp (R.A.C. 48·6) *Engine:* 4-cylinder, 140 × 150 mm, annular mechanical inlet valve (I.o.E.), L.T. magneto and dynamo and coil ignition. *Transmission:* Coil clutch, and as for 40 hp.

1911 50 hp (R.A.C. 35·7) *Engine:* 4-cylinder, 120 × 160 mm, S.V., H.T. magneto and coil ignition. *Transmission:* Coil clutch, 4 speeds and reverse, shaft, bevel-geared live axle.

1914 15/25 hp (R.A.C. 15·9) *Engine:* (Knight type), 4-cylinder, 80 × 130 mm, double sleeve valves, dual ignition. *Transmission:* Cone clutch, 4 speeds and reverse, bevel-geared live axle.

Métallurgique   Belgium

The Société Anonyme La Métallurgique began building cars in their locomotive factory at La Sambre in 1898, and two years later they opened a special automobile works at Marchienne au Pont where they made 2-cylinder and

4-cylinder Panhard type cars (76 × 80 mm in each case) with chain drive and low tension magneto ignition. They adopted Renault-type shaft and live axle transmission in 1902, and in the following year Ernst Lehman became chief designer. By 1905, two Lehman-designed 4-cylinder cars were added to the range; these had engines of 90 × 140 mm and 100 × 150 mm. They were fast cars and beautifully made. Warwick Wright and Moore-Brabazon (Lord Brabazon of Tara) were the English concessionaires and the latter raced Métallurgiques at Brooklands and elsewhere.

During the whole pre-1914 period Métallurgique, though certainly in the 'luxury car' market (even the little 2-cylinder models were notably refined), never built a 6-cylinder car. They argued, not without justification, that a big 4-cylinder engine could be made just as smooth running as a six and of higher thermal efficiency. A patented form of spring coupling, to absorb torsional shock, was used in the transmission and for many years the cars had an ingenious form of expanding clutch which was of very small diameter and consequently had little inertia: this made for easy gear-changing. A particularly handsome pointed radiator was used from 1908 onwards.

The inherent soundness and fine engineering of the Métallurgique is demonstrated by Mr Douglas FitzPatrick's famous Métallurgique-Maybach. This started life in 1907 as a 60 hp car with a Métallurgique engine of a mere 10 litres capacity. Some few years later a 1910 6-cylinder 180 hp Maybach engine of 21 litres was installed in the chassis, which was lengthened 6 in. to accommodate it. Otherwise no changes were made, and the Métallurgique's original clutch, gearbox, back axle, etc. have all proved capable of coping with more than twice the power they were designed for. The result may be a hybrid but it is undeniably magnificent with better-than-100 mph performance and perfect road manners.

1910 14 hp 4-cylinder sports two-seater

Though most of their standard models had orthodox side-valve engines the Company did sell what we should now call sports models and many of these were technically advanced. The 1912 Prince Henry model, for example, had a 4-cylinder engine of 105 × 165 mm with a single overhead inlet valve of 85 mm diameter to each cylinder, and four inclined exhaust valves per cylinder also. With a compression ratio of approximately 6:1 this engine developed 110 bhp at 2,200 rpm. With full touring body the gear speeds were 35 mph in 1st, 65 in 2nd, 80 in 3rd and 95 in top—a performance not to be despised in 1912 or 1963.

1905 10/12 hp (R.A.C. 11·2)
Engine: 2-cylinder, 95 × 110 mm, S.V. (M.O.I.V.), trembler coil ignition. *Transmission:* Cone clutch, 3 speeds and reverse, shaft, bevel-geared live axle.

1906 40/45 hp (R.A.C. 35·1)
Engine: 4-cylinder, 119 × 140 mm as above but H.T. magneto and coil ignition. *Transmission:* As above but expanding clutch and 4 speeds.

1908 40/45 hp, 50/60 hp and 60/80 hp
All as 1906 models but I.o.E. valves. Dimensions: 125 × 140 mm, 140 × 130 mm and 150 × 140 mm respectively.

1910 10/12 hp (R.A.C. 13·96)
Engine: 4-cylinder, 75 × 96 mm, S.V., H.T. magneto ignition. *Transmission:* As 1906/8 but cone clutch.

Metz   see Orient Buckboard

Minerva   Belgium

The Minerva was one of the best known Belgian makes, memorable not only for their fine quality but for their *Circuit des Ardennes* triumph. Doyle gives 1904 as the starting date and certainly the first cars seem to have appeared in that year, but Minerva engines for bicycles, tricycles and so on had been well known for some years before. It appears that M. de Jong, the founder of the firm, had started about 1897/8 as a De Dion Bouton concessionaire and then progressed, as so many did, to making his own engines.

The first full-scale motor cars were a 2-cylinder 10 hp, a 3-cylinder rated at 15 hp, and a 4-cylinder of 90 × 115 mm described as a 14 hp but apparently developing about 22 bhp. On all three the cylinders were separate, T-headed and furnished with mechanical inlet valves. No features of the chassis and transmission (side chain) departed from the standard practice of the time except that the springs were rather longer and softer than usual—the easy ride of the Minerva was a good selling point.

By 1906/7 the 3-cylinder models had disappeared together with the chain drive, and the models made included one with the old engine of 90 × 115 mm, a 16 hp of 92 × 115 mm, a 22 hp of 100 × 115 mm and a fine 6-cylinder 40 hp of 105 × 120 mm; this differed from the 4-cylinder models in having a plate clutch instead of cone, and a *désaxé* engine. This is believed to be the first *désaxé* six in production. A short-lived innovation of 1906 was a short-chassis motor brougham with the engine under the driver's seat, the centre of the chassis dropped very low and the gearbox mounted on a cranked 'dead' axle (so as to bring the propellor shaft low) and with final drive by half shafts and pinions meshing with internal-toothed drums on the back wheels in the Chenard Walcker manner.

The first English concessionaire for Minervas was the Hon. C.S. Rolls who entered one for the 1905 T.T., but as the Rolls-Royce business grew larger the Minerva concession was taken over by C.T. Moore-Brabazon (Lord Brabazon now) and Warwick Wright who also handled the Métallurgique. In 1907 they entered a team for the *Kaiserpreis*, in which they did not figure prominently, but soon after they really brought home the bacon in the *Circuit des Ardennes*. Twenty-three cars started, of which four were Minervas, and seven cars finished—of which four were Minervas which took first, second, third and sixth places. Lord Brabazon's winning car covered the 371 miles in 374 minutes and was subsequently used for many years as an ordinary touring car.

No startling mechanical novelties came from the Minerva works and by 1911 they had followed English Daimler practice and gone over to Knight sleeve-valve engines and Lanchester worm-geared back axles. This did not stop their sporting proclivities, however, and the trail of blue oil smoke laid by the Minervas was to be seen at many a pre-war race meeting. Their *Circuit des Ardennes* triumph was not repeated, but their score in the 1914 T.T., finishing second, third and fifth, gave the lie to those who said the Knight engine would never make the grade under racing conditions.

1904 10 hp (R.A.C. 10) *Engine:* 2-cylinder, 90 × 115 mm, M.O.I.V., trembler coil ignition. *Transmission:* Cone clutch, 3 speeds and reverse, bevel-geared countershaft, side chains, dead axle. L.T. magneto ignition available as an extra.

1911 16 hp (R.A.C. 16·7) *Engine:* Knight type, 4-cylinder, 82 × 110 mm, double sleeve valves, dual ignition by H.T. magneto and coil. *Transmission:* Cone clutch, 4 speeds and reverse, shaft, bevel-geared live axle.

26 hp and 38 hp as above, dimensions 102 × 125 mm and 124 × 130 mm.

M.M.C. England

One of Harry J. Lawson's most grandiose attempts to monopolise the English motor industry was embodied in the Great Horseless Carriage Company Ltd, which was founded in 1896 with a flourish of trumpets and authorised capital of £750,000. Numerous advertisements appeared promising immediate production of a great variety of motor vehicles ranging from heavy lorries to motor bicycles and tricycles. None of these, in fact, materialised and within a couple of years, most of the capital having evaporated (or found haven in the pockets of Lawson and his cronies), the concern was re-financed and re-formed as the Motor Manufacturing Company with headquarters in Bond Street.

For some time, however, the works were still housed in the 'Motor Mills' at Coventry and it is hardly surprising therefore that the first M.M.C. cars were virtually indistinguishable from the contemporary English Daimlers which were assembled under the same roof. That is to say they were Daimler-engined, Panhard-Levassor type cars which had put on a lot of weight and lost a good deal of performance. Unfortunately for the shareholders, there was too much shilly-shallying on the part of the board, and too much abortive experimenting on the part of successive works managers (none of whom stayed long), for any reasonable number of models to be standardised. In addition to cars the Company supplied outside firms with single-cylinder engines assembled from Cannstatt-Daimler components and rather inferior home-made De Dion engines. Further financial and managerial disasters overtook the concern which was again reconstructed.

After 1900 the M.M.C. did find its feet for a short while, though the legacy of its past haunted it in the shape of demands for spares for a wholly uneconomic range of more-or-less experimental models. Under the direction of George Iden, 7 hp 1-cylinder, 8 and 10 hp 2-cylinder and 20 hp 4-cylinder cars were made *c.* 1901/4. They were proudly advertised as 'All British' but the unprejudiced eye might observe that the axles, differential gears and some other parts were French and that the engines were recognisably based upon the Panhard-Levassor type. Many models had the Iden patent gearbox in

left 1914 18 hp 4-cylinder sleeve-valve tourer

right 1902 10 hp 2-cylinder tonneau

which the wheels were always in mesh and brought into use as required by a system of sliding keys: this certainly obviated wear and damage to gear teeth, but as owners found the shafts and keys only lasted about 7,000 miles it seems that Mr Iden's ingenuity was rather misplaced.

M.M.C. cars earned the reputation of being as massive and indestructible as the Forth Bridge and they did well in Reliability Runs. Unfortunately they were also notorious for being as old-fashioned in design as they were lethargic in performance, and despite heroic attempts at resuscitation the concern became moribund by 1905 and finally disappeared in 1908.

1900 6 hp (R.A.C. 10) *Engine:* Phoenix Daimler type, 2-cylinder, 90×120 mm, A.I.V., hot-tube and trembler coil ignition. *Transmission:* Cone clutch, 4 speeds and reverse, bevel-geared countershaft, side chains, dead axle.

(Some 1900 6 hp models retained the old system of reverse gear by two bevels on countershaft thus having 4 speeds forward and 4 speeds reverse; later models had Iden gearbox, constant mesh, gears actuated by sliding keys.)

1903/4 20 hp (R.A.C. 24·8) *Engine:* 4-cylinder, 100×130 mm, A.I.V., early models and M.O.I.V.

on later type, trembler coil ignition. *Transmission:* Cone clutch, 3 speeds and reverse, and as 1900.

Morris-Oxford England

It is fashionable to sneer at the little car William Morris put on the market late in 1912 as 'an assembled job'. So it was, and a very good assembled job too; for Morris had sufficient faith in his engineering knowledge and business flair to place big enough orders with his suppliers to allow him to impose fairly stringent specifications as to machining tolerances and materials. He also followed the plan of selling his cars absolutely complete so that there were no 'extras' for the buyer to fork out. Though becoming more common, this was by no means universal practice in 1912/13, and at £175 the smooth-running and well equipped little Morris was good value. Its success laid the foundation for the great post-war expansion when Morris, obviously lost to all decent feeling, scooped the cream of the motor trade into his cup by sticking to the unfashionable belief that the best way to expand business, in time of depression, is by lowering rather than raising prices.

The Morris-Oxford was a very well made small car, with a wheelbase of 7 ft and track of 3 ft 4 in., propelled by a 10 hp White and Poppe monobloc 4-cylinder engine of 60×90 mm; this engine may have been a thought old fashioned, in that it was T-headed and splash lubricated, but it was a very sweet-running and efficient unit which gave the car a top speed of 55 mph and consumption of about 45 mpg. The engine was assembled in unit with the housing of the multiplate clutch and 3-speed gearbox, and final drive was by enclosed propellor shaft to a Wrigley worm-geared axle mounted on exceptionally long three-quarter-elliptic springs.

Only minor modifications were made for 1914/16, such as fitting a slightly bigger radiator and lengthening the wheelbase by 4 in. to allow for a dicky seat. Incidentally, the name *Bull-nose Morris*, about the origins of which people argue from time to time, was originally *Bullet-nose Morris*. The radiator is much more like a ·303 rifle cartridge than it is like a bull's muzzle.

1913 10 hp (R.A.C. 8·92) *Engine:* White and Poppe, 4-cylinder, 60 × 90 mm, S.V. (T-head), H.T. magneto ignition. *Transmission:* Multiplate clutch, 3 speeds and reverse, shaft, worm-geared live axle.

1912 10 hp 4-cylinder two-seater

Mors
France

The Mors concern was founded in 1851 to make electrical instruments, telegraph equipment, etc. and Emile Mors began experimenting with motor cars in 1895. His first efforts were rather Benz-like with rear-mounted engines and belt-and-pulley change-speed mechanism, but though these characteristics remained until 1899 Mors looked askance at Benz's slow running horizontal engine and produced a remarkably advanced V-4 engine in 1896. This had air-cooled cylinder barrels and water-cooled heads, an effective carburation system with, in effect, a separate carburettor and throttle for each cylinder (all fed from a vast communal float chamber) and low tension electric ignition from dynamo and battery. This was probably the first successful small dynamo for motor car work; after 1899, however, the Simms-Bosch low tension magneto was used.

These rear-engined 4-cylinder cars were quite lively performers, but by the end of 1899 Mors saw the writing on the wall and hired Brasier to design a more modern car on modified Panhard lines. The first of these were powered by the old V-4 engine, a few were fitted with horizontally opposed twins but by late 1900 the vertical in-line type of engine was standardised—but the air-cooled barrels and water-cooled heads remained in use for another year. The 1903 season saw the introduction of a completely new engine design with mechanical inlet valves, detachable T-heads and aluminium water jackets—

the engines were now fully water cooled. The carburation was now more conventional though there was still a separate throttle (governor controlled) in each inlet tract.

With their adoption of the *système* Panhard the Société Mors also began to join in the racing game and were soon showing the older participants the way home. In particular, Gabriel's exploit in covering the 342 miles from Paris to Bordeaux (in the abortive Paris–Madrid Race of 1903) at an average of 65·3 mph is truly remarkable by any standard. His car, a 12 litre 70 hp Mors, was fitted with spring rebound dampers, or shock absorbers, which undoubtedly contributed greatly to the car's good handling qualities—though nothing can detract from Gabriel's achievement—and here one undoubtedly sees the hand of Brasier who was one of the first designers to appreciate the importance of adequate damping at high speeds.

Another Mors innovation, on their early chain-driven models, was the use of a direct-drive-on-top gearbox so contrived that the indirect gears only entailed the use of one pair of gear-wheels instead of two as on the usual type of direct-drive gearbox. The arrangement was quite widely copied but improvements in gear-cutting gradually made it an unnecessary refinement.

Gradually and inevitably the other distinctive features disappeared as car design became more uniform. The aluminium water jackets and L.T. ignition disappeared by 1906 for example, but an unusual form of contracting band clutch, which was very light in use, remained unaltered for many years. Mors cars of the Edwardian period also had full pressure lubrication although many of their contemporaries got by with drip and splash systems until surprisingly late. Knight-type double-sleeve valve engines were used for some Mors models in 1913/14 and one model was listed for a short while with a cuff-valve engine.

1899 7 hp (R.A.C. 12·1) *Engine:* Transverse, V-type, air-cooled barrels and water-cooled heads, rear mounted, 4-cylinder, 70 × 89 mm, A.I.V., L.T. ignition by dynamo. *Transmission:* Primary drive and 2 speeds by flat belts and two sets fast and loose pulleys to cone clutch on countershaft, epicyclic reversing gear, final drive by side chains to dead axle.

1901 10 hp (R.A.C. 15·84) *Engine:* Air-cooled barrels and water-cooled head, 4-cylinder, 80 × 120 mm, A.I.V., L.T. magneto ignition. *Transmission:* Cone clutch, 4 speeds forward, 4 speeds reverse, bevel-geared countershaft, side chains, dead axle.

1911 10/12 hp (R.A.C. 13·9) *Engine:* 4-cylinder, 75 × 120 mm, S.V., H.T. magneto ignition. *Transmission:* Contracting band clutch, 3 speeds and reverse, shaft, bevel-geared live axle.

1901 10 hp 4-cylinder tonneau

Motobloc

France

For the first twenty-five or so years of the century the majority of motor cars were arranged as Levassor had laid down in 1891. That is, engine and gearbox were separate entities with quite a long shaft between the clutch and the change-speed mechanism. There were, of course, exceptions and the modern concept of having the clutch enclosed in a housing which, together with the gearbox and crankcase is rigidly and compactly bolted together was not unknown in the earliest years. Many makes claim priority for this but the palm must probably go to Motobloc whose first cars of 1903 went a stage further and had the change-speed gears inside the crankcase (*à la* B.M.C. Mini-cars) with the second-motion shaft doing double duty by serving also as the valve camshaft. This system was used with a twin cylinder engine, inclined and placed transversely with final drive by single chain to a live axle.

More conventional models followed, with longitudinally placed engines and shaft drive. These no longer had the change-speed mechanism actually in the crankchamber but the gear and clutch casings were made in one piece together with the engine crankcase. Furthermore, the flywheel went in the centre of the crankshaft, to keep torsional vibration at a minimum, supported by a main bearing on either side, and Motoblocs earned an excellent reputation for silence and freedom from vibration.

Apart from the central flywheel and unit construction the cars were otherwise conventional and they were not very well known outside France.

1903/4 8 hp (R.A.C. 10) *Engine:* Inclined, transverse, forward mounted, 2-cylinder, 90 × 130 mm, I.o.E. Mechanical inlet valves, trembler coil ignition. *Transmission:* 3 speeds and reverse (direct on top), gears in crankcase, cone clutch, single chain, live axle.

1912 12/22 hp (R.A.C. 15·84)
Engine: 4-cylinder, 80 × 120 mm,
S.V., H.T. magneto ignition.

Transmission: Multiplate clutch, 4
speeds and reverse, shaft, bevel-
geared live axle.

Napier
England

For the first six or seven years of this century Napier could justly claim to be
Great Britain's leading *marque*: Montague Napier's engineering skill was
combined with S.F. Edge's forceful showmanship to demonstrate that
'Todgers' could do it'.

The story began in 1898 when the ebullient Australian, then London
Manager of Dunlops, took the Paris–Marseilles-winning Panhard (built in
1896), which he had bought from H.J. Lawson, to Napier's works at Lambeth
to be converted from tiller to wheel steering. Other improvements followed,
and finally Napier made a new engine for the car, basically the same as the
original Panhard, but with the cranks in the same plane instead of at 180°, and
with more efficient induction and exhaust arrangements. This was a great
success and the logical step of building complete Napier cars soon followed.
Financed by Harvey du Cros (who had the controlling interest in Dunlops),
Edge set up a sales organisation to handle Napier products in the autumn of
1899, and placed a preliminary order for three 2-cylinder and three 4-cylinder
cars. The first 2-cylinder, sold before completion to Edward Kennard, was

ready just in time to take part with distinction in the 1,000 Miles Trial of 1900.
Apart from the engines, these first Napiers were but little different from the
contemporary Panhards on which they were modelled, but Montague Napier
soon developed his own designs of chassis and transmission systems, whilst
Edge embarked upon a brilliant, if somewhat unscrupulous, publicity cam-
paign based upon a long series of letters, claims, challenges and assertions
which were usually tendentious and sometimes outrageous but which ensured,

at least, that never a week should pass without the name of Napier coming before the public. He was thought to have gone a bit too far when he sent for publication in *The Autocar* a photograph of a grandiose building, allegedly the headquarters of The Napier Motor Company of America, which turned out to be the premises of the Boston Automobile Club.

The first full-scale English racing car was the Napier built for the Gordon Bennett race of 1901. Three were built; they were rated at 50 hp, probably developed about 70 hp, had 4-cylinder engines of $6\frac{1}{2} \times 7\frac{1}{2}$ in., and were not very successful. Edge withdrew from the Gordon Bennett as the English tyres (required by the regulations) would not stay on the rims; consequently his car was fitted with French tyres and ran in the Paris–Bordeaux Race (run concurrently with the G.B.), but retired with clutch trouble. Much of the disappointment with the car was ascribed to its being too heavy, but it is now apparent that Edge's statement (in *My Motoring Reminiscences*), that it weighed $3\frac{1}{4}$ tons, is the outside Edge of enough as Jane Austen might have said, and contemporary estimates of $28\frac{1}{2}$ cwt seem nearer the mark. Be that as it may, in the following year Napier struck the exact balance between speed and reliability and Edge won the Gordon Bennett for Great Britain by being the only surviving entrant with his 1,000 kilos, 30 hp Napier, which had a 4-cylinder engine (5 in. bore and stroke), 3-speed gearbox, shaft drive and live axle. An important feature was that the sliding pinion gearbox was designed to give a direct drive in top with all intermediate wheels out of mesh. Edge's claim that this was the first time such a thing had been done cannot be substantiated but

left 90 hp 6-cylinder racing car, built for 1904 Gordon Bennett Race, later rebuilt as 'Samson'

right 1907 40 hp 6-cylinder landaulette

in longevity, ease of manipulation and quietness Napier direct-drive gearboxes were soon admitted to be in a class of their own. Thereafter, contrary to the usual practice, though many standard Napier models were chain driven, several of the racing cars had shaft drive.

Perhaps Edge's greatest personal triumph came in 1907 when he drove a 60 hp 6-cylinder Napier for 24 hours at an average speed of 65 mph on the newly opened Brooklands track, and certainly the Napier Company's most important contribution to the development of the motor car was the introduction of a 6-cylinder model, first of a long line, towards the end of 1903. Certainly not the first six-in-line engine, and almost certainly (by a few weeks) not the first 6-cylinder car, this fine machine sparked off a controversy which raged for years and in which Edge and his opponents often verged upon the ridiculous; in particular Edge weakened the case for the 6-cylinder by so often arguing from the wrong premises. Despite a certain amount of crankshaft failure at first, the early 6-cylinder Napiers were almost as important historically as the first Panhards and Mercedes, and their standards of flexibility and smooth running set other manufacturers on their toes.

The early Napier chassis and engines have a rather crude and 'blacksmith-made' appearance which is misleading, as in fineness of internal finish and closeness of working tolerances Napier insisted on very high standards. Also, the complete cars, particularly the early sixes, with their radiators mounted ahead of the front axles, were rather ugly and lumpish in appearance: the underlying reason being, perhaps, that Napier was an engineer first and a motorist a long way second. He did not, himself, enjoy driving and hated being driven fast. The later Napiers, however, were as handsome as you please.

Private cars marketed between 1903 and 1914 ranged from 12 hp 4-cylinder models up to the 90 hp 6-cylinder *Grand Prix* type which had an engine of 126×154 mm in a 9 ft 8 in. wheelbase and sold for £1,500 chassis price in 1910. Technical innovations included the Napier 3-port inlet valve (in the days of automatic valves), a system of synchronised ignition which was widely copied, hydraulically controlled carburettor and many detail refinements of chassis parts, steering gear linkages and so forth.

In 1912, following a rather unedifying disagreement, Edge severed his connection with Napier and accepted a handsome 'golden handshake' in return for which he agreed not to take any part in the motor trade for another ten years. The renown which he had done so much to enhance remained undimmed until, to the regret of many, the Napier company decided to stop making motor cars in 1925.

1900 8 hp (R.A.C. 12·8) *Engine:* 2-cylinder, 4×6 in., A.I.V., trembler coil ignition. *Transmission:* Cone clutch, 4 speeds forwards, 4 speeds reverse (reverse gear on countershaft), bevel-geared countershaft, side chains, dead axle.

1902 12 hp (R.A.C. 19·6) *Engine:* 4-cylinder, $3\frac{1}{2} \times 4$ in., A.I.V., Napier 'synchronised' coil ignition. *Transmission:* Cone clutch, 4 speeds and reverse, bevel-geared countershaft, side chains, dead axle.

1904 30 hp (R.A.C. 38·7) *Engine:* 6-cylinder, 4×4 in., Mechanical I.o.E. valves, Napier 'synchronised' ignition. *Transmission:* Metal cone clutch, 3 speeds and reverse, and as above.

1909 10 hp (R.A.C. 8·4) *Engine:*
2-cylinder, 3¼ × 5 in., S.V., H.T.
magneto ignition. *Transmission:*

Cone clutch, 3 speeds and reverse,
shaft, bevel-geared live axle.

1914 30/35 hp (R.A.C. 29·4)
Engine: 6-cylinder, 3½ × 5 in., S.V.,
H.T. magneto ignition.

Transmission: Single plate clutch,
and as 10 hp but worm drive.

New Orleans   (Vivinus)   England

M. Vivinus of Brussels began experimenting with horseless carriages about
1896 but it was not until 1899 that his neat little voiturette was in production.
Georges Richard (who had hitherto built Benz-type cars and was later to
produce the Unic) was so impressed with the design that he arranged to build
1,000 cars under licence in France. Similarly the De Dietrich concern undertook to build 750 in Germany and Messrs Burford & Van Toll, who had been
part of Lawson's *ménage*, set up a factory at Orleans Road, Twickenham to
build the New Orleans.

The Vivinus, or New Orleans, voiturette had a fan-assisted air-cooled engine
of 3½ hp set transversely across the frame. A contemporary report gives the
dimensions as 95 mm bore × 90 mm stroke, but as over-square engines were
distinctly uncommon before 1900 and actual measurement of a surviving 1900
model gives 95·5 × 98·5 mm it seems likely that the original reporter was
mistaken and that the dimensions were intended to be 95 × 100 mm. This
engine had an overhanging crank and two large gauze-covered openings in the
crankcase to help the cooling. Transmission was by single flat belt to a counter-

1900 7 hp 2-cylinder two-seater with spyder

shaft integral with the back axle; on the countershaft was a loose pulley for neutral, and two fixed pulleys meshing by spur gears of different ratios with the axle. As on the Benz, guiding the belt from loose to fixed pulley provided a clutch action for starting. The whole axle and countershaft assembly could be shifted backwards by a sort of giant gear-lever in order to take up stretch in the belt. Although its top speed was only 16 mph, and the slightest gradient brought it down to a slow walking pace, the little New Orleans sold well because it was reliable and simple. In 1900 a 2-cylinder model, on exactly the same lines (indeed, the engine was virtually two of the singles coupled together), made its appearance and this was capable of about 25 mph.

However, public opinion was hardening against belt-drive, and in 1901 a new 7 hp car was produced on conventional lines. This had a tandem-twin water-cooled engine of 95 × 100 mm, dual radiators outside the side panels of the bonnet something like the contemporary Renault, an expanding clutch, 3-speed and reverse Panhard type gearbox and shaft drive. With a well-equipped 4-seater tonneau body this model was good value at £240.

More and larger models on the same general plan followed and were warmly praised; yet the firm did not survive beyond 1907 despite *The Autocar's* commendation of a new 6-cylinder model, and the appointment of the Company to the dignity of Suppliers of Motor Cars to the Amir of Afghanistan.

1900 3½ hp (R.A.C. 5·62) *Engine:* Transverse, air-cooled, vertical, forward-mounted, 1-cylinder, 95·5 × 98·5 mm, A.I.V., trembler coil ignition. *Transmission:* Belt to fast and loose pulleys on countershaft, clutch action by shifting belt from loose to fast, 2 speeds, no reverse, by spur gears direct to live axle.

Oldsmobile (Reo) America

Although Ransom E. Olds was experimenting with petrol motor cars from 1896 onwards, and had built a steamer many years before that, it was not until 1901 that he started series production of the famous 'curved dash' Oldsmobile which was the archetype of the American gas-buggy. Most of the early American light horseless vehicles, steam, petrol and electric, had unsprung 'reach-bar' underframes with the mechanism and bodywork supported by full-elliptic springs on a separate tubular framework. In the Oldsmobile, however, two long springs served both as supplementary chassis side-members and suspension units making, in effect, a pair of laminated steel frame members with quarter-elliptic springs sticking out at the four corners. A light channel iron framework mounted upon these springs carried the simple bodywork, and a slow-running horizontal 5 hp engine which drove via 2-speed and reverse epicyclic gearing and single central chain to the divided rear-axle. The whole affair was extremely simple, rather too frail for serious long distance work and commendably quiet. Maximum speed was about 20 mph, and hill climbing, though very slow, was excellent except that the first models were apt to strip the rawhide pinions of their epicyclic gear on steep hills.

left 1904 Oldsmobile 7 hp single-cylinder curved-dash runabout

right 1907 Reo 18 hp 2-cylinder limousine

The 1902 and later models were more strongly made and some were fitted with 7 and 9 hp engines supplied by Henry Leland who founded the Cadillac Company. These had, from 1904, dummy bonnets and wheel steering, in place of the tiller and curved dash; the runabouts were produced up to 1906/7 alongside more up-to-date models. These first appeared in 1905 and were built on European lines—4-cylinder 20 hp ($4\frac{1}{2} \times 4\frac{3}{4}$ in.) and 2-cylinder 12 hp (5×5 in.)—with 3-speed sliding-pinion gears, shaft transmission and pressure lubrication.

Late in 1904, R.E. Olds sold out his interest in the original company and set up a new concern to build Reo cars which were at first, as one might suppose, very similar to Oldsmobiles. The Reo range included single cylinder 9 hp runabouts, a very tough 18 hp horizontally opposed twin cylinder version of the original type, and, a little later on, 4- and 6-cylinder vertical-engined cars which never quite achieved the reputation of the contemporary Oldsmobiles: this seems less than fair as they were at least as good if not rather better.

1903 Oldsmobile 5 hp (R.A.C. 8·1)
Engine: Horizontal, transverse, centrally mounted, 1-cylinder, $4\frac{1}{2} \times 6$ in., M.O.I.V., trembler coil ignition. *Transmission:* 2 speeds and reverse epicyclic gear. Clutches: for low speed and reverse, by contracting brakes on epicyclic gear drums, for high speed by metal cone which operated a form of plate clutch; single chain to live back axle. Tiller steering.

1905 Oldsmobile 20 hp (R.A.C. 28·9)
Engine: 4-cylinder, $4\frac{1}{4} \times 4\frac{3}{4}$ in.,
A.I.V., trembler coil ignition.

Transmission: Cone clutch, 3 speeds
and reverse, shaft, bevel-geared live
axle.

1909 Reo 18/22 hp (R.A.C. 22·5)
Engine: Horizontally opposed,
transverse, centrally mounted,
2-cylinder, $4\frac{3}{4} \times 6$ in., M.O.I.V.,
trembler coil ignition. *Transmission:*
As Oldsmobile 1903 above.

Opel   see Lutzmann

Orient Buckboard   (Metz, Waltham   America
Orient)

If extreme simplicity is the supreme virtue then the Orient Buckboard might
well claim to be the most virtuous automobile in the world. It was designed by
L.B. Gaylor and made by the Orient Cycle Co. of Waltham, Mass.

Two hickory wood 'reach bars' coupled the axles together and served both
as suspension springs and chassis frame. A slatted wood floor was fixed to
these bars and carried a light channel-iron framework aft to support the motor.
This was air-cooled, $3\frac{1}{4}$ in. bore $\times 4\frac{1}{4}$ in. stroke, and could run up to 3,000 rpm.
Drive was by exposed spur gears and clutch direct on to the live axle; there
was only the one gear and the ratio was $7\frac{1}{2}$ to 1. An extension of the crankshaft
opposite to the driving pinion carried a small fan which blew into the mouth
of an affair shaped like an old-fashioned ear-trumpet the narrow end of which
was curled over the cylinder head. Not surprisingly, this cornucopia effectually
throttled the air-stream and it was soon found that the engine ran just as well
with the ear-trumpet removed.

These simple little runabouts weighed only 4 cwt and their 4 hp engines

1904 4 hp single-cylinder runabout

could whirl them along at 25 mph on a smooth road, but as there were then few smooth roads in America, outside the towns, the Company supplemented the Buckboard in 1909 with a sturdier and more conventional 4-cylinder air-cooled car called the Waltham Orient. The firm was later (*c.* 1910) re-organised as the Metz Company and sold a Metz car in Do-It-Yourself kits or factory-assembled to choice. The first Metz had a 9 hp 2-cylinder vertical engine and friction disc transmission. In 1912 a 4-cylinder 22 hp geared car was offered but not, apparently, in Do-It-Yourself form.

1904 Orient Buckboard 4 hp **(R.A.C. 4·2)** *Engine:* Vertical, transverse, air-cooled, rear-mounted, 1-cylinder, $3\frac{1}{4} \times 4\frac{1}{4}$ in. *Transmission:* Cone clutch and spur gear to live axle. (Late 1904 and subsequent models had 2-speed gear without reverse, 1906 had variable friction-disc transmission and side chain final drive.)

1906 Waltham Orient 14/16 hp **(R.A.C. 17·1)** *Engine:* Air-cooled, 4-cylinder, $3\frac{1}{4} \times 4\frac{1}{4}$ in., O.H.V., coil ignition. *Transmission:* Cone clutch, 3 speeds and reverse, shaft, bevel-geared live axle.

Packard   America

In 1898 Alexander Winton was one of the foremost automobile builders in America: he had actually sold a dozen motor cars. According to a story so delightful that one hopes it is true the twelfth car was delivered on August 13th to James Ward Packard. Unfortunately this particular car was a stumer which broke down repeatedly on the 50 mile trip to Packard's home town and the journey was ignominiously finished with the car being towed by a 'hay motor'. The following day Packard and Winton, both irascible men, had a row the upshot of which was that Winton said '. . . if you're so smart Mr Packard, why don't you build your own automobile?' To which Packard replied 'That's a good idea. By God, Mr Winton I will.' Whereupon he did, with the help of his brother William and aided by the inspiration of the unsatisfactory Winton plus an admixture of the De Dion Bouton tricycle brought back from a holiday in Paris. Further help came when W.A. Hatcher, Winton's machine shop superintendent, joined the Packard brothers in 1899 just before their first 'Ohio' models emerged.

The earliest Packards fitted into the accepted American pattern with centrally placed, slow-running, transverse, horizontal engines and single chain transmission to a live axle. Unlike most of their kind they had 3-speed transmission.

Packards immediately started entering their cars for competitive events of one sort and another, largely, one suspects, for the pleasure of wiping Winton's eye—a project in which they were very often successful. In their first venture, the New York to Buffalo 475 mile endurance test, all five Model C one-lunger Packards finished, although more than half the eighty-nine entrants failed.

Model C was followed by Models D to F, all basically the same except that F had a transverse front spring. One of these, named 'Old Pacific' broke Winton's transcontinental record by making the coast-to-coast journey, in August/September 1903, in sixty-one days: a record that says all that needs to be said of American roads at that time.

1906 20 hp 4-cylinder sports two-seater

Model K, Packards' first 4-cylinder, vertical-engined, European-style car came out in 1904. This had an engine of 4 in. bore × 5 in. stroke which developed 20 hp at 1,000 rpm, and 3-speed sliding-pinion gearbox. A lightweight, 2-speed version 'Gray Wolf' (bore enlarged to $4\frac{3}{16}$ in.) was capable of 90 mph on the track. About 500 Model K's were sold at a slight loss, but the slightly smaller Model L which followed it put the firm on its feet financially. Models K and L had honeycomb radiators very similar to those of the contemporary Mors and recognisably the ancestors of the handsome and distinctive Packard shell of the 'twenties. Indeed the whole aspect of the new models was more than a little French, which is hardly surprising as they were largely the work of Charles Schmidt who came to Packards from the Mors work.

The Packard brothers were not much concerned with anything but the best, and made no attempt to compete with Ford and the rest in low-priced cars for the multitude. Their range of models after 1905 included 4-cylinder cars of 20, 24, 30 and 40 hp, and 6-cylinder models of 38 and 48 hp. The last named was thought by many (not without reason) to be the American answer to the Silver Ghost Rolls-Royce which it much resembled in specification.

By 1913 the 4-cylinder models had been dropped, and the famous 'Double-six' was under development late in 1914.

1906 20/24 hp (R.A.C. 25·8)
Engine: (Imported parts, probably Mors, finished in Packard works), 4-cylinder, 4 × 5 in., S.V. (T-head),

H.T. magneto and coil ignition.
Transmission: Mors-type band clutch, 3 speeds and reverse, shaft, bevel-geared live axle.

1913 38 hp (R.A.C. 38·7) *Engine:* 6-cylinder, 4 × 5½ in., S.V., dual ignition. *Transmission:* Band (?) clutch, 4 speeds and reverse, shaft, bevel-geared live axle.

Panhard et Levassor France

The history of Panhard et Levassor's entry into the motor business is too well known to need much explanation. The bare bones are: Edouard Sarazin granted French agency and manufacturing rights for Daimler engines early 1887. To satisfy legal needs engines had to be made in France. Arrangements made with Panhard et Levassor, makers of woodworking machinery, to do this. Sarazin died December 1887. Gottlieb Daimler confirmed his widow's entitlement to the patent rights. Emile Levassor married Mme Sarazin, May 1890. First experimental P.-L. cars soon after. The *système* Panhard evolved early 1891.

The *système* Panhard (*système* Levassor would have been kinder and more truthful) provided the foundation on which the twentieth-century motor car was built—largely fortuitously it is true. Levassor took the new 3½ hp V-twin Daimler engine (patented 1888) and mounted it in the front of a wooden chassis, with the crankshaft in the longitudinal line, driving through a foot-controlled friction clutch to a sliding-pinion change speed mechanism, bevel-geared transverse countershaft and then by chain to the back axle. The usual Daimler hot-tube ignition was used, there was no radiator so a large water tank was required and the Ackermann steering, so far with no castor action, was controlled by a bath-chair tiller. The whole affair was pretty crude, particularly the combination of a constant-speed engine with sliding change-speed gears, but it worked and was capable of almost unlimited improvement as time has shown. Within a few months cars on this *système* were being sold to the public (one of the very first was still in daily use in 1912), and when

left 1903 15 hp 4-cylinder tonneau
right 1903 Paris-Madrid 80 hp 4-cylinder two-seater racer

motor racing started the Panhard-Levassor products soon towered over all rivals.

So much has been written about the motor-races of the 'nineties it is only necessary to say here that each year from 1894 onwards saw the P.-L. concern competing in everything competitive, each year saw improvements to their design, which remained basically unaltered, and by the time motoring caught on with the general public (at least, with those who could afford it) Daimler engines and Panhard cars were right at the top of the tree. Levassor adopted Daimler's new 2-cylinder in-line engine design in 1895 and with his first car so fitted performed his memorable feat of driving single handed for $48\frac{3}{4}$ hours to be first home in Paris–Bordeaux–Paris race. In 1896 a 4-cylinder engine of 8 hp was used for the first time in the Paris–Marseilles race; like the tandem twin this was known as the Daimler-Phoenix type, but 4-cylinder cars were not sold to the public until some two years later by which time, sadly enough, Levassor had died from the delayed effect of being thrown out of his car in the course of the race. It was now found that the great speeds of 25/30 mph being attained were too much for the tiller-steering and the firm started fitting wheel steering. At about the same time they began to use rather ineffectual radiators hung behind the back axles, but they stuck to tube ignition and all-indirect gearboxes.

After 1900 Panhard et Levassor began to find their position assailed. Peugeots, their chief rivals in the early races, abandoned their rear-engined layout, a host of new makes began to catch up and in 1901 the Cannstatt-Daimler concern brought out the Mercedes which made the P.-L. look old fashioned—just as the first *système* Panhard car had made all else obsolete ten years earlier.

1905 50 hp 6-cylinder detachable-top tourer

During the next few years Panhard-Levassor cars were no longer, perhaps, in the first rank technically but the firm could still sell all they could produce and their racing efforts, though no longer quite so all-conquering, were impressive by any standards. The racing car engines were now very different from those supplied to the public: they grew bigger each year, reaching in 1902, for example, the magnificent folly of a 70 hp, 13-litre, 4-cylinder engine crammed into a chassis so exiguous that the complete car just came into the 1,000 Kilo limit.

Standard models were now fitted with trembler coil ignition, and production included very popular 7 hp 2-cylinder models, and 4-cylinder cars from 12 to 40 hp. A 6-cylinder 11-litre car of terrifying ferocity was shown in London in 1905 but this was, apparently, only done to show that P.-L. could do what Napier, Sunbeam, Brooke and the rest were doing. Only a few were made and none were sold in France. In view of the crankshaft failures which so often beset early 6-cylinder cars P.-L. were probably wise to stick to 2-, 3- and 4-cylinder models in the main. They did, however, fall in line with a pressed-steel chassis in 1905 and the direct-drive gearbox and live axle transmission followed soon after.

From 1905 to 1914 Panhard cars grew steadily more refined and luxurious but no very striking technical changes were made until 1912 when some, not all, of their cars were supplied with Knight double-sleeve-valve engines. Once again the wheel had come full circle; the first English Daimler cars had been copied from the P.-L., and now the French company copied the English in their adoption of an American invention. Amongst the many detail improvements was a method of expanding the brake shoes by a wedge and roller mechanism (remarkably like the Girling brake of the 'thirties): this appeared in 1911 and was soon followed by a patent plate clutch, a new form of universal joint and seven-eighths-elliptic back springs of which the upper portions were cantilevered.

Panhard et Levassor obviously put a great deal of care and thought into the sleeve design and porting of their Knight engines which performed extremely well. Apart from the tell-tale plume of smoke the sleeve valvers could be distinguished from the poppet-valve cars by the letters 'S.S.' on the radiators. These stood for 'sans soupapes'—only French logic could get away with describing as valveless an engine which, in some quarters, was thought to consist of more valve than engine.

1891 3 hp (R.A.C. 6·1) *Engine:* Daimler V-type (Built by P.-L. under licence.), (2-cylinder, 70 × 110 mm, A.I.V., hot-tube ignition, surface carburettor.

Transmission: Brush clutch, 3 speeds forward, 3 speeds reverse (gears not enclosed) bevel-geared countershaft, single chain, live axle. Tiller steering. Iron tyres.

1895 4 hp (R.A.C. 6·98) *Engine:* As above, but dimensions 75 × 150 mm and Maybach spray carburettor. *Transmission:* Cone clutch, 3 speeds forward, 3 speeds reverse (enclosed gears), bevel-geared countershaft,

side chains, dead axle.

(The 'Phoenix' tandem twin engine was first used 1895 but the older V-type was not immediately supplanted.)

1900 12 hp (R.A.C. 20) *Engine:* 4-cylinder, 90 × 130 mm, A.I.V., hot-tube and trembler coil ignition.

Transmission: As 1895 model, but 4 speeds.

1906 15/20 hp (R.A.C. 20) *Engine:* Dimensions as 1900 12 hp but M.O.I.V. and no tube ignition.

Transmission: As 1900 but reverse gear no longer on countershaft, hence only one reverse speed.

1913 25 hp (R.A.C. 24·8) *Engine:* (Knight type), 4-cylinder, 100 × 140 mm, double sleeve valves, H.T.

magneto. *Transmission:* Single plate clutch, 4 speeds and reverse, shaft, bevel-geared live axle.

Perry

England

Perry was a company with one of the simplest combinations of models in production prior to the first world war. The small output was manufactured from 1913 to 1915, and only two models were made.

The 8 hp 2-cylinder car was produced first, and several hundred were made in the short space of two years. These small cars, invariably fitted with two-seater bodies, were never noted for their performance, and probably sold quite well due to their low price of £135 (which was half the price of most other cars).

Just before the outbreak of war a 4-cylinder 11·9 hp car was put into production, and only a few were produced. After the cessation of hostilities, the 11·9 was again in production, but this time by Bean who had bought out the company.

1913 8 hp (R.A.C. 6·4) *Engine:* 2-cylinder, 72 × 108 mm, thermo-syphon cooling, H.T. magneto. *Transmission:* metal-to-metal clutch, 3-speed gearbox with bevel-gear rear axle.

1914 8 hp 2-cylinder two-seater

Peugeot

France

Armand Peugeot, who had been sent to England for engineering and commercial training, added bicycle-building to the other activities of the Peugeot family's old-established ironmongery business. This was in 1885, and four years later, in collaboration with Serpollet, he built a large 3-wheeled, 4-seater

left 1902 6½ hp 2-cylinder detachable-top tonneau
right 1913 6 hp 4-cylinder two-seater 'Bébé Peugeot'

carriage powered by a Serpollet flash boiler and engine. With many vicissitudes this made a trial trip from Paris to Lyons in June 1890 with Peugeot, Serpollet and Ernest Archdeacon aboard. The last named was clad impeccably but incongruously in gent's natty suiting, high stick-up collar, bow tie and curly-brimmed bowler all of which, one opines, were something less than *soigné* at the end of the five-day 300-mile journey.

After this venture Peugeot forswore steam and built his next car, a 4-wheeler, round a V-twin Daimler engine built and supplied by Panhard et Levassor. It was a rear-engined vehicle in the Benz fashion but, after a few experiments with belt and pulley gearing, endowed with cone clutch and 3- or 4-speed sliding-gear transmission in the Panhard fashion: and in the fashion of Gottlieb Daimler's experimental quadricycle the cooling water was circulated round the tubular chassis which thus served as a radiator.

From 1891 to 1901 the rear-engined Peugeot recipe was only altered in detail by continual process of improvement; up to 1896 Panhard-Levassor engines were used, placed vertically and longitudinally, but thereafter Peugeots developed their own engines, which were still recognisably Daimler-cum-Levassor in spirit but arranged to be placed horizontally and transversely so as to do away with the need for bevel gears in the transmission. During the decade Panhard and Peugeot were keen rivals in all the French trials and races, and the honours were fairly evenly divided between them. By the end of the period, when Panhard-Levassor had adopted the 4-cylinder engine for their racing cars, Peugeot had enlarged their 2-cylinder engines to formidable proportions. The 1900 Paris–Toulouse Peugeot, for example, had an engine rated at 30 hp with cylinders of 140×190 mm. With this engine, for the first time, the firm used electric ignition in place of hot-tube.

Vertical forward-mounted engines, Panhard style, were adopted for 1902 and Peugeots soon got one jump ahead with steel chassis and direct-drive gearboxes, whilst their old rivals still had wooden frames and all-indirect gears.

Nearly fifty models were made between 1901 and 1915, ranging from the 5 hp, single cylinder, tubular framed 'Baby Peugeot', first seen in 1902, up to a 50 hp 6-cylinder chain-driven car. In 1912 the 'Baby' was re-introduced, this time in the form of a miniature 4-cylinder car designed by Ettore Bugatti. This had a monobloc T-head 856 cc engine of 55 × 90 mm: dimensions which were thought absurdly small and impractical then, but it was soon apparent that the small 4-cylinder engine was destined to supplant the big singles and twins which had served so long for light car work. The first *Bébés* had a form of 2-speed gear consisting of two concentric propellor shafts so contrived that the bevel pinions on the business ends of each could be engaged as necessary with two rows of teeth on the crown wheel.

At the other end of the scale, in 1913, was a 40/50 hp sleeve-valve car and the advanced *Grand Prix* machines, with twin overhead camshaft engines designed by Henry, which marked a new stage in the evolution of the high-efficiency, high-speed engine.

Peugeots were also exponents of the long-stroke engine in the middle period of the voiturette races. These Peugeots, like the contemporary Sizaire-Naudins reached truly heroic dimensions, and the V-twin 80 × 280 mm Peugeot of 1910, for instance, besides being extremely fast must have been more than a little terrifying as the head of the driver and the head of the engine were roughly equidistant from the ground.

1895 4 hp (R.A.C. 6·96) *Engine:* Panhard-Levassor (Daimler V-type), vertical, rear-mounted, 2-cylinder, 75 × 150 mm, A.I.V., hot-tube ignition. *Transmission:* Cone clutch, 3 speeds and reverse, bevel-geared countershaft, side chains, dead axle. Handle-bar steering.

1899 8 hp (R.A.C. 11·4) *Engine:* Horizontal transverse, rear-mounted, 2-cylinder, 96 × 132 mm, A.I.V., hot-tube ignition. *Transmission:* Cone clutch, spur gears to first-motion shaft of 4 speed and reverse gearbox, side chains from second motion shaft to dead axle. Handle-bar steering.

1909 60 hp (R.A.C. 62·8) *Engine:* 6-cylinder, 130 × 140 mm, S.V., H.T. magneto ignition. *Transmission:* Multiplate clutch, 4 speeds and reverse, shaft, bevel-geared, live axle.

1914 40 hp 4-cylinder tourer

1913 6 hp (Bébé Peugeot) (R.A.C. 7·5) *Engine:* 4-cylinder, 55 × 90 mm, S.V. (T-head), H.T. magneto ignition. *Transmission:* Cone clutch, 2 speeds and reverse by two concentric shafts and two pairs of bevel-gears on live axle. Late 1913 onwards with 3-speed gear.

Phänomobile
Germany

Until somebody produces evidence to the contrary it will be generally accepted that the first automobile to run under its own power was Joseph Cugnot's steam truck of *c*. 1769. In this interesting and necessarily primitive machine a single front wheel acts as both driver and steerer, and the whole massive power plant is mounted above and in front of the steering pivot and has consequently to be moved with the front wheel when the latter is pivoted for steering.

At various times from the late nineteenth century onwards this layout has been revived, though usually without much success until the coming of the Bond Minicar—if that rather nasty little creature could have been called successful. Well-deserved success, however, attended the odd-looking Phänomobile which was made from 1906 onwards by Gustav Hiller A.G. who were also responsible for the Phänomen car.

The Phänomobile started life as a 2-seater 'sociable' tricar with tiller steering and a fan-assisted air-cooled engine perched a-top the front-wheel forks and with petrol and oil tanks, controls and sundries clipped to the tiller bar. The transmission was looked after by chain and 2-speed epicyclic gear. The Phänomobile quickly grew up into a twin cylinder affair with a full scale 2- or 4-seater touring body. The disadvantages were that all the weight of machinery was on the single front wheel, that front-tyre life was consequently short (and puncture mending a worse-than-usual chore), that it was difficult to prevent the engine from being smothered in dust or mud, that the noise was considerable and that the works were so placed that, like a sort of locomotive eye-level grill, hot oil was spat straight in the driver's eye. Nevertheless the Phänomobiles sold well for a number of years and seem to have been extremely reliable and cheap to run. Many were fitted with van bodies and sold to the German post-office.

Flown with success the makers even produced 4-cylinder air-cooled models, many of which were equipped with large limousine or landaulette bodies. By 1912 the smallest model had an 8 hp V-twin engine and tubular frame, whilst the tandem twin 10/12 hp and the 14/18 hp 4-cylinder had pressed-steel chassis and coachbuilt bodies. A curiously old fashioned feature was that the inlet valves were automatic even at that late date. The sprung telescopic front forks were distinctly ingenious and so was the control system. The long tiller handle had a 'spade grip' at the driver's end which could be locked in the horizontal position, to give a free-engine whilst starting, and could then be twisted one way to engage the low-speed clutch and t'other way to bring the high gear into action. Throttle air and spark controls were also mounted on the tiller bar.

1910 8 hp 2-cylinder two-seater

1910 8 hp (R.A.C. 8·34) *Engine:* V-type, air-cooled, transverse, 2-cylinder, 82 × 84 mm, A.I.V., H.T. magneto ignition. *Transmission:* 2 speeds epicyclic gear (no reverse). Clutches: low speed by brake on epicyclic gear drum, high speed by metal cone, two stage chain drive to front wheel.

1911, 12 hp as above but 4-cylinder in-line engine 74 × 90 mm.

Phoenix
England

As his name suggests, Mr J. Van Hooydonk hailed from the Low Countries and he began his career in the motor business in this country as a concessionaire for the Belgian Minerva motor bicycles, tricycles and engines. In 1903 the Phoenix Motor Co.[1] was founded with Van Hooydonk as chief engineer and general manager, and the earliest products were 'Phoenix Trimo' and 'Phoenix Tricar' 3-wheelers. These were much less nasty than most 3-wheelers of the period and were amongst the first vehicles to be fitted with front wheel brakes. These were followed by the 'Phoenix Quadcar', which had tandem seats like the 3-wheelers, and this in turn evolved into the 'Quadcar Runabout' with side-by-side seating and a dummy bonnet in place of the front seat. Both types were powered by inclined transversely mounted Fafnir engines cooled by two cylindrical vertical radiators carried one on each side of the dashboard. They had internal-expanding front wheel brakes.

The next design was altogether bigger and sturdier and a complete breakaway from the quadricycle tradition. It appeared late in 1908 and, though outwardly conventional, it had various features which singled it out from its contemporaries. Transverse engines and two-stage chain transmission, as on the Quadcars, were used at a time when such things were supposedly out of date. Two-cylinder engines were used, now placed vertically, behind a distinctive triangular-topped radiator and beneath a steeply roofed bonnet which greatly resembled a dog-kennel. Some mystery attaches to these engines, as it is not quite clear whether they were made by Fafnir or Minerva—but as both concerns had started on the well-tried De Dion lines (Fafnirs, indeed, under licence originally) the point is not of great importance.

[1] Not to be confused with a Southport firm of the same name which succeeded Felix Hudlass who made the first motor cars native to Lancashire.

If one accepts *The Autocar*'s word for it the 1909 models, at least, had 2-cylinder Minerva engines, and these were praised for being exceptionally smooth running, and able to pull at very low speeds. What is indisputable is that primary drive was by Renold's silent chain to a plate clutch and 3-speed gearbox amidships, and final drive by another Renold's chain to a massive live axle. This system, reminiscent of the Austin-designed Wolseleys, made possible the use of two stages of reduction between engine and road wheels, consequently, as the primary gear shaft ran at less than engine speed, gear changing was easy; also large differences in sprocket wheel diameter were avoided to the benefit of the chains. R.A.C.-observed tests of a 12 hp Phoenix showed that transmission efficiency was 93 per cent. Other features which were praised were the exceptionally large and powerful metal-to-metal brakes and modest thirst for petrol. Maximum speed was, perhaps, unduly restricted in the interests of top-gear flexibility and hill climbing, and at anything over 25 mph the cars became a little fussy—but they were able to carry bodies of a roominess and comfort usually only found on cars of twice the horsepower and three times the price.

1910 8/10 hp 2-cylinder two-seater

In 1913 a conventional 4-cylinder shaft-driven model with Lanchester worm-geared axle was added to the range. This had an 11·9 hp 69 × 100 mm engine and cost £230 complete. A dashboard radiator and coal-scuttle bonnet distinguished it outwardly from the older type which continued to be made in two sizes: these were an 8/10 hp 90 × 100 mm at £195, and the sturdy favourite 2-cylinder 12 hp 102 × 115 mm which sold for £220.

1909 8 hp (R.A.C. 7·9) *Engine:* Minerva (or, possibly, Fafnir), transverse, vertical, 2-cylinder, 80 × 80 mm, I.o.E., H.T. magneto ignition. *Transmission:* Multi-plate clutch, Renold's chain to 3 speeds and reverse gearbox, final drive from second-motion shaft by Renold's chain to live axle.

1913 11·9 hp (R.A.C. 11·8)
Engine: 4-cylinder, 69 × 100 mm,
S.V., H.T. magneto ignition.

Transmission: Cone clutch, 3 speeds
and reverse, shaft, worm-geared
live axle.

Pick

England

The Pick Motor Co. of Stamford seem to have used commendable restraint in avoiding the obvious slogan 'The Pick of the Bunch'. Had they done so, to judge from an indignant writer to *The Autocar*, the rejoinder might well have been on the lines of '. . . never do well if you pick it'.

The Company started in 1900 with a tubular-framed light car powered by a 2¾ hp De Dion engine mounted at the back: single or twin cylinder models followed with the engines mounted transversely in front. Transmission was by flat belt and loose-and-fixed pulleys; there were two fixed pulleys, one for low speed, one for high, driving direct to the differential carrier on the back axle by spur gears. Despite *The Autocar*'s furious correspondent, these belt-driven runabouts, at £160 apiece, for the smaller model, were no worse than many early voiturettes, and rather better than some to judge from the performance of the surviving 1901 model.

By 1904 the Company was selling a 6 hp single cylinder car and a 10 hp horizontal-engined twin. Both had transverse engines driving by chain to the gearbox amidships and then by central chain to a divided live axle. A distinctive feature was an automatic extra-air valve in the induction pipe which could be put out of action by a pedal to give a richer mixture which increased the power on hills—though one doubts whether a carburation expert today would approve.

left 1901 4 hp single-cylinder
two-seater

right 1911 Pierce Arrow 66 hp
6-cylinder tourer

Vertical engined 2- and 4-cylinder cars with conventional lay-out and shaft drive were made after 1906, and the Pick Co. also supplied hoods and body fittings, etc. to other manufacturers. Proprietary engines were used, some of the first cars having Simms or Fafnir motors and many of the later ones being fitted with White and Poppe units. The marque survived the first German war and Mr Pick himself survived the second, having given up the motor business and become a greengrocer in 1925.

1901 Pick 4 hp (R.A.C. 4·91)
Engine: Transverse, vertical, forward-mounted, 1-cylinder, $3\frac{1}{2} \times 4$ in., A.I.V., trembler coil ignition. *Transmission:* Belt to fast and loose pulleys on countershaft, 2 speeds (no reverse) direct to spur gears on live axle.

1910 New Pick 14/16 hp (R.A.C. 20)
Engine: 4-cylinder, 90×102 mm, S.V. (T-head), H.T. magneto ignition. *Transmission:* Cone clutch, 3 speeds and reverse, shaft, bevel-geared live axle. (Worm-gear optional after 1911.)

Pierce (Pierce-Arrow) America

The De Dion Bouton influence on engine design for small cars both in France and England was very marked at the beginning of the century, but most American 'runabout' makers favoured a modernised Benz-type of slow running horizontal engine. A notable exception was the George N. Pierce Company whose later cars were as fine as anything produced either in Europe or America.

The first Pierce model, of 1901, was virtually a quadricycle, with 'sociable' bodywork, fitted with $2\frac{3}{4}$ hp De Dion engine, and Didier 2-speed gear. The 'Motorette' as it was called soon grew up into a $3\frac{1}{2}$ hp and then a 5 hp machine,

typically American in appearance with the sensible provision of a buggy-type hood, but recognisably based upon the rear-engined De Dion voiturette, except that the back axle was unsprung. (Unsprung back axles were to be found on American light cars until surprisingly late.) Some of the later versions of the Motorette may have had American-built De Dion engines, though it has been said that the Pierce Company merely chiselled and filed away the cast lettering on their imported De Dion engines. A larger version of the Motorette, a Stanhope model of 6 or 8 hp, came out late in 1903.

Also in 1903, the first 'Arrow' model appeared with a 2-cylinder 12 hp De Dion engine in front, cone clutch, 3-speed and reverse sliding-pinion gearbox, steering column control, shaft drive and sprung live axle. This admirable car was supplemented in 1904 with the first of the famous 'Great Arrows'—a 24 hp 4-cylinder model for which the engines, though still on De Dion Bouton lines, were made by the Pierce Company. The next two years saw the addition of 28/32 hp and 40 hp 4-cylinder cars, which were re-classified as 30 and 45 hp in 1907 when the first 6-cylinder model appeared. This was first called the '65', then '60' and finally '66': it remained in production, with only detail and body-work changes until 1918.

Various new smaller models replaced the earlier ones, and in 1909 the name Pierce Great Arrow was simplified to Pierce-Arrow, and the designation of the Company followed suit a little later. By 1910 production had settled down to three basic types, which remained virtually unaltered for eight years. These were the '36' (later '38'), and '48' and the '66'. To the regret of many the 4-cylinder 24 hp was finally dropped in this year.

Flexibility, silence and lightness of controls were hall-marks of the Edwardian Pierce-Arrows. The Company never raced officially but they were great contestants in reliability trials of all kinds; they took more first places in the Glidden Tours than all other manufacturers combined and in 1905 a Pierce Great Arrow scored 996 points out of a possible 1,000.

1903 Pierce 'Motorette' 5 hp (R.A.C. 4·37) *Engine:* De Dion Bouton, transverse, vertical, rear-mounted, 1-cylinder, 84 × 90 mm, A.I.V., coil ignition. *Transmission:* 2 speeds, no reverse, constant mesh gears, expanding clutches, final drive by spur gears to unsprung live axle.

1916 Pierce Arrow 66 hp (R.A.C. 60) *Engine:* 6-cylinder, 5 × 7 in., S.V., dual ignition. *Transmission:* Cone clutch, 4 speeds and reverse, shaft, bevel-geared live axle.

Renault
France

In the early days a lot of young enthusiasts built their own motor cars, and one of these was the twenty-year-old Louis Renault who, in 1898, took the 1¾ hp engine off his De Dion Bouton tricycle and mounted it, Panhard fashion, vertically at the front of a tiny tubular chassis. In this very first effort Renault introduced two innovations which are still in use in the majority of motor cars —a gearbox giving direct drive in high gear (thereby avoiding the frictional loss and noise of the Panhard all-indirect system) and a spring suspended, gear-driven live axle. The idea of a bevel- or worm-gear driven live axle was not new, but in previous examples such axles had been attached rigidly to the chassis to avoid complication. This inevitably produced worse complications in use, and Renault got over the difficulty by using a modern form of universally jointed propellor shaft which allowed the back axle to rise and fall on springs in the usual way. So many people wanted a little car like Renault's that he and his two brothers set up a factory at Billancourt and went into business.

The Renault business grew very quickly, helped by the publicity earned by

left 1899 1¾ hp single-cylinder voiturette (Louis Renault driving)
right 1910 10 hp 4-cylinder two-seater

participation in racing. De Dion Bouton engines were used until 1903 when Renaults wanted to climb into the 2- and 4-cylinder markets. The Marquis de Dion, however, did not want to sell them his new 2-cylinder engines and was not then building a 4-cylinder, consequently the Renault brothers first bought a batch of 4-cylinder engines from M. Viet, Georges Bouton's brother-in-law, and subsequently managed to coax Viet into their own fold and away from his allegiance to De Dion Bouton. This occasioned some hard feelings but Renault gained a first class engine designer. During the next dozen years, though the firm produced nothing startlingly new, their cars were never so agricultural and old-fashioned as many recent writers have said. For accessibility and ease of maintenance they were outstandingly good, and the famous dashboard radiator (first used in 1904, earlier water-cooled models had dual radiators in the sides of the bonnet) was quite widely copied. The firm was one of the first to adopt high-tension magneto ignition.

In common with many of their contemporaries Renaults produced a great variety of models—from 6 to 90 hp. The little 'Renault à six chevaux', known as the 8 hp in England, was one of the pleasantest light cars of all time, and a larger 2-cylinder engine propelled many hundreds of London taxicabs and the majority of those used in Paris; the famous fleet of cabs which rushed the troops to the Marne in 1914 were mostly Renaults. These cabs—indeed all Edwardian Renaults—seemed incapable of wearing out.

The firm officially withdrew from racing after the death of Marcel Renault in the Paris–Madrid race in 1903, but private owners continued to race Renaults and the firm were back again to win the *Grand Prix* of 1906, against some much larger cars, with a 13-litre, 4-cylinder 96 hp side-valve car which averaged 63 mph over 770 miles at the hands of the ebullient and unpronounceable M Szisz.

1911 20/30 4-cylinder limousine

1898 1¾ hp (R.A.C. 2·78) *Engine:* De Dion Bouton, air-cooled, 1-cylinder, 66 × 70 mm, A.I.V., coil ignition. *Transmission:* Cone clutch, 3 speeds and reverse 'tumbler action' direct drive gearbox, shaft, bevel-geared live axle. (Probably only three or four built with 1¾ hp engines; series production started 1899 with 2½ hp De Dion engines.)

1901 4½ hp (R.A.C. 4·38) As above but water-cooled De Dion engine 84 × 90 mm.

1903 10 hp (R.A.C. 12·4) *Engine:* 2-cylinder, 100 × 120 mm, A.I.V. (variable lift), trembler coil ignition. *Transmission:* As above.

(Mechanical inlet valves 1904 et seq. 'tumbler' gearbox discontinued 1906.)

1908 20/30 hp (R.A.C. 24·8) *Engine:* 4-cylinder, 100 × 140 mm, S.V., H.T. magneto ignition.

Transmission: Cone clutch, 4 speeds and reverse, shaft, bevel-geared live axle.

Renault specifications unaltered except for detail improvements 1906 onwards, 2- and 4-cylinder models only until 1911; two 6-cylinder models thereafter of 18/20 and 40 hp.

Reo   see Oldsmobile

Riley   England

The Riley Cycle Co. Ltd first manufactured an air-cooled $2\frac{1}{4}$ hp De Dion engined quadricycle in 1899. The De Dion based single-cylinder single-gear tricycles subsequently manufactured have been described as being slow, clumsy, rather ungainly, with insufficient power for anything but gentle inclines without pedal assistance. Bearing in mind that one either walked or found oneself a horse for local journeys at this period in time, the Riley tricycle, being no worse and certainly less tiring than the alternatives, established a flourishing market for such machines in competition with such firms as Star and Swift. One curious feature of some of the early machines was a sort of transvestite arrangement whereby the quadricycle could be converted into a tricycle and vice versa.

By 1903 a new company called the Riley Engine Co. started life by manufacturing single-cylinder air-cooled engines with a patented mechanically-operated inlet valve. A subsequent development was a twin-cylinder V engine of $4\frac{1}{2}$ hp which was water-cooled. According to one contemporary report on the 1904 2-speed tri-car, the ignition coil was thoughtlessly mounted in a wooden box clipped to the rear of the water-cooler. The water frequently boiled, and on such occasions the internal insulation of the coil naturally melted, causing the ensemblage and pillion to come to a halt.

By 1905 the tri-car had developed into a three-wheeler of more conventional appearance, with bucket seats, a 3-speed and reverse box. A conventional steering wheel was fitted, and 4 hp air-cooled, $4\frac{1}{2}$, 6 and 9 hp (V twin) engines could also be fitted to choice. The 9 hp, of which several examples survive, is on record as being an extremely competitive car of its type, and was a curtain raiser of the Riley car of the future. The by-now popular 9 hp sprouted another wheel, and drove via a leather-faced cone clutch and a Riley quadrant-change 3-speed constant-mesh gearbox (of notable sweetness) a differentially-geared back axle. The engine was placed amidships beneath the seats, with the engine and gearbox being across the chassis, the drive to the rear being by chain. Once again competitive success was achieved by this new Riley design.

A notable Riley first was scored in 1907 when the Riley detachable wheel became a standard fitment to 9 hp cars. The Riley wheel became the subject of many patent actions which the company was able to defend.

By 1908 a 12/18 car had appeared, and this sported a 'squashed' circular radiator which enclosed a developed 9 hp engine driving (via a metal-to-metal clutch) a Riley patent gearbox in a conventional arrangement. The rear axle was shaft driven. For around 200 guineas a most elegant open two-seater could be purchased.

The 9 hp still continued in production (unlike the tri-cars) and developed into a 10 hp with similar features to the 12. A speed model version of this car was produced in 1910, when the 9 hp ceased production. From 1910 to 1913 Riley produced only the 10 and 12/14 models with detail changes only. At the 1913 Motor Show, a new 4-cylinder side-valve in-line engine appeared of nearly 3 litres capacity, and was fitted to a new 17 hp car. This car had at first a 3-speed gearbox which was soon to become a 4-speed with a constant mesh twin-top feature. Final drive featured the Lanchester worm gear, and production of this car was resumed after the first world war until 1923.

At the same time an in-line development of the 10 hp car was produced with the 1914 Show in mind. A 3-bearing pressure lubricated crankshaft engine of 1,390 cc powered the car, and conventional bevel gears prevailed over the brief change to worm power of the 17 hp. Only 3 test cars were completed before the outbreak of war and the narrowly abandoned 1914 Motor Show. This model never reappeared.

1907 9 hp two-cylinder two-seater

1905 9 hp (R.A.C. 9·2) *Engine:* 2-cylinder, V twin, water-cooled, battery ignition. *Transmission:* Cone clutch, 3-speed gearbox, chain final drive with differential.

1908 12/18 (R.A.C. 12·9) *Engine:* 2-cylinder, V twin, 65 × 105 mm, thermo-syphon cooling, magneto ignition. *Transmission:* Leather-faced cone clutch, 3-speed gearbox and bevel-gear final drive.

Robinson
England

Although it was intended to put the Robinson in production things went awry and only three were made. This was in 1907 and, miraculously, one vehicle survives to prove that there are more ways of killing a cat than kicking it in the kidneys, for the Robinson uses its own exhaust gases to cool the engine which, at first sight, seems comparable with an overheated stoker fanning himself with his red-hot shovel.

1907 12 hp 2-cylinder two-seater

What happens is this: the exhaust pipe extends to the rear of the car in the usual way and then turns back on itself, for the whole length of the chassis, and enters the bottom tank of a 'radiator' which contains no water. The radiator acts as a combined silencer and cooler; the exhaust gases pass upwards through copper tubes to the equivalent of the normal 'header tank' being partly cooled on their way by fan-assisted draught. The mouth of a funnel-shaped pipe in the face of the 'header tank' admits fresh air to a sheet iron casing over the finned cylinder heads of the 4-cylinder engine, and the final stage in the tortuous progress of the exhaust gases is to emerge into this fresh-air-collecting-funnel so as to accelerate the flow of air on the principle of the blast-pipe of a railway locomotive. Obviously this takes a good deal of the 'coolth' away from the cool air scooped into the funnel—and if the car had a closed body could it be that the occupants might notice some exhaust fumes?

Apart from its eccentric cooling system the Robinson is as conventional as it is beautifully finished.

1907 12 hp (R.A.C. 14·4) *Engine:* Air-cum-exhaust-cooled, 4-cylinder, $3 \times 4\frac{1}{2}$ in., S.V., H.T. magneto ignition. *Transmission:* Cone clutch, 3-speeds and reverse, shaft, bevel-geared live axle.

Roger (International)   France/England

Emile Roger of 52 Rue des Dames was probably the world's first motor agent, for in 1887 Carl Benz showed one of his horseless carriages at the Paris Exposition where it was seen by Roger who became, it is said, the first person to buy one. Shortly afterwards he was granted sole agency and manufacturing rights in France. He sold the cars under his own name to overcome French antipathy to all things German: he soon started assembling cars in his own workshops and may, indeed, have manufactured some of the parts himself. Roger cars took part in many of the earliest French races and trials and though they did well enough Roger does not seem to have prospered. A very early example, bearing his name-plate and believed to have been made in 1888, is in the Science Museum and in 1959 it demonstrated that it had lost little of its vigour in seventy years by covering the London to Brighton course at an average speed of 9 mph.

In 1894 Gascoine L'Hollier of Birmingham imported a Roger-Benz and subsequently started an English agency which ultimately developed into the International Motor Co. with offices in Marylebone. They, at first, imported cars through Roger and then started building under licence. Roger seems to have faded out of the motor business in 1898 but the International Co. struggled on until 1904, their last product being the Charette (or International Charette) which was a version of Benz's last attempt to modernise his original design by using a vertical forward-mounted engine but retaining his beloved belt primary-drive.

Roger Specifications: as for Benz q.v.

1888 1½ hp single-cylinder Victoria

Rolls-Royce England

From a strictly 'engineering' point of view there is much in the design of Rolls-Royce cars to justify the old gibe of 'a triumph of workmanship over design', but this leaves out of account the all-important factor that F.H. Royce was that rare being: an artist-craftsman. He openly admitted that he never originated anything new, but he was never satisfied with anything less than perfection.

The Rolls-Royce story began in 1903 when Royce, then in business making electric cranes in Manchester, being displeased with his Decauville, built a small 2-cylinder car from imported parts for his own use. This had a 10 hp engine of 95 mm bore × 27 mm stroke which was astonishingly quiet, flexible and smooth running. Two similar cars were then made and the last of the trio was demonstrated in 1904 to the Hon. C.S. Rolls, a pioneer motorist, who was then in partnership with Claude Johnson importing large luxury cars from the Continent. Though inclined to dislike 2-cylinder machines, Rolls was so impressed by the refinement of the little Royce that an agreement was made for Rolls & Co. to take the entire output of cars made by Royce & Co. By the end of the year they agreed to market them as Rolls-Royces and a new company, Rolls-Royce Ltd, was formed in March 1906.

During 1905 several models were made, including the 10 hp 2-cylinder, a 15 hp 3-cylinder, a 20 hp 4-cylinder (the famous 'light twenty') and a 30 hp 6-cylinder. All these cars were outstandingly good and many major components were interchangeable between models, which simplified machining of cylinder blocks, pistons, etc. There was also a brief flirtation with a V-eight cylinder machine, which had the engine placed below the floor so that the outward appearance of an electric brougham could be obtained. Another version of the V-eight had the engine in the usual place and this model was designed to be incapable of exceeding 20 mph: it was called the 'Legalimit' and, not surprisingly, it did not sell very well.

In 1906 Royce brought out a new 6-cylinder 40/50 hp car which is so famous as scarcely to need description. This was the 'Silver Ghost'. Cylinder dimen-

right 1905 10 hp 2-cylinder tourer

below 1905 20 hp 4-cylinder tourer

sions were 114 × 114 mm, increased in 1909 to 114 × 121 mm. The output of 48 hp at 1,700 rpm was not, perhaps, very impressive by today's standards, but the combination of brisk performance with complete silence and watch-like perfection of finish was beyond praise. Repair costs, in terms of miles run, were very low and after a 15,000 miles R.A.C. observed trial, without any attention, one of the first of the type was found to require only fifty shillings-worth of replacements to bring it to as-new condition. Although the Silver Ghost was not cheap, reliability of this sort probably made it better value for money than anything before or since.

In 1907 Claude Johnson, now Managing Director, persuaded his fellow directors to drop all models but the Silver Ghost. Various detail modifications were made, chiefly to the transmission and rear suspension; the first models had a 4-speed gearbox, the fourth speed being an overdrive, then came a four-year interlude of 3-speed models followed by a reversion to 4-speed—but without the geared-up fourth of the early days. Apart from these alterations the Silver Ghost remained basically unchanged during its nineteen years production life; it also remained, and remains, a monument to the genius of one who was content to call himself merely—Henry Royce, mechanic.

1904 10 hp (R.A.C. 11·2)   *Engine:* 2-cylinder, 95 × 127 mm, mechanical I.o.E. valves, coil ignition. *Transmission:* Cone clutch, 3 speeds and reverse, shaft, bevel-geared live axle.

1905 20 hp (R.A.C. 24·8)   *Engine:* 4-cylinder, 100 × 127 mm, and as above. *Transmission:* As above, 4 speeds, direct on third, overdrive fourth.

1906 30 hp (R.A.C. 38·4)   As 20 hp but 6-cylinder engine. 100 × 130 mm.

1906 20 hp Landaulet or Legalimit (R.A.C. 34·1)   *Engine:* V-type, 8-cylinder, 83 × 83 mm, S.V., coil ignition. *Transmission:* As above, 3-speeds.

1910 40/50 hp Silver Ghost (R.A.C. 48·6)   *Engine:* 6-cylinder, 114 × 121 mm, S.V., H.T. magneto and coil ignition. *Transmission:* As above, 3 speeds.

(Silver Ghost gearboxes 1906/9
4 speeds, direct on 3rd and overdrive
4th. 1910/12 3 speeds. 1913/14 3 or 4
speeds optional, 4 speed box direct
on 4th. 1915 et seq. 4 speeds only.)

Rover

England

J.K. Starley of Coventry was the first cycle builder to make the modern form of 'safety bicycle' in quantity, and 'Rover' bicycles soon became world famous. This, more than anything else, led to the bicycle boom of the 1890s which, in turn, produced the mental atmosphere which helped to make the motor car acceptable. Starley also patented the differential gear in 1877, though, in essentials, this mechanism had been known for centuries. Although he

left 1910 40/50 hp 6-cylinder
torpedo tourer

right 1904 8 hp single-cylinder
two-seater

experimented with a motorised tricycle in 1889 Starley's company did not go into the motor business until 1903 when they made a few 2¼ hp bicycles.

A single-cylinder 8 hp car (114 × 130 mm) followed in 1904 and this was soon supplemented by a 95 × 110 mm 6 hp model on the grounds that the bigger fellow was 'too powerful'. The earliest models had an interesting form of chassis-less backbone construction, largely made of aluminium, extremely advanced except that the back axle was unsprung. This was soon given up in favour of a sprung axle and an ash chassis reinforced with steel flitch-plates. Also the first cars were offered with wire and bobbin steering or, at extra cost, rack and pinion, but the latter soon became standard equipment. A steering column lever looked after the 3-speed and reverse gearbox; maximum speed was about 30 mph for the 8 hp and slightly less for the 6 hp. Petrol consumption of better-than-40 mpg was obtained from the Rover patent carburettor which lurked under the floor a long way away from the engine.

Another patented feature was the engine braking system, in which the brake pedal shifted the camshaft to alter valve timing so as to convert the engine into an air-compressor; this worked well and was also to be found on the 16/20 hp 4-cylinder cars which came out in 1906. The 6 and 8 hp singles were produced up to 1912: they did well in many Trials, were deservedly popular and were particularly favoured by doctors. They were designed by E.W. Lewis who had been with Daimler.

Four-cylinder cars included a not-very-effective 10/12 hp in 1906 and the very effective 95 × 110 mm 16/20 hp referred to. One of these won the 1907 T.T. This model was normally supplied with a 3-speed gearbox but for £50 extra could be had with an overdrive 4-speed version, as used on the Tourist Trophy car. The rather feeble 10/12 hp grew up into an admirable 15 hp in 1908.

For 1912, when the original 'singles' were dropped, Owen Clegg, from Wolseleys, designed a splendid 12 hp 4-cylinder model (75 × 130 mm) which had an advanced monobloc sv engine with silent chain drive for the camshaft and auxiliaries, multiplate clutch, worm-geared axle and dynamo electric lighting. It was an excellent car at £350, not very fast but smooth running and indestructible. Many of them were fitted with a particularly elegant and comfortable 'Doctor's Coupé' body, which was built by the Company as, indeed, were nearly all their bodies.

For 1911 Rovers succumbed to Knight's Disease in the form of single- and twin-cylinder sleeve-valve cars. These were, in fact, excellent but, except for cycle-car work, single and twin engines were now out of date, and only a few sleeve-valve Rovers were sold.

1906 8 hp (R.A.C. 8·1)   *Engine:* 1-cylinder, 114 × 130 mm, S.V. (M.O.I.V.), trembler coil ignition and/or H.T. magneto optional.

Transmission: Single plate clutch, 3 speeds and reverse, shaft, bevel-geared live axle.

1906 10/12 hp (R.A.C. 13·96)   As above but 4-cylinder. 75 × 100 mm.

1911 12 hp (R.A.C. 11·4)   *Engine:* Knight type, 2-cylinder, 96 × 130 mm, double sleeve valves, H.T.

magneto ignition. *Transmission:* As above but worm-gear.

1915 12 hp (R.A.C. 13·96)   *Engine:* 4-cylinder, 75 × 130 mm, S.V., H.T. magneto ignition. *Transmission:* As 1911 model above.

1910 8 hp single-cylinder two-seater

Russo-Baltique Russia

Russia has not, until recently, been thought of as a motor car producing country, but according to Doyle at least seventeen makes of car have been made in Muscovy and at least one of these was in being before 1914.

The Russko-Baltyskij Waggonyi Zawod of Riga began toying with car production in 1909. Apparently, even then, the Russian Government foresaw the war and were planning to mechanise their army, in so far as armies were mechanised in those days. Hence the Russian Trials and other sporting events (in which several English firms such as Austin, Lagonda and Vauxhall participated), Russian Army tests of heavy lorries and tractors (in which the energetic Mr Coleman helped the White Co. to score a bull's-eye) and hence, finally, official support for the Russo-Baltique in order to acquire a nucleus of automobile know-how.

The cars are said to be fairly direct copies of the little-known Rex-Simplex which was built by Richard und Hering, Automobilwerk A.G. of Thuringia. The Rex-Simplex was, in its turn, based upon the Mercedes as, indeed, were all the many makes in which the word 'Simplex' formed part of the name. Richard & Hering's chief designer went to Riga to supervise production which was, apparently, well under way by 1911. Another theory is that the car derived from an obscure make called the Fondu, but the Rex-Simplex evidence seems stronger although M. Charles Fondu from Belgium was hired to supervise engine erection. General works management was in the hands of Jules Potterat, a Swiss. It is not known how many Russo-Baltiques were made nor whether any survive.

Specification: Not known, but from the evidence of the decayed remains of a Rex-Simplex, the Russo-Baltique is believed to be but little different from the contemporary 25 hp Mercedes. Two models were made: a 24/30 hp 4-cylinder of 105×130 mm, and a 15 hp of 80×110 mm.

Sheffield-Simplex   (Brotherhood) England

The Brotherhood Engineering Co. had, as it were, a vested interest in the high-speed engine having produced, in 1875, a light 3-cylinder radial steam engine able to run at 700 rpm—an unprecedented speed for those days. The firm began making motor cars towards the end of 1904 under the name of Brotherhood-Crocker, and the first car to be finished covered 23,000 trouble-free miles on test and demonstration runs before being sold; the buyer was still using it ten years later. The Brotherhood car was a straightforward 4-cylinder chain-driven affair, strongly influenced by Mercedes practice, with a pressed steel chassis and one very distinctive feature which was that the bulb for the horn stuck out of the boss of the steering wheel.

In 1908 the car-making business was separated from the rest of the Brotherhood affairs, a factory was taken in Sheffield, the name of the car changed to Sheffield-Simplex and Earl Fitzwilliam enlarged his financial and directorial interest with the avowed object of making 'the best car in the world'. By 1909 a 25 hp 6-cylinder live axle car replaced the 4-cylinder chain-driven model, and a 45 hp 'gearbox-less' car came on the market. Actually it was not entirely gearbox-less as there was an emergency low-gear in the back axle, but the object was that all normal running should be done on the direct drive. There was nothing new in this; C.G.V., for example, had made an 8-cylinder one-gear-only car in 1902, but the matter had come to the fore again owing to the craze for London-to-Edinburgh top-gear runs made by Rolls-Royce, Napier, Daimler *et al*. These were a great talking point in 1908 though really proving nothing—except that a car with a big enough engine could go from London to Edinburgh in top-gear, or that a 1-mouse power engine could haul St Paul's Cathedral to the top of Snowdon if suitably geared for the job. The latter point was overlooked by most of those who engaged in such pastimes.

Undoubtedly the 45 hp Sheffield-Simplex was a very fine car, and one duly made a Land's End to John o' Groats run without using its emergency gear, but it became apparent that the car would be even better with a gearbox and consequently the 1911, and subsequent, models had a 3-speed box. This was integral with the back axle—an indefensible arrangement which was just coming into fashion.

An unusual minor feature was that, up to 1912, the accelerator pedal was very wide and flanged at the sides to prevent the foot slipping off; it was moved laterally by using the heel as a pivot, and the claim that this avoided fatigue of the ankle muscles was probably justified. Both clutch and foot-brake were worked by the same pedal and the cars therefore had a form of 2-pedal control in the best modern style.

From 1909 to 1913 a smaller car than the 25 and 45 hp models was marketed:

1912 45 hp 6-cylinder two-seater with dickey seat

this was an almost exact copy of the contemporary 14/20 hp Renault for, with perfect truth, the Sheffield-Simplex Company pointed out that it was one of the best of its kind, and they felt no compunction about making what was in effect, a high-grade Sheffield-steel Renault.

For the 1913 Motor Show the Company announced a one-model policy. The new car was a 30 hp 6-cylinder, 4,741 cc machine with the same bore and stroke as the original 25 hp—89 × 127 mm. It had a very clean design of engine placed in an up-to-date rigid chassis. The seven-bearing crankshaft had journals 70 mm in diameter, and for silent vibrationless running nothing but a Rolls-Royce could touch it. Electric lighting and starting were looked after by a U.S.L. flywheel-dynamotor which foreshadowed the D.K.W. Dynastart by some twenty years. The back-axle-cum-gearbox was abolished in favour of a close ratio 4-speed box in the normal position with final drive by Lanchester worm gear.

After 1919, alas, Sheffield-Simplex never quite made good the impetus lost during the war and the firm sank into limbo by 1925: their last fling was to make that odd, but remarkably safe and comfortable motor bicycle, the Ner-a-Car to the design of Mr Neracher.

1906 Brotherhood 20 hp (R.A.C. 24·8) *Engine:* 4-cylinder, 100 × 130 mm, S.V., H.T. magneto and coil ignition. *Transmission:* Multiplate clutch, 4 speeds and reverse, bevel-geared countershaft, side chains, dead axle.

1909 Sheffield-Simplex 'gearless' model 45 hp (R.A.C. 48·3) *Engine:* 6-cylinder, 114 × 114 mm and as above. *Transmission:* Multiplate clutch, shaft, bevel-geared live axle with emergency low gear and reverse incorporated with final drive mechanism.

1914 Sheffield-Simplex 30 hp (R.A.C. 29·4) *Engine:* 6-cylinder, 89 × 127 mm, S.V., H.T. magneto ignition only. *Transmission:* Multiplate clutch, 4 speeds and reverse, shaft, worm-geared live axle.

Siddeley and Siddeley-Deasy   see Wolseley

Singer   (Lea-Francis)   England

The name Lea-Francis suggests to most people a successful light car of the 'twenties, motor bicycles before that and bicycles first of all. In fact, Messrs Lea & Francis built motor cars before they went in for motor bicycles, and in

1904, after two years experimenting, they put a 15 hp 3-cylinder horizontal-engined car on the market. The designer was Alexander Craig and one of the most remarkable features was that the connecting rods were 39 in. long: the object of this was to have a long stroke without excessive side-thrust of the pistons and it was, by all accounts, a very efficient and smooth-running engine. Mechanical inlet valves were operated by an overhead camshaft, and an ingeniously simple arrangement provided 3-speed transmission with direct drive on both second and third speeds: final drive was by alternative single chains to a live axle.

Before going into partnership with Francis, R.H. Lea had served seventeen years with the Singer Cycle Company, and late in 1904 Singers stopped building their remarkable motor bicycle (which had the engine built into the back wheel) and started making motor cars under licence from Lea-Francis, who soon stopped making cars themselves and went in for motor bikes.

The Lea-Francis type of Singer was superseded for 1907 by a line of vertical-engined cars with shaft drive. Two- 3, or 4-cylinder White and Poppe engines were fitted, all of 80 × 90 mm and rated at 8, 10 or 12 hp: two larger models were powered by Aster engines of 84 × 110 mm (12/14 hp) and 95 × 130 mm (22 hp). Great attention was paid to designing these cars to be easy to erect, dismantle and adjust.

With the addition of a 'bonnetless' car for town work the Singer range remained virtually unaltered for some years, though of course improvements were made from time to time, and Singers developed their own engines, which were still recognisably derived from the White and Poppe; that is, as far as the production cars were concerned, but Singers entered trials and speed events from an early period and evolved some special types for racing. Many of their successes, however, were achieved with hotted-up production cars, and these included the 15 hp record at Brooklands in 1911 at 77·108 mph, and first place both at Aston and Shelsley Walsh in the same year.

From the sporting proclivities came a very effective side-valve 10 hp light

1907 12/14 hp 4-cylinder tourer

car in 1912. Except that it was bedevilled by the then-fashionable combined gearbox-cum-back-axle, it was probably one of the best light cars of the period —though it did not really come into its own until after the War—and B. Haywood took the 'cyclecar' record at Brooklands in May 1913 with a flying mile at 65·85 mph and the flying kilometre at 66·5 mph. The classification of cyclecar is a little misleading as it was far removed from the crudity of most of that breed, but the classification was based upon weight: whatever name was used, it was a creditable performance for a 1,096 cc engine at that time.

1907 12/14 hp (R.A.C. 15·84)
Engine: White and Poppe, 4-cylinder, 80 × 90 mm, S.V. (T-head), trembler coil ignition.

Transmission: Cone clutch, 3 speeds and reverse, shaft, bevel-geared live axle.

1912 20 hp (R.A.C. 20·1)   *Engine:* 4-cylinder, 90 × 130 mm, S.V.

(L-head), H.T. magneto ignition. *Transmission:* As above, 4 speeds.

1914 10 hp (R.A.C. 9·8)   *Engine:* 4-cylinder, 63 × 88 mm, and as 1912 above. *Transmission:* Cone clutch,

shaft, 3 speeds and reverse gear integral with live back axle.

Sizaire-Berwick   (Sizaire et Naudin)   France/England

Sizaire et Naudin entered the motor business in 1905 with a voiturette powered, it is said, by a De Dion Bouton engine (how strange). By 1906 they were making their own engines, the dimensions of which were slightly different from the standard De Dions on which they were obviously based. Apart from which there were some refreshingly original features including a fearsome but effec-

1909 12 hp Sizaire-Naudin single-cylinder two-seater

tive 3-speed and reverse mechanism in the back axle. This had straight toothed pinions of different diameters made to mesh as required with a straight-toothed contrate wheel by an improbable combination of lateral and longitudinal movements. The acute reader will observe that only one of the pinions could have been correctly pitched with the contrate ring, but despite this drawback, and its very considerable unsprung weight, the affair worked very well. The chassis was a homely ash and channel-iron structure with independent front wheel suspension provided by a sliding-pillar and transverse spring arrangement similar to that used on the Critchley-Daimler and Decauville cars in 1899. The merits of i.f.s. went unnoticed at that time and the Sizaire-Naudin suspension was commended (or condemned) by contemporary observers solely on the grounds of cheapness and lightness. On the first Sizaires, although the radiator was in front of the bonnet, the header tank was behind the engine and formed part of the dashboard. Much of the impressive bonnet was occupied by the petrol tank which was placed between radiator and engine.

1914 20 hp Sizaire-Berwick 4-cylinder torpedo tourer

The brothers Sizaire were avid participants in the Voiturette races and developed their 'big single' engines (still recognisably based upon the standard De Dion units) to a state of remarkable effectiveness—ferocity is perhaps the better word. To suit the regulations of the *Coupe de l'Auto* events this necessitated constant increase in stroke/bore ratio. The winning Sizaire-Naudin in 1908, for example, though nominally rated at 12 hp had a 100 × 250 mm engine which developed a most creditable 42 bhp at 2,400 rpm—at which pace piston speed reached the terrifying figure of 3,937 ft per minute. The cars sold to the public, naturally, had more normally dimensioned and tempered engines but the standard models were, none the less, much faster than most contemporary light cars. They were usually endowed with handsome 'sporty' bucket seat bodies in marked contrast to the usual sit-up-and-beg auntification of the time. There are those who say that more wrists were broken in starting

Sizaire-Naudins than by any other car but the Model T—which, however, had a great advantage in numbers.

In 1910/11 the big singles were gradually supplanted by less interesting, but still distinctive, cars with 4-cylinder engines. Two versions were made: a 70 × 140 mm rated at 12 hp and a 15 hp of 70 × 170 mm. They were remarkably 'clean' engines, very square-cut almost in the Bugatti manner, and the carburettors and magnetos were contained in extensions of the crank-chamber castings which also acted as engine bearers. These features disappeared by 1913, as did the i.f.s. which was replaced by a normal beam axle and half-elliptic springs.

The English agents were F.W. Berwick & Co. of Acton, and in 1913 a new car called the Sizaire-Berwick was put on the market. This Franco-English hybrid (French chassis, part-English assembly and finish, English coachwork), was an extremely silent, refined luxury carriage, with a side-valve engine and Rolls-Royce-like radiator. This involved a law suit with R.-R., and Sizaire-Berwick had to alter their radiator. But Rolls-Royce had to pay them a handsome consideration, for it transpired that Sizaire-Berwick had registered the design, whilst Rolls-Royce had not: one opines there were some red faces in Derby and Couduit Street when this became known.

1910 Sizaire-Naudin 12 hp (R.A.C. 8·93) *Engine:* 1-cylinder, 120 × 140 mm, I.o.E. valves with variable duration of inlet opening, H.T. magneto ignition with coil optional.

Transmission: Plate clutch, shaft, 3 speeds and reverse gear integral with live back axle. Independent front wheel suspension.

1911 Sizaire-Naudin 12 hp (R.A.C. 12·1) *Engine:* 4-cylinder, 70 × 120 mm, I.o.E. valves (no variable control) H.T. magneto ignition. *Transmission:* As 1910 above.

1914 Sizaire-Berwick 20 hp (R.A.C. 20) *Engine:* 4-cylinder, 90 × 160 mm, S.V., H.T. magneto ignition.

Transmission: Multiplate clutch, 4 speeds and reverse, shaft, bevel-geared live axle.

Spyker   Holland

Until the coming of the D.A.F. in 1957 (apart from a few 'specials') the only cars to have been made in any quantity in the Netherlands were those produced by the Spijker brothers of Amsterdam from 1900 to 1925. From their small beginnings with a 2-seater voiturette on De Dion lines the Dutch firm quickly progressed to a long line of exquisitely made and technically adventurous models. Though it was hotly denied by S.F. Edge, it is probable that Spykers were first in the field with regular production of 6-cylinder cars. One was certainly shown in England in November 1903 together with a 10 hp 2-cylinder, and 4-cylinder models of 12, 20 and 30 hp. These greatly impressed the motoring press, and the Elsworth Automobile Co. of Bradford contracted to take the entire output for the next three years.

A peculiarity of the early models was that the cylinder blocks were encased in barrel-shaped water jackets, and the firm adopted a handsome circular radiator to correspond. Mechanical inlet valves were used and the lower halves of the crankcases and gearboxes were pressed as part of the rigid chassis structure. Ball bearing crankshafts were fitted to the early 4-cylinder models, with the inner races ground directly upon the journals. One of the most talked about exhibits at the Paris show in 1903 was a 50 hp 6-cylinder car with 4-wheel drive which was said, probably with some truth, to be immune from the dreaded side slip. It was rather ahead of its time and very few were made, though a 60 hp racing version competed in the Paris–Madrid.

The Spyker Company took the dust nuisance very seriously, and equipped their later cars with full-length undershields specially designed to avoid eddy currents below the chassis; these Dustless Spykers, as they were called, were much appreciated in the pre-tarred-road period.

One of Spyker's most intriguing innovations appeared on their 1911 models. These had short *transverse* camshafts, worm-driven from the crankshaft, passing between the cylinders—one camshaft to each pair of cylinders and each camshaft carried only two cams to operate the four valves for which it was responsible. No prize is offered for the first correct solution.

1905/6 12/18 hp (R.A.C. 20)
Engine: 4-cylinder, 90 × 100 mm, S.V. (M.O.I.V. T-head), trembler coil ignition, plus H.T. magneto optional. Ball bearing crankshaft.
Transmission: Cone clutch, 3 speeds and reverse, shaft, bevel-geared live axle.

1905 14/18 hp 4-cylinder tourer

Standard England

If the copy writers are to be believed the 'over-square engine' is something completely new. Needless to say they are quite wrong and one of the earliest exponents of the over-square engine is the Standard Motor Company, of

Coventry, whose first production models of 1903 had 8 hp single-, or 16 hp twin-cylinder engines of 5 in. bore × 3 in. stroke. Both were L-head engines with mechanical inlet valves and the patent Standard carburettor allowed them an abnormally wide range of speed—250 to 2,000 rpm—which was a remarkable degree of flexibility in 1903. The chassis of these first Standard cars had seven generously proportioned cross members in marked contrast to many more famous makes, such as the Napier, which were scarcely more rigid than a tape worm. Cone clutch, 4-speed gearbox and bevel-geared live axle completed the layout, and the extremely squat compact engines were placed very low down. This was of advantage in some of the later 4-cylinder models which had the engines mounted far back in the chassis, with steering column and controls in front of them, so as to accommodate the fashionable bonnetless type of town carriage bodywork. This practice was followed by many firms at that time, but the Standard design was much more accessible and satisfactory than most.

1907 20 hp 6-cylinder Roi-des-Belges tourer

A 6-cylinder 3-speed model came out in 1906, this had more conventional dimensions of 4 × 4 in. (or 4 × 4¼ in.—contemporary lists disagree); it was rated at 24/30 hp and was most successful, as was an even smaller, 15 hp 3½ × 3½ in., 6-cylinder model which came out in 1907. Less well known was a 50 hp luxury car. The bonnetless cars went out of fashion about 1909 and Standards introduced a new model with a small 4-cylinder monobloc engine, rated at 12 hp, placed in a wide-tracked chassis designed to carry spacious closed coachwork. Spacious, that is for an engine then thought scarcely big enough for a 2-seater. As turned out with landaulette bodies they had to be very low-geared (6½ : 1) and their maximum speed was only about 25 mph. But they were good cars and the famous 9·5 hp light car of 1913 onwards was developed from them.

As the name implies, the Company was largely concerned at first in producing a limited number of models, to standardised patterns and with interchangeable parts, at moderate cost. The founder was R.W. Maudslay (whose cousin designed the contemporary ohc Maudslay cars) and he is usually given credit for designing the Standard cars. This is certainly not true of the original models which were the work of a consulting engineer called Craig. Standards competed in the T.T. Races and consistently did well in reliability and hill climbing trials.

1913 9.5 hp 4-cylinder two-seater 'Rhyl' model

1907 20 hp (R.A.C. 29·4) *Engine:* 6-cylinder, $3\frac{1}{2} \times 3\frac{1}{2}$ in., S.V., coil ignition, plus H.T. magneto optional. *Transmission:* Single plate clutch, 3 speeds and reverse, shaft, bevel-geared live axle.

1907 15 hp as above, cylinders $2\frac{3}{4} \times 3\frac{1}{4}$ in. 30 hp as above, cylinders $4 \times 4\frac{1}{4}$ in. 50 hp as above, cylinders $5\frac{1}{2} \times 5$ in.

1910 12 hp (R.A.C. 11·4) *Engine:* 4-cylinder, 68×114 mm, S.V., H.T. magneto ignition. *Transmission:* As above but worm-gear.

was that rare being
1913 9·5 hp *Engine:* 4-cylinder, 62×90 mm, 1096 cc, side valve, water-cooled, thermo-syphon, trough lubrication, Zenith carburation. *Transmission:* Disc clutch and 3-speed gearbox to shaft-driven worm axle.

Stanley   see Locomobile

Star England

The ancestry of the Star concern is rather complicated. The Star Motor Co., The Star Cycle Co., The Star Engineering Co. and trade names Star, Starling, Stuart and Briton are all interlinked with such names as Benz, De Dion, Panhard and Mercedes, together with the production of a large variety of motor cars. For example, no fewer than 33 models were listed between 1908 and 1914 under the trade names of Star, Stuart and Briton. It was claimed that the company was the sixth largest in the U.K. before the first world war.

A De Dion engined tricycle appeared in 1898, followed by a well-made Benz-powered car of 3½ hp in 1899. By 1904 a 6 hp voiturette, 6 and 7 hp 2-cylinder cars, 15 hp and 20 hp cars were in production. The 20 hp developed 24 bhp at 800 rpm from a motor weighing 5 cwt. A Panhard-type 4-speed gearbox was used, and this combination propelled a car weighing 18 cwt, bodied by Star.

In 1908 a 9 hp (R.A.C. 11·2) 2-cylinder, a 12 hp (R.A.C. 17·5) 4-cylinder, 16 hp (R.A.C. 22·4), 18 hp (R.A.C. 43·4) and 30 hp (R.A.C. 43·4) 6-cylinder cars were on offer to the public at chassis prices ranging from £185 to £525. By 1909 the 30 hp 6 had become the 40 hp 6 of the same cylinder dimensions as before (108 × 127 mm), and continued in production until 1911. A 25 hp appeared from 1909 to 1913, together with a new 20 hp, which replaced the 16 and 18 hp models.

Also in 1909 the Star Cycle Co., which had previously manufactured under the trade names of Stuart, then Starling, became Briton. They pursued a more or less separate existence in new premises, and the company essentially covered the light car end of the market.

By 1913 a 10/12 hp, a 12/15 hp (with identical bore and stroke) together with a 15·9 hp (all of R.A.C. formulae 15·9 hp) and a 20·1 hp were being manufactured alongside two 6-cylinder cars. By 1914 only the 4-cylinder cars remained.

Star cars were well made and popular, but it is doubtful if many of the larger cars were made in any numbers, particularly the 6-cylinder cars, as none seem to have survived.

No mechanical innovations are attributed to Star; they largely gained a good reputation for reliable, well-made cars by copying the best of their continental competitors.

1908 30 hp (R.A.C. 43·4) *Engine:* 6-cylinder, 108 × 127 mm, dual ignition. *Transmission:* Leather cone clutch, 4-speed gearbox, final drive by propeller shaft or chains.

1913 15·9 hp (R.A.C. 15·9) *Engine:* 4-cylinder, 80 × 150 mm, pump cooling, magneto ignition. *Transmission:* Leather cone clutch, 4-speed gearbox, shaft driven bevel-gear rear axle.

1899 3½ hp single-cylinder vis-a-vis

Stellite   see Wolseley

Stephens   England

A complete Stephens car still exists, and the remains of a second has accompanied it through several ownerships. The car was in production from 1898 to 1900, and was manufactured in Clevedon, Somerset, by a local engineer who gave his name to the car. About 10 cars were made, together with the odd charabanc.

Featuring independent front suspension, the car was advanced for its time. The engine was based on the Benz design of the period, but was much more refined, and developed 10 bhp. The engine design incorporated a cylinder screwed into the head (to avoid gasket problems) and steel water jackets which were welded onto the barrel. Stephens developed methods of keeping the drive belts under tension (one of the curses associated with most other belt-drive systems was slipping, when the belt invariably stretched), and his own electric ignition system. A surface carburettor was used. Top speed was around 25 mph; due to its independent suspension the car handled well, despite tiller steering and solid tyres.

Evidence of the roadworthiness of this car is given by its completion of the 1927 Brighton run and its ascent, in 1951, of the Dorking Hill speed climb in a mere 142·1 seconds.

1898 dog cart   *Engine:* two-cylinder Benz-based engine, water cooled with electric ignition. *Transmission:* via belt drive.

1898 8 hp 2-cylinder dog cart

Straker-Squire   England

The old and established Bristol engineering firm of Sidney Straker and Squire first entered the transport market with the manufacture of steam waggons in 1901. In 1906 a 25 hp motor car of French ancestry appeared under the Straker Squire badge, followed in 1907 by a 16/20 hp car of no particular merit, being not entirely of their own manufacture. Also in 1907 a small (87 × 87 mm) 4-cylinder, of just over 2 litres, appeared under the guise of a Shamrock. Possibly the similarity of the coats of arms of Bristol and Dublin inspired this choice of name. This first wholly home-made product gave way in 1909 to a slightly smaller 14/16 hp car which was only produced for one year. In 1910 the best performing car produced prior to the war emerged first as the 15 hp of 87 × 100 mm, with a cubic capacity of 2,377 cc, then from 1911 to 1914 as the 87 × 120 mm 3 litre version (2,853 cc). This car finally developed again into the 15/20, with enlarged bore of 90 mm, for 1914. This car revived the company's fortunes after the war until 1922.

The 15 hp, as it was generally known, was a performance car often fitted with a smart 2-seater body by Mullet & Co. of Redcliffe, Bristol. It took records at Brooklands in 1912 at speeds in excess of 90 mph, which were achieved by Messrs R.S. Witchell and R. Fedden. Fedden designed the engine of the 15 hp, which was a monobloc side-valve design with patented self-adjusting tappets. Fedden, like W.O. Bentley, later distinguished himself in the design of aero engines.

1910 15 hp (R.A.C. 18·8) *Engine:* 4-cylinder monobloc, 87 × 100 mm, S.V. water-cooled thermo-syphon, patented self-adjusting tappets, trough lubrication. *Transmission:* Leather cone clutch with 4-speed gearbox, bevel-geared rear axle.

1910 15 hp 4-cylinder two-seater

Sunbeam England

At the height of the bicycle craze anybody who *was* anybody had a 'Sunbeam' bicycle—with the famous 'little oil-bath chain case'—made by Marston & Co. of Wolverhampton. After one or two experiments, which did not come to anything, the Sunbeam Company joined the motor movement by producing the odd Sunbeam-Mabley device (qv): this was in 1901. A year later the motor trade was booming (though very few of the new companies prospered), so Sunbeams decided to go into the business more thoroughly and called in Thomas Pullinger to organise full-scale manufacture of full-scale cars. Before this, Pullinger had been works manager for Teste et Moret in Paris, builders of light cars. To avoid unnecessary waste of time he advised importing a few 12 hp Berliet chassis and using them as a basis for Sunbeam's own production.

Though this seems to indicate lack of faith in his former employers, the advice was sound and the 12 hp Sunbeams of 1902/5 were virtually indistinguishable from Berliets, except that some of the later ones were fitted with the 'little oil-bath chain cases'. Specification of the first type included a 4-cylinder engine of 80 × 120 mm, atmospheric inlet valves, trembler coil ignition, exposed timing gears and drip-feed lubrication in the Victorian manner placed in a steel-reinforced wooden chassis and driving through an excellent 4-speed box and side chains. For 1905 Sunbeams brought out a new engine, very similar to the original Berliet, but with mechanical inlet valves and a 4-millimetre increase in the bore.

left 1904 12 hp 4-cylinder tourer

below 1913 12/16 hp 4-cylinder tourer

Sunbeams were only a short head behind Napiers in bringing out a 6-cylinder model in 1904, but it does not seem that very many were made. In 1905, Angus Shaw, the chief draughtsman, designed an admirable 4-cylinder 16/20 hp model to replace the earlier type. This did extremely well and went on without much alteration for some four years.

In 1909 Louis Coatalen was hired as chief engineer and in addition to redesigning the 16/20 he soon added a new 12/16 hp model which later formed the basis of the *Coupe de l'Auto* racing Sunbeams which came in first, second and third on the Dieppe circuit in 1912.

These fine 3-litre cars (80 × 149 mm), though classed then as *voitures légères*, were most impressive machines, and though their side-valve engines may have looked a thought old-fashioned by comparison with some, they were far from ineffectual. Specific output was nearly 33 hp per litre which makes the 4½ hp per litre of the original Berliet-Sunbeams look pretty puny. The 1913 *Coupe de l'Auto* cars had differential-less back axles—a feature also to be found on the firm's *Grand Prix* cars and the fabulous V-12 cylinder car also produced in 1913.

Apart from these special types the firm's standard models were among the best in their classes. Best known models were the 4-cylinder 12/16 and 16/20s and the fine 25/30 hp six. The best of all worlds were combined in these—sound design, the best possible finish procurable in an old-established, well-equipped and prosperous works and the *panache* which always attaches to success in racing. Small wonder the owners of Edwardian Sunbeams would not 'have the Queen for Auntie'.

1905 12 hp (R.A.C. 17·5) *Engine:* 4-cylinder, 84 × 120 mm, S.V. (T-head, mechanical variable-lift inlet valves), trembler coil ignition. *Transmission:* Cone clutch, 4 speeds and reverse, bevel-geared countershaft, side chains, dead axle.

(Engine etc. of Berliet type, many components imported: early models had, perhaps, French-built engines. 1903/4 12 hp model as above, but bore 80 mm and inlet valves automatic.)

1912 12/16 hp (R.A.C. 15·84) *Engine:* 4-cylinder, 80 × 150 mm, S.V., H.T. magneto ignition. *Transmission:* Cone clutch, 4 speeds and reverse, shaft, bevel-geared live axle.

16/20 hp as for 12/16 but dimensions 90 × 160 mm and dual ignition by H.T. magneto.

25/30 hp as 16/20 but with 6 cylinders.

1914 16/20 hp 4-cylinder cabriolet

Sunbeam-Mabley   England

Although it had no influence at all on the development of motor car design the Sunbeam-Mabley deserves a separate place because it was so funny.

The machine was designed by Mr Mabberley-Smith, built by the Sunbeam Company and sold from 1901 to 1904. The bodywork resembled an S-shaped Victorian 'sociable' settee; two fairly slim passengers could be seated in the forward curve of the S, facing the left-hand side of the road, and the driver occupied a seat right at the back of the S facing, more or less, the direction in which he essayed to aim the conveyance by means of a tiller. This tiller pivoted both the back and the front wheels (which were staggered one on either side of the centre line) and the Mabley could almost pivot about on its central driving axle. It is to be hoped the pictures makes all this clear.

A 2¾ hp De Dion Bouton tricycle engine, with water-cooled head, was carried on a shelf beside the front wheel and drove by flat belt to the counter-shaft amidships: two sets of chain and sprocket gear provided low or high speed final drive to the central axle. This was unsprung, but the front and back wheels were quite softly sprung and the Mabley had a peculiar lolloping motion. The object of the curious layout, according to the advertisements, was to obviate the 'dreaded side-slip'; in this it was wholly successful as a Sunbeam-Mabley could usually be relied upon to overturn before it started to skid.

1901 2½ hp (R.A.C. 3·39)   *Engine:* De Dion Bouton, transverse, air-cooled barrel, water-cooled head, forward-mounted, 1-cylinder, 74 × 76 mm, A.I.V., coil ignition. *Transmission:* Belt to fast and loose pulleys on countershaft, two fast pulleys each geared at different ratio by sprockets and chain to live central axle.

1901 2½ hp single-cylinder voiturette

Swift   England

The Swift Co. of Coventry, makers of sewing-machines and bicycles, was one of that numerous band who built their first motor cars round the famous De Dion Bouton engine. Their very first models were probably, like the contemporary Regal, built up from wholly French components but for 1902 a Swift-designed voiturette appeared. This had a 4½ hp De Dion engine, a light tubular chassis and an unsprung live back axle, in which two rings of teeth on the crown wheel could be selectively engaged by dog-clutch to one or another of two bevel pinions to provide the two speeds. There was no differential gear but the driving wheels had free-wheel mechanism in their hubs to allow for cornering. A rather haphazard reverse gear could be fitted as an extra and an engaging peculiarity was that the starting handle shaft stuck out of the back of the final drive housing; it engaged with the main propellor shaft via a short jack-shaft and a pair of spur gears. Within a year the Swift Company, and their hapless customers, had discovered what happens to the gears and bearings of an unsprung live axle mounted on a rather floppy chassis and their later models had a conventional transmission system.

Proprietary engines—De Dion, Simms or Aster chiefly—continued to be used for the single-cylinder models for some years, but by 1906 a 10 hp 2-cylinder Swift engine was being fitted to a larger type of car. This was quite advanced and its large well-designed valve ports and exhaust manifold could have served as examples to some manufacturers thirty years later. A 1906 10 hp Swift won a Gold Medal in the Scottish Reliability Trials, and two 15 hp 4-cylinder cars were entered for the Tourist Trophy. A 3-cylinder White-and-Poppe engined model was also made which earned itself a good reputation.

Twin-cylinder light cars were the Company's mainstay during most of the Edwardian period, but an excellent small 4-cylinder 10 hp was brought out in 1912. The motoring public were still rather suspicious of small multi-cylinder engines, however, and Swifts wisely continued their well-known twins. Single-cylinder 7 hp models were also continued until quite late and were almost as popular as the contemporary Rover. In 1909 the Swift Company made an arrangement whereby the newly-introduced single-cylinder Austin also served as the single-cylinder Swift. In other words the Austin factory made 7 hp Austins and Swifts which were identical except for the radiators, bonnets and nameplates. They were rather nasty little cars, with horribly wide-ratio 3-speed gears, and they did not remain on the scene very long being, really, quite out of date by 1911. They had cast-iron bearings for the crankshafts and gearbox shafts.

1907 9/10 hp twin-cylinder
two-seater

1904 7 hp (R.A.C. 5) *Engine:* De Dion Bouton, 1-cylinder, 90 × 110 mm, A.I.V., coil ignition. *Transmission:* Cone clutch, 3 speeds and reverse, shaft, bevel-geared live axle. (By mid-1904 the Swift Co. were making De Dion type engines at home.)

1910/11 7 hp (R.A.C. 6·85) Specification identical with single cylinder 7 hp Austin of the same period.

1914 15·9 hp (R.A.C. 15·9) *Engine:* 4-cylinder, 80 × 130 mm, S.V., H.T. magneto ignition. *Transmission:* As above.

Talbot   see Clément

Thornycroft

England

John Thornycroft built a steam carriage in 1862 and, in 1895/6, when the abolition of the old restrictions was in sight, he built an experimental light steam van which still performs admirably. It is often said that it was once used to deliver Queen Victoria's laundry to Windsor Castle—a piece of picturesque fiction which can be believed only by those who can also believe that the Great and Good sent her smalls out to the local bagwash. What is indisputable, however, is that the van is propelled by a 2-cylinder compound launch engine, has front wheel drive, steers with its back wheels and requires thirty-two turns of the steering handle to go from lock to lock.

By 1903 the Thornycroft Steam Wagon Co. Ltd, as they were then called, put two types of petrol car into production: one was a 10 hp twin and the other a 4-cylinder 20 hp. Both were well designed and carefully made, with pressed steel chassis of much greater rigidity than was common then. The footbrake, as usual, worked on the transmission, but the drum was placed on the pinion shaft of the live back axle instead of just aft of the gearbox, so as to relieve the universal joints of stress. Both models had automatic inlet valves and trembler coil ignition, but the larger car had a belt-driven dynamo which was an uncommon luxury in 1903.

Clearly influenced, as so many were, by Mercedes practice the firm produced a 24 hp model for the 1905 season with low tension magneto ignition, mechanical inlet valves and honeycomb radiator; this had separate cylinders but the smaller 14 hp Tourist Trophy model of the following year had a monobloc casting and overhead valves—as did the new 36 hp 6-cylinder model.

Throughout the Edwardian period Thornycroft design ran on conventional lines but managed always to be up to date if not actually a little way ahead. Specific output was on a par with the best of their contemporaries, and care-

left 1904 20 hp 4-cylinder tonneau
right 1909 30 hp 4-cylinder landaulette

fully designed and beautifully finished transmission, braking, and steering systems allowed far from despicable performances. The firm competed in the T.T. Races of 1905 to 1908 and Tom Thornycroft was fifth in 1908 at an average speed of 44·1 mph. In the hands of private owners Thornycrofts often did well in reliability trials and hill climbs: in 1911, at Brooklands, an 18 hp car was timed to cover 60·1 miles in 59·9 minutes and reached 30 mph in 12·45 seconds.

In 1908 the 14 hp model became a 20 hp, though bore and stroke remained unaltered, and in 1909 the stroke was increased from 3¾ in. to 4½ in. whereupon, by some curious reasoning, the hp rating was reduced to 18. In 1911 the bore was increased from 3¾ in. to 4 in., and the nominal hp was still quoted as 18 though in view of the car's performance it was probably developing some 40 bhp. In the 1909/11 period the 36 hp 6-cylinder model was gradually dropped in favour of a 45 hp model which was very similar to the contemporary Rolls-Royce in specification and price.

For 1912/13 only the 18 hp was listed and private car production stopped at the end of 1913, to allow for increased production of the famous Thornycroft lorries.

1903/4 10 hp (R.A.C. 12·9) *Engine:* 2-cylinder, 4 × 4⅜ in., A.I.V., trembler coil ignition. *Transmission:*

Cone clutch, 3 speeds and reverse, shaft, bevel-geared live axle.

1903/4 20 hp (R.A.C. 25·8) *Engine:* As 10 hp, but with 4-cylinder and dynamo for ignition current.

Transmission: As 10 hp but with multiplate clutch.

1906 14 hp (R.A.C. 22·4) *Engine:* 4-cylinder, 3¾ × 3¾ in., O.H.V., L.T. magneto ignition. *Transmission:*

Multiplate clutch, 3 speeds and reverse, shaft, bevel-geared live axle.

1908 20 hp As 1906 14 hp but with
H.T. magneto ignition.

1911 45 hp (R.A.C. 43·4) *Engine:*
6-cylinder, $4\frac{1}{2} \times 5$ in., S.V., H.T.
magneto ignition. *Transmission:* As
above.

Turner-Miesse
Belgium/England

J. Miesse et Cie. of Brussels began making steam cars in 1896 which were
recognisably inspired by the contemporary Serpollet. In 1902 Thomas Turner
& Co. of Wolverhampton began importing Miesse steamers and two years
later started manufacture of the Turner-Miesse.

The Miesse design, like the Gardner-Serpollet, had a paraffin-fired 'flash'
boiler and a single acting engine with trunk pistons and poppet valves. The
furnace and generator went under the bonnet and the 3-cylinder engine was
placed horizontally and transversely amidships, geared direct to the differential, which was contained in the crankcase. Final drive was by side chains up
to 1907, and thereafter by shaft and bevel-geared live axle.

One of the many difficulties steam car designers had to contend with was to
make a burner which could quickly be varied to accord with the constantly
changing demands of the engine. This was bad enough with petrol burners
(early Locomobile, Weston, etc.), but worse still with the paraffin burners
which the English market demanded. The variety of perverse ways in which
paraffin burners could blow back, blow out, blow dense clouds of black smoke
from unexpected quarters, flare up and generally cause alarm and despond-
ency, if suddenly called upon to work at less than full bore, are beyond
description. The Miesse solution to the problem was masterly—they merely
ignored the problem and designed their burners to work either at a minimum,
as a pilot-light, when the car had to stand for any time with steam up, or at any
unvarying maximum while the car was running. Rises in temperature and
pressure when the demand for steam was small were boldly and coldly disregarded, and the makers claimed their flash boilers could stand full heat
without water for 20 minutes. And, in any case, if the bottom section of the
generator did burn out it could easily be side-tracked to allow the car to
proceed at reduced power. This arrangement overcame many difficulties
though odd things could still happen; a few years ago a well-known steam
enthusiast and maker of musical instruments (who might, one feels, astonish
the world at any moment with a high-pressure harpsichord) remarked with
delight that his Turner-Miesse had surpassed itself by directing a five-foot jet
of flame at a policeman's boots.

Although orthodox engineers shook their heads at the crudity of the system
it worked well, and Turner-Miesse steamers sold in fair numbers until it

became quite clear that despite all their advantages and sweetness of action, the simplest steam car needed far more skilled attention than the most complex petrol car. Once the motoring public realised this they made it quite clear they were going to buy petrol cars or else. Turner and Co. wisely paid heed to the straws in the wind, removed the straws from their hair and started making conventional, rather dull, petrol cars in 1910—though they continued to supply their steamers until 1913.

1904 10 hp (R.A.C. 4·64) *Engine:* Horizontal, transverse, centrally mounted, single-acting, simple, 3-cylinder, 50 × 80 mm, poppet valves. *Boiler:* Serpollet-type flash generator, pressure variable from 50 lb sq in. to 400 lb sq in. according to load on engine. *Transmission:* By spur gear direct from crankshaft to differential-countershaft enclosed with cranks, side chains, dead axle.

1904 10 hp 3-cylinder tonneau

Unic   see Brasier

Valveless   (Lucas, Lucas Valveless, Simple Valveless)   England

In the early days of the gas engine the new-fangled 4-stroke system had many rivals and various forms of 6-stroke, 3-stroke and 2-stroke engines all had their advocates. By the end of the nineteenth century the big 2-stroke, pump-scavenged, stationary engine had reached a high state of efficiency and the modern type of light high-speed affair with crankcase induction/compression had made a hesitant appearance. However, it was many years before the small 2-stroke engine made much headway and it was seldom used for anything but bicycles or small motor launches. It was almost universally condemned by 'expert' writers on motoring matters—which should have been in its favour.

The only 2-stroke car of the early period to achieve much success (apart from some light American runabouts) was known at various times as the Lucas, the Lucas Valveless, the Valveless or, occasionally, the Simple Valveless. Under the last two names production was in the hands of David Brown and Sons who were also then responsible for the Sava and Dodson cars; the Dodson, incidentally, was so remarkably like a Renault as to provoke the thought that somebody was cribbing something from someone. It is sometimes said that the David Brown Valveless had no connection with the Lucas Valveless but as the engines were virtually identical this seems unlikely. It was also said that Mr Lucas had drawn his inspiration from the 3-cylinder 2-stroke *La plus Simple* cars made at Fécamp early in the century and this is probably true.

The Lucas, or Valveless, engines had two cylinders, two pistons, two crankshafts and one combustion chamber which the cylinders shared. The cylinders and cranks were side by side, the latter counter rotating and geared together. On the up stroke of the pistons only fresh air was drawn into the crankcase, through a non-return valve, and on the down stroke it was compressed; towards the end of the down stroke one piston uncovered the exhaust port in one cylinder and, fractionally later, the other piston uncovered the inlet port in the other cylinder whereupon the compressed air in the crankcase rushed in to fill the common combustion space and carried with it a charge of petrol from a spraying nozzle in the inlet tract. As with Leslie Hounsfield's famous Trojan engines of the 'twenties (but without his flexible connecting rods) this duplex cylinder arrangement gave much better exhaust scavenging than the usual 2-stroke system.

As at first made (in very small numbers) by Mr Lucas's Valveless Motor Co. of Blackheath the cars had the engines placed with their crankshafts athwart and with transmission by 2-speed chain and sprocket gear (selection by dog-clutches) direct from clutch shaft to back axle. Reversing was at first provided for by advancing the ignition, when the engine was idling, beyond its normal point so as to reverse the engine itself by making it backfire. This system was soon found to be not without hazard and an epicyclic reverse gear was provided. However, the arrangement for reversing the engine was retained so that, in emergencies, with the engine made to turn backwards, the erstwhile reverse gear could be made to do duty as a very low-geared forward speed.

1909 25 hp 2-cylinder tourer

By 1909 the Valveless cars had the engines normally placed, crankshafts in the longitudinal line, driving via a normal clutch, 3-speed, shaft and bevel live axle. Under the D.B. régime they blossomed out with four speeds and worm final drive. The cars were warmly praised for their simplicity, and silent vibrationless running. They had the characteristic 2-stroke virtue of excellent torque at low speeds and, to a very high degree, the 2-stroke vice of extreme reluctance to re-start with a hot engine.

1907 20 hp (R.A.C. 20·2) *Engine:* Duplex, 2-stroke, cylinders longitudinal, crankshafts transverse, 2-cylinder, 133 × 140 mm, coil ignition. *Transmission:* Cone clutch and epicyclic reverse gear, 2 speeds by independent chains to live axle, speeds selected by dog-clutches.

1909 25 hp (R.A.C. 20·2) *Engine:* As above, but cylinders transverse and crankshafts longitudinal, H.T. magneto ignition. *Transmission:* Cone clutch, 3 speeds and reverse, shaft, bevel-geared live axle.

1914 15 hp and 19·9 hp (Makers' and R.A.C. rating) *Engines:* As 1909 but 113 × 127 mm *or* 127 × 140 mm. *Transmission:* As 1909 but 4 speeds and worm-geared final drive.

Vauxhall England

F.W. Hodges of the Vauxhall Ironworks began experiments with opposed-piston petrol engines for launches in 1896 and followed these by making one or two experimental belt-driven light cars, but it was not until 1903 that the Vauxhall Company put their first car on the market. It was a 5½ cwt runabout with a transverse horizontal engine under a pointed bonnet in front; this engine was rated at 5 hp and had 4 in. bore × 4¾ in. stroke. It was controlled both by a governor (unusual on small engines), which could be over-ridden by the accelerator, and by hand-controlled variable lift of the automatic inlet valve. Transmission was direct on the high speed from engine shaft to back axle by single central chain, a crypto gear provided a low speed but there was neither reverse nor differential gear—differential action was provided by free-wheel clutches in the back hubs. Suspension was by coil springs all round and the controls were particularly neat: a side-tiller, worked by the driver's left hand, steered the vehicle whilst his right hand rested on a short lever on the side of the steering post opposite to the tiller-bar. Moving this short lever backwards brought the epicyclic low gear into action, and moving it forwards released the low speed and engaged the direct-drive clutch whilst twisting the lever throttled the engine by increasing the tension of the inlet valve spring.

This was all very neat and simple and cost £130–£150, according to body-work. Fewer than half a dozen of the 5 hp cars were made and a 6 hp version

(4 × 5 in.) came out in 1904 and this had a reverse gear. These little cars soon became popular and made their mark in trials of various kinds.

For 1905 the Company brought out three models of 3-cylinder cars (7, 9 and 12/14 hp) with vertical engines and side-chain final drive. In view of their greater speed they were given normal half-elliptic springs all round and wheel steering (also now fitted to the single-cylinder cars which were still produced). These new Vauxhalls were smooth-running and endowed with well-chosen gear ratios, good brakes and adequate radiators; the Company continued their active competition policy and entered a 12 hp model (95 × 114 mm) for

left 1904 6 hp single-cylinder two-seater

below 1911 20 hp 4-cylinder tourer

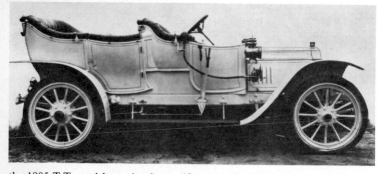

the 1905 T.T., and by a simple modification their standard 3-speed gearbox was made to provide six speeds for the occasion. Despite this refinement A.J. Hancock had to retire half way round the second circuit with coil failure, but, generally, Vauxhall cars did well in hill climbs and reliability trials and, later on, outright speed events.

Good though the 3-cylinder cars were, the demand for ever bigger and heavier bodies brought about their demise. A conventional shaft-driven 18/20 hp 4-cylinder model came out for 1906/7, and was the chief Vauxhall product for some while; plans for a 2-cylinder hansom-cab, complete with driver's seat perched above the back of the roof, were mercifully laid aside. One of the 20 hp cars won its class handsomely in the 1908 2,000 miles R.A.C. Trial.

Amongst the many contests in which Vauxhalls distinguished themselves were the *Coupe de l'Auto* races, the Prince Henry Trials and numerous Brooklands events. As a result both Vauxhall and Sunbeam became interested in seeing what they could squeeze out of their standard 16 hp 3-litre cars, hotted-up for the purpose but not materially altered. In 1909 a Vauxhall covered the half mile at 88·62 mph, in 1910 they improved this to 100·83 (the first time the 'ton' had been cracked by a 3-litre car) and by 1912 they reached 101·24.

With some chassis modifications the 3-litre Vauxhalls put up a stout performance against much larger cars in the 1910 Prince Henry Tour (the last P.H. event with any competitive element), and in 1911 the Prince Henry type of car was put into production for sale to the public. In 1913 engine size was increased from 90 × 120 mm to 95 × 140 mm and a handsome pointed and fluted radiator was fitted. These 4-litre cars were still sold as 'Prince Henry' models though, as the purists point out, no 4-litre Vauxhalls had ever run in a Prince Henry event. They were splendid cars with the beautiful balance and road-holding of the best Edwardians, and their apparently old-fashioned side-valve engines could accelerate impressively or slog away at low rpm; late in 1913 an even more famous successor was evolved from them by L.H. Pomeroy, works manager. To meet a customer's requirements for Shelsley Walsh L.H.P. bored out a cylinder block to 98 mm and stretched a crankshaft forging to make the stroke 150 mm. Thus the famous '30/98', which was not to reach the public until the 'twenties, was actually born before the war.

1903 5 hp (R.A.C. 6·4) *Engine:* Horizontal, transverse, forward-mounted, 1-cylinder, 4 × 4¾ in., A.I.V. (with variable lift), trembler coil ignition. *Transmission:* 2 speeds (no reverse) epicyclic, clutches: for low speed by contracting brake on epicyclic gear drum, for high speed by pressing low-gear drum against flywheel-face, final drive by single chain to live axle. 1904 6 hp, as above but stroke increased to 5 in., and reverse gear added.

1905 7/9 hp (R.A.C. 10·7) *Engine:* 3-cylinder, 3 × 3¾ in., S.V., trembler coil ignition. *Transmission:* Cone clutch, 3 speeds and reverse, bevel-geared countershaft, side chains, dead axle.

1914 (Prince Henry type) 25 hp (R.A.C. 22·4) *Engine:* 4-cylinder, 95 × 140 mm, S.V., H.T. magneto ignition. *Transmission:* Multiplate clutch, 4 speeds and reverse, shaft, bevel-geared live axle.

1914 25 hp 4-cylinder 'Prince Henry' tourer

Vertex   see James and Browne

Vivinus   see New Orleans

Vulcan

England

From its origins in 1903 to obscurity as a car-producing firm on amalgamation with Tilling Stevens in 1928, the Vulcan Company produced no fewer than 42 different models. Of these, 29 were listed before 1915. All the early cars were of side-valve configuration, varying in capacity from a 628 cc single-cylinder in 1903 to a 5,885 cc 6-cylinder in 1908. This latter car of R.A.C. 38 hp (and also referred to as a 40 hp) was marketed for the then reasonable sum of £500, being £100 less than a comparable Austin.

The company began modestly enough in Southport, and from a parentage of founders it became the Vulcan Manufacturing and Engineering Co. The first example of the marque was the single-cylinder 6 hp, which had mechanically-operated inlet valves and was shaft-driven, a feature of the marque. A belt-driven single-cylinder voiturette had preceded it, but it is doubtful if serious production was undertaken, and none survives.

By 1904 a 2-cylinder 10 hp was in serious production, and like the previous model was water-cooled. Cars of 12, 14, 18 and 25 hp rapidly followed, until in 1907 the first 6-cylinder car of 30 hp was produced. This was followed in 1908 by a 102 × 120 mm known as the 35 hp, which was of nearly 6 litres capacity. These cars were intended to carry formal coachwork as among the five or so early Vulcans to survive is a 35 hp landaulette.

From 1910 onward smaller cars were favoured, and whilst a 25/30 6-cylinder car was produced until 1914, the mainstay of production were cars of between 12 hp (2 litres) and 20 hp (4 litres), fitted with 4-cylinder engines and featuring worm-drive rear axles. The car radiators became more rounded in profile, and all were topped by the now much sought after mascot of Vulcan, blacksmith to the gods.

1904 10 hp (R.A.C. 10·5)   *Engine:* 2-cylinder, 3·625 × 4·75 in., water-cooled with pump, pump and drip-feed lubrication, Vulcan carburettor, H.T. coil ignition. *Transmission:* Leather-faced clutch, 3-speed gearbox and shaft to bevel drive rear axle.

1908 35 hp (R.A.C. 38)   *Engine:* 6-cylinder, 102 × 120 mm, pump lubrication, accumulator and magneto ignition. *Transmission:* Leather-faced cone clutch, 4-speed gearbox to shaft-driven rear axle.

1913 10/15 hp (R.A.C. 15·9)
Engine: 4-cylinder, 80 × 150 mm,
thermo-syphon cooled, trough
lubrication, Longuemare

carburettor, magneto ignition.
Transmission: Leather cone clutch,
4-speed gearbox to worm-drive axle.

Waltham Orient   see Orient Buckboard

White   America

The White Sewing Machine Co. of Cleveland, Ohio began making steam cars
in 1901. Their first efforts were very similar to the contemporary Stanley/
Locomobile steam buggies but by 1903 they had forward-mounted engines and
were fitted with condensers as standard equipment. (Condensers were optional
extras on Locomobiles, fitted only to avoid showing visible exhaust steam.)
Owing to the amount of oil carried over with the exhaust it was not possible to
use the condensate in the Locomobile type of fire-tube boiler, and in order to
overcome the objection of very heavy water-consumption, Whites also adopted
a semi-flash type of generator, on Serpollet principles, which was not so fussy
about a little oil in the tubes and consequently allowed them to give their cars
a 100 miles radius on a filling. They also adopted a compound engine in place

of the 'simple' variety, although most steam engineers considered compounding of little value except for fairly large installations.

The White layout, therefore, from 1903 onwards consisted of a flash-boiler under the driver's seat, double-acting vertical compound condensing engine under the bonnet, condenser in the usual 'radiator position' and shaft drive to a live axle. From 1905 a 2-speed gear was fitted in the back axle which besides providing an emergency low-gear for starting on steep hills, allowed the engine to run free, and thus drive the boiler pumps, when standing in traffic. By this means steam could be kept up without laborious hand pumping.

The English branch of the White Co. was headed by the energetic and appropriately named Mr Coleman who staged many impressive demonstrations of White reliability and performance, and who competed, when possible, in hill climbs and speed trials. Much controversy arose over the virtual ban on steam cars imposed, at one time, by the Automobile Club and other bodies, in competitive events. Their argument was that a steamer could raise a great head of steam whilst standing and thus a 10 hp nominal engine could develop 30 to 40 hp, say, for a brief spurt and thus make nonsense of the classifications; this reasoning hardly applied to machines with flash boilers and Mr Coleman had a genuine grievance. When able to compete, the White cars usually gave a good account of themselves, as at the Shelsley Walsh Hill Climb in 1906 when Coleman took a 20 hp White up faster than all the petrol cars, being 24½ seconds better than the runner-up, a 60 hp De Dietrich driven by Charles Jarrott.

Despite this and other successes nothing could disguise the fact that as petrol cars grew every year quieter and more flexible the disadvantages of steamers grew more apparent. More skill in driving was needed despite the absence of clutch and gearbox, maintenance was more expensive, fuel consumption greater and the best steamers took, on average, about fifteen minutes to start from cold. Also there was a large body of people who thought poorly of riding on a machine which had some thirty or forty pipe and flange joints of various kinds under high pressure, and a live furnace blazing away within eighteen

1909 15 hp 2-cylinder (compound steam) double phaeton

inches of their backsides. For the 1910 season the White Co. began making petrol cars and in 1911 the steamers were discontinued.

The petrol cars were based upon the Delahaye design, and by 1911/12 the 20/30 hp, the only model, was proving so successful that it was continued for the next few years. Electric lighting and starting equipment was added in 1913 supplied from a dynamotor almost as big as the engine. This was a very smooth running 3,680 cc unit (95 × 130 mm), 4-cylinder monobloc side-valve, driving the live axle via a plate clutch and 4-speed gearbox which had direct drive on third and overdrive fourth, in the manner of the early Rolls-Royces.

1903 White (steam) 10 hp (R.A.C. 13·6) *Engine:* Double acting, condensing, compound, 2-cylinder, bore, high-pressure cylinder 3 in., low-pressure cylinder 5 in., stroke $3\frac{1}{2}$ in., slide valves, Stephenson's link motion. *Boiler:* Flash generator. Average working pressure 300 lb sq in. *Transmission:* Shaft, bevel-geared live axle.

1908 18/20 hp (R.A.C. 13·6) *Engine and Boiler* as 1903 10 hp but pressure increased to approximately 450 lb sq in. *Transmission:* As 1903 but 2-speed gear in back axle.

1908 30 hp (R.A.C. 18) *Engine:* As above but bore, high-pressure cylinder 3 in., low-pressure cylinder 6 in., stroke $4\frac{1}{2}$ in. Piston valve to H.P. cylinder. *Boiler:* As above, average working pressure approximately 650 lb sq in.

1914 White (petrol) 20/30 hp (R.A.C. 22·4) *Engine:* 4-cylinder, 95 × 130 mm, S.V., H.T. magneto ignition. *Transmission:* Cone clutch, 4 speeds and reverse, shaft, bevel-geared live axle.

Winton

America

Although Elwood Haynes, the Duryea brothers and many more were in the field slightly before him Alexander Winton was one of the first American manufacturers to sell home-brewed petrol cars to the public and the first to take part in European racing.

Winton went to America from Scotland in 1879 and after a spell as ship's engineer and superintendent of a marine engineering works he started the Winton Bicycle works, in collaboration with Thomas Henderson, in 1890; seven years later, after many experiments, he built his first satisfactory horse-less carriage which astounded the sceptics by covering the mile circuit at the Glenville Track, Cleveland, at an average speed of 33·8 mph—a most praise-worthy performance. This and other feats impressed local business men, finance was forthcoming and by 1898 the Winton Motor Carriage Company was firmly established with $200,000 capital, and the first production single-cylinder 'phaeton' was sold on April 29th. Therefore, although the Duryea Motor Wagon Co. was established some months earlier, there seems some basis for Winton's claim to have sold America's first home-designed and home-built production petrol car.

Between 1898 and 1900 in addition to supervising production of his standard single-cylinder cars (twenty-two were sold in the first eight months) Winton took advantage of every possible opportunity to display his reliable machines to the public. In 1900 he decided to have a go against the European manufacturers on their own ground and entered a large single-cylinder tiller-steered car for the first Gordon Bennett race. Despite its $6\frac{1}{2} \times 7$ in. pot the 14 hp Winton was nowhere in it against the 24 hp 4-cylinder Panhards driven by De Knyff, Giradot and Charron, and Winton was soon left behind. His gallant effort came to an end with a buckled front wheel before reaching the half-way mark.

As a result of this experience Winton produced his first vertical-engined 4-cylinder model in 1901, but the horizontal-engined cars which had earned so good a reputation were not dropped—indeed the single-cylinder models were supplemented by a 15 hp horizontally opposed twin. Wheel steering was now fitted to all models. A racing version of the 20 hp, 4-cylinder model, rated at 40 hp, was named Bullet I and from it originated the unorthodox Bullet series of racing cars.

Winton's production models, broadly speaking, followed the then typical American style. That is, they had centrally placed, slow-running horizontal transverse engines and single chain drive to a live axle. They differed from most in being larger and sturdier, in having very respectable power to weight ratios (the 15 hp 2-cylinder model was enlarged to 20 hp by 1903 but weighed less than a ton), and in having variable-lift mechanical inlet valves controlled by a unique compressed air system. They shared with many of their compatriots the shortcoming of having no intermediate speed between a very high top-gear and very low bottom-gear.

Though they had nothing in common with the production cars, Bullet II

1903 20 hp 2-cylinder tonneau

and Bullet III, which were entered for the 1903 Gordon Bennett, were spectacular and unconventional. Both had their engines placed horizontally and very low down so as to allow the use of flat wind-cheating bodies. Bullet III had a 4-cylinder engine derived from that of the previous year but Bullet II had two of these engines coupled in line, thereby, with the exception of the C.G.V. of 1902, making one of the first straight-eights in the world. Neither car was very successful in the event and both retired early.

The original horizontal-engined type was discontinued for the 1905 season and the firm concentrated on 4-cylinder models of high quality. More and more compressed air devices were used for engine speed control, fuel feed, lubrication and so on. The Model K of 1906 was curious in having only 2-speed transmission; Model M of late 1907, however, had a 4-speed box with direct third and overdrive fourth. The first 6-cylinder Winton—Model XVI— appeared soon after and in the following year the company dropped the 4-cylinder models.

Model XVI was rated at 48 hp and had 3-speeds; it grew up in 1909 to 60 hp (5 in. bore and stroke) and was endowed with a 4-speed box. The compressed-air-for-everything system, by 1911, included starting and tyre pumping equipment, but by 1915 Winton had to bow to pressure from his agents and offer air or electric starting to choice.

1903 20 hp (R.A.C. 22) *Engine:* Transverse, horizontally opposed, centrally mounted, 2-cylinder, $5\frac{1}{4} \times 6$ in., pneumatically controlled variable-lift inlet valves, trembler coil ignition. *Transmission:* Combination plate and cone clutch, 2 speeds and reverse, single chain, live axle.

1913 40 hp (R.A.C. 48·4) *Engine:* 6-cylinder, $4\frac{1}{2} \times 5$ in., S.V., H.T. magneto and coil ignition. *Transmission:* Multidisc clutch, 4 speeds and reverse, shaft, bevel-geared live axle.

Wolseley (Siddeley, Wolseley-Siddeley, Deasy, Siddeley-Deasy, Stellite) England

The Wolseley with its various affiliations and offshoots affords many pitfalls for the would-be historian, and the story starts with the Wolseley Sheep-Shearing Machine Company becoming interested in the motor business in 1895 and giving scope to Herbert Austin, who had worked for them in Australia, to start experiments. The first fruit of his labour was a tandem tricar obviously inspired by Léon Bollée's voiturette and almost identical as far as the final drive arrangements were concerned, but with a much superior design of engine with horizontally opposed twin cylinders, mechanical inlet valves, electric ignition and throttle control. Austin would then have no part of the automatic inlets, tube ignition and governor-controlled exhaust valves of most early designers, though in his production models he took the retrograde step of using automatic inlet valves. Another experimental tricar followed the first effort, and the first 4-wheeled prototypes appeared late in 1899, firstly a single-cylinder 3½ hp which succeeded in completing the 1,000 Miles Trial and a hardly finished 8 hp 2-cylinder car which broke down and was withdrawn.

This first type of 4-wheeler was tiller-steered, powered by a 4½ × 5 in. horizontal transverse engine mounted forward which drove to a centrally placed 3-speed and reverse gearbox by flat leather belt. The gearbox was arranged to tilt in trunnion bearings in order to slacken or tighten the belt when starting from rest or changing gear: final drive was by chains. By the

left 1902 Wolseley 10 hp 2-cylinder tonneau

below left 1904 Siddeley 6 hp single-cylinder two seater
below right 1909 Wolseley-Siddeley 16/20 hp 4-cylinder rotunde phaeton

time series production started late in 1900 wheel steering had replaced the tiller and the belt primary drive gave way to a cone clutch and Renolds silent chain from engine to gearbox. Otherwise the original Austin-Wolseley remained virtually unchanged for the next five years—though, of course, many detail improvements were made. Models included the original 4½ × 5 in. single-cylinder (now re-rated at 5 hp), a 10 hp twin of the same dimensions which was very popular, a 20/24 hp 4-cylinder (very rare) and, c. 1903, a new single-cylinder model with single chain and live axle final drive instead of the side chains and dead axle of its larger brothers. These horizontal-engined Wolseleys were warmly praised for their efficiency, simplicity and reliability and criticised adversely for excessive noise, rather small margin of safety in their lubricating arrangements, and poorly chosen gear-ratios; the last failing has been a fairly consistent feature of Austin products until quite recently.

The Wolseley Company, and Herbert Austin in particular, were keen supporters of racing and built a number of racing cars on their horizontal-engined plan. These reached their peak with the 96 hp 4-cylinder 'Beetles' with their underslung chassis, streamlined bonnets, wire-braced wood wheels and general air of efficiency and speed. They were fine cars but prone to steering wander at high speeds and, unfortunately, often beset by lubrication and bearing failures.

By 1905 Wolseleys were anxious to break away from their horizontal-engined design as sales were dropping, but Austin, an obstinate man, was convinced that vertical engines were wrong and that shaft and live axle transmission on the Renault plan (then making great headway) was utterly indefensible. At this point Colonel Siddeley comes into the picture both as a director of Wolseleys and an importer of Continental cars. There was already a small 'Siddeley' car in production in 1903/4, and that this was practically identical, except for the bonnet and radiator, with the contemporary small Wolseley is hardly surprising as it was made to the Wolseley plan in the Wolseley works; in addition, the Siddeley Autocar Co. began selling a few 2- and 4-cylinder vertical-engined Siddeley cars late in 1903: these were, almost certainly, imported Peugeot chassis furnished with new names and English

coachwork. In due time a compromise was reached whereby vertical-engined Siddeleys (or Wolseley-Siddeleys) and the old horizontal-engined models were built side-by-side in the same works; like so many compromises this was not a very happy arrangement and in 1906 Austin set up in business on his own, whereupon he too began making the vertical-engined cars he had hitherto frowned upon, leaving Wolseleys to continue with various new Siddeley models.

By 1907 Siddeley cars (known indiscriminately as Siddeleys, Wolseley-

Siddeleys or, occasionally, as Siddeley-Wolseleys) had marched on from their Peugeot origin at the hands of Charles Rimmington. The range included a 10 hp twin, 4-cylinder cars of 15, 18, 30 and 40 hp and a 6-cylinder of 45 hp. The 10 and 15 hp models were shaft driven, the 18 hp shaft or chain to choice, the 30 and 40 hp shaft driven only and the 45 hp chain only. These last three models also had a direct drive on third with a geared-up fourth *à la* early Rolls-Royce—although Col. Siddeley claimed to have thought of the idea first. Another distinctive feature of the early Wolseley-Siddeleys was their mechanically operated I.o.E. valve gear.

The link between Siddeley and Wolseley lasted until 1910, after which Wolseley cars showed no startling changes except for the adoption of Lanchester-type worm-geared axles. Large 4- and 6-cylinder models continued to be made (the twin-cylinder was dropped in 1909) and a particularly successful newcomer was the famous Stellite in 1913. This was a new light car, powered by a remarkably efficient and flexible 4-cylinder sv engine of 62×89 mm, and with a 2-speed and reverse gear integral with the back axle. It was a handsome little car, very well made to Wolseley specification by the Electric and Ordnance Accessories Co. which, like the Wolseley Motor Company itself, was a Vickers subsidiary. The standard model only weighed 11 cwt and as the engine developed 22 bhp it had a lively performance despite the 2-speed gear: the slightly heavier De Luxe model had three speeds.

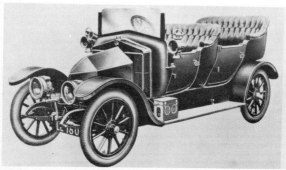

1909 Siddeley-Deasy 14/20 hp 4-cylinder tourer

In 1911 the new amalgamation of Siddeley and Deasy took place. Captain H. Deasy had been concerned with Rochet-Schneider and Martini cars at first and had set up in business as a manufacturer in 1906. The standard 24 hp Deasy car which appeared in time for the 1907 season was the work of E.W. Lewis who designed the contemporary Rovers; indeed, the Deasy was pretty well straight-forward Rover throughout. Despite their many good qualities, and their appearance in the T.T. and numerous other events, Deasy cars never became very well known. Siddely-Deasys, however, enjoyed considerable popularity and were a nice blend of good features from various sources, such as Knight double sleeve-valve engines, Renault-style dashboard radiators, Lanchester worm-geared back axles and Lanchester-type cantilever rear suspension complete with the parallel-motion radius links. Either Siddeley or Deasy (or their designer) realised that much of the merit of the Lanchester suspension lay in the link-work which ensured that the springs were only concerned with springing, and that the axle could only move vertically in relation to the chassis instead of describing part of a circle as was usually the case. Most of the firms who copied the cantilever springs failed to appreciate this point and largely nullified the virtues of the arrangement by using the springs to transmit driving and braking effort.

1901 Wolseley 5 hp (R.A.C. 8·1) *Engine:* Transverse, horizontal, forward-mounted, 1-cylinder, $4\frac{1}{2} \times 5$ in., A.I.V., trembler coil ignition. *Transmission:* Cone clutch. Renold's silent chain to 3 speeds and reverse gearbox, final drive from second-motion shaft of gearbox by side chains to dead axle.
    1902 10 hp as above but 2-cylinder and 4 speeds.

1906 Wolseley-Siddeley 15 hp (R.A.C. 25·6) *Engine:* 4-cylinder, 4×4 in., M.O.I.V. (I.o.E.), H.T. magneto ignition. *Transmission:* Cone clutch, 3 speeds and reverse, shaft, bevel-geared live axle.

1909 Siddeley (or Wolseley-Siddeley) 50 hp (R.A.C. 51) *Engine:* 6-cylinder, $4\frac{5}{8} \times 5$ in., S.V., dual ignition by H.T. magneto. *Transmission:* Metal cone, 4 speeds and reverse, bevel-geared countershaft, Renold's silent chains to dead axle.

1913 Siddeley-Deasy 18/24 hp (R.A.C. 20) *Engine:* Knight-type, 4-cylinder, 90×130 mm, double sleeve-valves, H.T. magneto and coil ignition. *Transmission:* Single plate clutch, 4 speeds and reverse, shaft, worm-geared live axle.

1914 Wolseley 16/20 hp (R.A.C. 20·3) *Engine:* 4-cylinder, 90×121 mm, S.V., H.T. magneto ignition. *Transmission:* Multiplate clutch, 4 speeds and reverse, shaft, worm-geared live axle.

Y.A.X.A. Switzerland

If the reader thinks the Y.A.X.A. is included so as to have something to put under the letter Y he is not far short of the truth, for it is the only one of the odd half-dozen machines beginning with this letter which survived for any length of time. Also, with Martini, Piccard Pictet and Dufaux it shares the distinction of being made in Switzerland, which was then a strongly 'anti-motoring' country.

The Y.A.X.A. was produced by Charles Baehin et Cie. of Geneva nominally from 1905 to 1914. It appears, though, that for the first two or three years the concern chiefly functioned as an importing agency and thereafter produced limited numbers of voiturettes built up from imported proprietory components.

By 1911/12 these had developed into neat 4-cylinder light cars of which a few were exported. The engine was a side valve monobloc of 67 × 120 mm with magneto ignition and Claudel carburettor. Transmission was by cone clutch and 4-speed gearbox to a bevel-geared live axle. Distinctive features were the central gear lever (then very rare) and what was describeed as a progressive braking system.

According to M. Baehin's own explanation in 1958 the strange name stood for '*Y'a qu'ca*' which is a corruption of '*il n'y a que cela*' or 'it's the one and only'.

1914 10/15 hp (R.A.C. 11·1)
Engine: 4-cylinder, 67 × 110 mm, S.V., H.T. magneto ignition.

Transmission: Cone clutch, 4 speeds and reverse gearbox, shaft and live axle.

Zebra   (Le Zèbre)   France

The Zebra started in 1908 at the point many older concerns were abandoning; that is, it was a light single-cylinder runabout. The first models only weighed $5\frac{1}{2}$ cwt complete with a neat 2-seater body, therefore the Zebra was classed as a cycle car though its design was that of a scaled-down 'real' car and the specification included a pressed steel chassis, automatic, constant-level splash lubrication, excellent multidisc clutch, shaft drive and bevel-geared live axle.

Though rated at only 6 hp the 88 × 120 mm engine was lusty enough to disguise the nastiness of the 2-speed gearbox fitted at first, and the little cars

1911 6 hp single-cylinder two-seater

had a good turn of speed. From 1910 onwards a 3-speed box was fitted, the engine stroke was reduced to 106 mm and the weight had increased by 1½ cwt. Thereafter the 6 hp single remained much the same and was supplemented in 1912 by a new 8 hp car which was almost identical except for a longer chassis and a 4-cylinder 50 × 100 mm engine.

The Zebra was a French car and the English importers, Messrs F.B. Goodchild & Co., showed their cosmopolitan instincts and zoological interests by importing also the German-built Oryx cars, which were notable for their ball-bearing crankshafts and an unusual form of carburettor most of the body of which was cast integrally with the cylinder block.

1912 Zebra 6/8 hp (R.A.C. 4·8)
Engine: 1-cylinder, 88 × 106 mm, S.V., H.T. magneto ignition.

Transmission: Multidisc clutch, 3 speeds and reverse, shaft, bevel-geared live axle.

1913 8 hp (R.A.C. 6·2) As above but 4-cylinder 50 × 100 mm engine.

Zust (Brixia-Züst) Italy

Züst was the name of a Swiss engineer who set up in business in Northern Italy making hydro-electric machinery and machine tools towards the end of the nineteenth century; by 1904 he had subsidiary works at Milan and Brescia and in 1906 he began making motor cars at the last named. Hence the 'Brixia-Züst' such being the accepted spelling during, and for long after, the Austrian domination of Italy.

At first sight Züst might very easily have been mistaken for Fiats, and they shared with Fiats and Italas the use of low tension magneto ignition until fairly late. Also Züst was one of the last firms to produce a 3-cylinder car, and the firm's 10 hp 3-cylinder model was still current in 1911; two years, that is, after *The Autocar* had pronounced the 3-cylinder to be extinct, despite the fact that

1913 25/30 hp 4-cylinder tourer

at least one English firm (Clyde) were using White and Poppe 3-cylinder engines for their smaller models. The only mechanical peculiarity of the Züst design lay in the use of full pressure lubrication of the gearbox, by a separate pump, after the manner of the contemporary Lanchesters. Quite a number of the Züst models, towards the end of our period, were fitted with Gnome engines, but it is not clear whether these were imported or built under licence.

Many of the smaller Züst models served as taxicabs and some of the larger made an impact in sporting events. After considerable squabbling a 40 hp Züst was accorded second place in the New York to Paris Race in 1908—a triumph for European design as the Thomas Flyer which won was really an American-built Brasier and in the previous year the Pekin to Paris affair had been won by Prince Scipio Borghese's Itala.

1907 40 hp (R.A.C. 41·9)   *Engine:* 4-cylinder, 130 × 140 mm, S.V., L.T. magneto ignition. *Transmission:* Multiplate clutch, 4 speeds and reverse, bevel-geared countershaft, side chains, dead axle.